Towards Integration

Towards Integration

*A Study of Blind and Partially Sighted
Children in Ordinary Schools*

*Monika Jamieson, Malcolm Parlett
and Keith Pocklington*

NFER Publishing Company Ltd

Published by the NFER Publishing Company Ltd.,
2 Jennings Buildings, Thames Avenue,
Windsor, Berks. SL4 1QS
Registered Office: The Mere, Upton Park, Slough, Berks. SL1 2DQ
First published 1977
© National Foundation for Educational Research in England and Wales
ISBN 0 85633 119 8

Printed in Great Britain by
Staples Printers, Love Lane, Rochester, Kent
Distributed in the USA by Humanities Press Inc.,
Atlantic Highlands, New Jersey 07716 USA.

Contents

PREFACE

This book reports a study of educational provision for one group of handicapped children — the visually impaired. It is the result of an 18-month inquiry (September 1974 to February 1976), funded by the NFER, in which the integration of visually impaired children into ordinary schools was the central concern.

Our research was not intended to replicate the exhaustive survey and discussion carried out by the Vernon Committee on The Education of the Visually Handicapped, which reported in 1972. Instead, we have deliberately sought to be selective, pursuing an intensive study of a major area of uncertainty in educational policy that concerns the relative merits of ordinary and special schooling.

In writing this book, we have not seen it as our task to make explicit policy recommendations. Our aim is altogether more modest: that by collecting information, summarizing arguments, displaying the issues, and undertaking our own interpretive analyses, we may add to the substance of the ongoing discussion about how best to educate children with impairment of vision.

Both the research and this report have been undertaken with various 'target' audiences in mind. One of these is the Warnock Committee set up in September 1974 'to review educational provision in England, Scotland and Wales for children and young people handicapped by disabilities of body or mind, taking account of the medical aspects of their needs together with arrangements to prepare them for entry into employment: to consider the most effective use of resources for these purposes, and to make recommendations'. We hope our study will usefully contribute to their work, and be a timely contribution to the discussions that will inevitably follow the Committee's reporting. We recognize that while we have concentrated solely upon the visually impaired, many issues selected in our study are shared in other areas of special education.

A brief word about the authors of this report who worked as a close team on all aspects of the research, sharing the fieldwork and report writing. However, there was inevitably some division of labour. Dr Malcolm Parlett, the project leader, worked in a half-time capacity, and was responsible for overall strategy and the final editing of this report. Monika Jamieson was responsible for a large section of the investigative fieldwork, the day-to-day management of the project, record keeping, and assembling of the report's numerous drafts. Keith Pocklington, who joined the team in January 1975, was also responsible for sections of the fieldwork, arrangement of data, and parts of the report writing.

We have used a few novel conventions in writing this book and would like to draw the reader's attention to them.

First, since much of the data used in this book are based on interviews and conversations, we have used double quotation marks to denote direct speech; single quotation marks are used to indicate material taken from written sources, or to emphasize and highlight words or phrases used in ways other than common usage.

Second, because the research design used in this study falls outside what is commonly regarded as traditional, we have provided a special account of the research approach (see Appendix 1). A second appendix gives methodological details germane to this study alone. Appendix 3 lists organizations visited.

Third, we have also included a glossary of medical and educational terms used in the book — many may be unfamiliar to readers not directly involved in the education of the blind or partially sighted.

Finally, the team would like to acknowledge their indebtedness to a great many people, whose help, advice, time, and interest made possible both the research and the book. First of all we thank the NFER Board of Management for providing funds for the project. We offer particular thanks to Dr David Hamilton and Mr Barry Hampshire who carried out important inquiries on our behalf; and also to Ms Carolyn Miller, University of Sussex, and Professor Ernest House, University of Illinois, who acted as occasional consultants to the project.

The research would clearly have been impossible without the support, interest, involvement, and practical assistance of many pupils, ex-pupils, families, teachers, head teachers, advisers, HM Inspectors, local education authority officials, ophthalmologists, and representatives of many different organizations and institutions. We extend our warm thanks to all in these groups who helped us so much. Unfortunately they are too numerous to mention individually. However, exceptions to any rule may be necessary and, accordingly, we single out for special mention here certain individuals who provided extensive and sometimes prolonged help to the project team, enabling us to set up and carry out major parts of the investigation. Special thanks, therefore, go to Mr Anders Arnör, Miss Joan Brown, Sister Clare, Mr R.J. Crosbie, Mr Iain Davidson, Dr Gerald Friedman, Mr D.W.F. Folley, Mr Leslie Frost, Mr Tore Gissler, Mrs Joan Kell, Miss Jeanne Kenmore, Mrs Hanne Lindau, Miss Janet Silver, Mr F. Tooze, Miss Brenda Watson, Mr J. Whittaker, and Mr J.G. Wilkinson.

We are also extremely grateful to the following who read and commented upon the manuscript in preliminary draft form: Professor R.A. Becher, Sir Edward Britton, Miss Joan Brown, Dr Clare Burstall, Mr Phil Clift, Mr M. Colborne Brown, Mr R. Crosbie, Mr R. Fletcher, Dr David Hamilton, Mr Barry Hampshire, Dr Seamus Hegarty, Mr George

Marshall, Ms C.M.L. Miller, Ms Joy Parlett, Miss Margaret Reid, Miss Janet Silver, Ms Daphne Such, Miss Monica Taylor, Dr M.J. Tobin, Professor M.D. Vernon, Mr John Wray, Mr Alfred Yates; representatives of the Association of Blind and Partially Sighted Teachers and Students; and a group comprising HM Inspectors and the Medical Officer from the Department of Education and Science. In no way, however, should the readers be held responsible for any errors that remain; nor should it be assumed that they agree with or endorse the views expressed.

Finally, our thanks go to Mrs Hilary Hosier and Ms Curtilia Thomas for their patience and technical ability in deciphering three different styles of handwriting and transforming them into an accurate manuscript.

Part One

Introduction

Chapter One

Origins, Background and Aims

This book is about the schooling of children who are partially sighted or blind. It concentrates on their education in ordinary primary and secondary schools where educational practices depend heavily on the use of sight, and also deals with how they are educated in special schools for the visually impaired.[1]

Inevitably, impaired vision presents problems for teaching and learning whatever kind of school attended — special or ordinary. When sight is extremely limited, braille becomes the basic educational medium. Even for those children who can still use print, reading and writing are often slow and difficult; and visual aids — notably the blackboard — are clearly not as useful for pupils who are visually impaired. Ball games and sports requiring rapid movements present difficulties; and so do woodwork, handicraft, and other practical subjects.

Much is taken for granted — visually speaking — by those with normal sight. They take in vast amounts of information through their eyes. In day-to-day functioning the world appears to them as structured and unchanging; it is recognizable and verifiable. Close and distant views, colours and physical features, can be examined either intensively or merely glanced at casually; complex relationships can be built up between them. Expressions and movements can be imitated. However, for those with severe interference of vision, none of this can be taken for granted. Sight may not be lost altogether, but the environment is less stimulating and more fragmented. It is more difficult to be confident about it. Accordingly, the visually impaired child may need deliberately to be taught how to analyse and think about his or her environment and encouraged to explore it.[2]

It is clear at once that the education of visually impaired pupils must differ from that of those with normal sight. Teaching the visually impaired occupies an area of 'special education' — until recently a term that was more or less synonymous with special schooling: the natural assumption was that teaching the handicapped was the province of the special schools alone. However, as a senior HMI recently stated: "special education is no longer restricted by place or method".[3] The trend is away from maintaining hard and fast divisions between ordinary and special schooling and towards greater flexibility in deciding where a handicapped pupil should go to school. Special education has acquired the wider meaning of providing for 'special educational needs'.

These shifts in thinking towards the schooling of handicapped children provided the original incentive for the study reported here. A research proposal was put forward that suggested the need for an 'evaluative study of educational provision . . . at present it is unclear whether integration of handicapped children into ordinary schools should be encouraged or not'.[4] It mentioned the educational alternatives — ordinary or special schooling — and concluded: 'there is as yet little evidence regarding the relative effectiveness of these various possibilities.' In short, the proposal was to study the integration of visually impaired children in ordinary schools and to collect evidence about how well it worked in practice.[5]

The investigation and whom it is for

It was understood that the study would also provide an opportunity to try out the 'illuminative' approach to educational evaluation and research (see Appendix 1),[6] on a larger scale than hitherto. Two principal features of the approach are that a study should be geared to the needs of its clients or audience; and, second, that the research design should evolve in the course of study rather than being fixed in advance. Both imply the need for flexibility. As the investigation unfolds, the preoccupations, puzzles, dilemmas, and policy questions of the target audiences become apparent. The researchers judge which predominate and then give greater concentration to these issues.

The investigation was divided into three phases. The first four months constituted the 'design phase' — a time for basic orientation, for fact-finding, for deciding whom exactly we were doing the research for (what was our constituency or readership?), and for deciding on areas to explore in depth. During phase one we read books and papers, studied published statistics, visited the Royal National Institute for the Blind, made some early school visits, went to meetings of teachers, followed up contacts suggested to us, visited and consulted other researchers in the field of visual handicap, and generally sought to immerse ourselves in the concerns, specialist terminologies, problems and history of this area of special education.[7]

The first phase in an illuminative research study is perhaps the most significant. It certainly was in the present research. None of us had previous experience in the study of visual impairment nor of special education; we were appointed for our general experience in educational research. We were therefore anxious to move ourselves from being uninformed to being knowledgeable in the shortest possible time.

In some ways our lack of directly applicable pre-knowledge was clearly a disadvantage. But in other ways it was beneficial. Thus, we found that we were probing controversial issues. We were also operating in a relatively small community where experts and influential voices tended to know each other's views already. It helped that we were newcomers to the group, without previously formed opinions or positions. Our inquiries, questions, and interviews were genuine requests for information and opinion, rather than a social scientist's conversational contrivances. We were received with friendly curiosity and given a great deal of assistance (perhaps being regarded as in need of it).

By the end of phase one we had established the general nature and direction of the study and which subsidiary in-depth investigations would occupy phase two — the major 'fieldwork phase'.[8] It was to be an investigation grounded in the study of schools, both special and ordinary, where blind and partially sighted pupils were being educated. It would be based on interviews and informal talks with head teachers, teachers, and pupils; and linked to observation of teaching and to the study of school documents and records. Secondly, there would be discussions and contacts with local authorities, advisers and HM Inspectors, representatives of national bodies, other professional and research groups. We decided, too, to make case studies of individual children in the contexts of home and ordinary school; to follow up certain groups of ex-pupils; and to make visits abroad to examine different countries' schemes of integrating the visually impaired.[9]

Also by this time — the end of the first phase — we had discovered that there were many separate constituencies and interest groups concerned with the subject matter of our research. We decided that we should try to reach a wide spectrum of these groups; we would not confine ourselves — as educational research seems to so often — to an audience of professionals and other researchers. It meant that our eventual report, as well as the research leading up to it, had to be geared towards concerns of interest to a broad readership.

We identified as our 'target' groups for this study: (i) those who are partially sighted or blind themselves, or whose children are; (ii) teachers, head teachers, and advisers associated with ordinary schools who are participating in a scheme of integration or who are thinking about it; (iii) teachers and head teachers of special schools for the visually impaired; (iv) committees of local education authorities, school governors, advisers and officials with responsibilities for special education; (v) paediatric ophthalmologists and consulting opticians; (vi) officers and members of the various supporting organizations and societies for (and of) the visually impaired; and (vii) other, more general readers intrigued by the numerous questions in which integration is embedded.[10]

Finally, in deciding the aims and directions of the study, there was one particular influence that we had not foreseen in advance. This we now discuss.

The integration debate

A recent pamphlet produced by the Department of Education and Science begins:

> 'It is generally agreed that if a handicapped child can manage successfully in an ordinary school he should go there; some now take the view that if handicapped children are to live within the normal community they should not be "segregated" for their education in special schools but should be educated alongside other children in ordinary schools. "Segregation" versus "integration" has become a major topic of educational debate today.'[11]

What we had not bargained for was the intensity of this debate. The issue, we found, like many controversies in education, had become polarized: there was a pro-integration lobby (self-typed as progressive reformers) and the anti-integrationalists (typing themselves as pragmatic realists) and they each decried the views of the other 'party'.

We thus found ourselves launched on a topic that appeared to divide sharply the professionals in the field. What was slightly unnerving was that we discovered a widespread expectation that our study would resolve the controversy. Since the study was under the auspices of the National Foundation for Educational Research, there was the legitimate expectation that the study would be impartial and objective, an independent appraisal without an axe to grind. No-one expected us to take an ideological position in favour of integration or against it at the beginning of our study. However, there *was* an expectation, widely held, that by the end of our project we would be in a position to come down on one side or the other, having found out whether integrated or special provision was the 'better method', which one was 'most effective'. In other words, we were expected to decide the debate and announce the winner.

This was completely at variance with the kind of study that we thought would be most useful, in the long term, to the target audiences we had selected. We also had strong theoretical objections. It would be misguided, we considered, for any study to claim 'to measure the educational effectiveness of integration': effective for what? effective for how long? what criteria are to be used for judging effectiveness? who chooses these criteria and on what grounds? These are just some of the complex questions that lurk behind the phrase 'measuring effectiveness'.[12] Of course, evaluators from more traditional research backgrounds might have attempted a systematic comparative study between the two alternatives — ordinary and special schooling — based on tests and questionnaires completed by matched samples of children, the results subjected to statistical comparison. However, given the small and dispersed samples, the immense variation between schools and kinds of integration, and the short duration of the study, even they would have encountered immense technical difficulties.[13]

Our aims in this research have been altogether different. They are *first*, to document an evolving educational movement and the controversy surrounding it; *second*, to investigate examples of schemes of integration at work; *third*, to elucidate questions about classroom life when blind or partially sighted children are taught alongside those with normal vision; *fourth*, to explore the relationships between school and home for the child who is integrated; *fifth*, to examine and spell out a variety of policy alternatives, teachers' concerns, childrens' adaptations, as well as a range of practical and philosophical dilemmas associated with implementing integration.

Our study has straightforward purposes: to collect information that is currently dispersed and to present it together in more concentrated form; to summarize and portray arguments, points of view, personal and professional convictions developed by those in the schools; and to elucidate a variety of basic underlying assumptions in the education of the visually impaired. The report does not claim to provide conclusive answers to questions about which type of educational provision is 'better', nor deliberately does it advance definitive policy recommendations or design an organizational blueprint. On the other hand, the report is grounded in the day-to-day practical problems and policy questions that relate to organization. It is not, we trust, a heavily academic document. Conversely, it does not over-simplify, which would be to avoid the complexities involved. Also, our commitment to present a scrupulously balanced presentation does not prevent us from expressing certain convictions of our own, developed in the course of study — and we make it clear at the points where we do so.

To summarize, our purpose is to examine integration — within the sphere of special education for those with impaired vision — in a way that proves informative, useful, and timely for many separate constituencies of concern. In this way we hope to contribute to the ongoing debates about integration by adding to their substance.

Outline of the book

The report is divided into six parts — each with a different emphasis and purpose. Part I (*Introduction*) includes this chapter and two others, each of which provides certain basic information about visual impairment. These are not written for the already knowledgeable, but rather for those (like we were at the beginning) who are relatively uninformed about the precise nature of blindness and partial sight, e.g. their definitions and incidence and how they are assessed. The information in the two chapters pertains specifically to educational issues: it is not a treatise on all aspects of visual impairment. Surprisingly, what is presented is not always readily accessible.

Part II (*Form and Practice*) has its own brief introduction and is concerned with reporting on organized schemes of integration in England and Wales and to some extent abroad. Our inquiries during phase one revealed how little information was publicly available about the various organized schemes. Even those directly involved or interested in integration seem to have little information at their fingertips about arrangements elsewhere. It was clearly one area for research concentration.

As in Part I it is not necessary for all the chapters of Part II to be read consecutively and with equal attention. The detailed reporting of schemes may not interest all readers equally, and the reader does not need to know them all in detail in order to follow later parts of the book.

Part III (*The Search for the Normal*) enters the realm where controversy mingles with fact, with differing interpretations being placed on the same observed phenomena to argue either the advantages or disadvantages of ordinary and special schooling. It draws on information gathered in visits to both special and ordinary schools and is based chiefly on interviews, group discussions, and numerous informal conversations with teachers, advisers, and pupils. It reports and summarizes arguments and discusses underlying assumptions, draws out areas of agreement and disagreement, and attempts to stir in some new ingredients to old themes.

Part IV (*The Experience of Individual Integration*) is altogether different. Four extended case histories of partially sighted pupils are included. It begins with a short general introduction that provides the rationale and basis for this portion of our work. It is not expected that all readers will want to read all four case histories (Chapters Thirteen to Sixteen) at one sitting — again they will interest some readers more than others. Each has been chosen to reveal particular relevant phenomena. It was decided in phase one that we should locate families with a child attending a local ordinary school and examine the interaction of home and school, finding out how institutional, psychological, and ophthalmological factors combine to promote a child's well-being (or lack of it) at school.

Part V (*Supporting and Coping*) — Chapters Seventeen to Nineteen — goes into the issues embedded within Part IV's case histories. Drawing on these — as well as on those of a further 18 children studied in the same way — it probes issues to do with the child's individual adaptations to being integrated. Parts IV and V perhaps bring alive some of the issues raised in Parts II and III.

Finally, Part VI (*Towards Integration*) attempts to draw together certain points in summary and conclusion. What does it all add up to? What has been learned from the study? What are the implications, policy questions, and major problems requiring most attention? What becomes clear is that the study unearths many different levels and contexts for policy discussion and decision. They range from shifts in society's general thinking to the use made of low vision aids in ordinary classrooms; from organizational and financial deliberations at the town hall to interactions of sighted and partially sighted children in school playgrounds; from questions of training and provision of services to the coping of confident and not so confident pupils in different school milieux. A proper appreciation of the issues surrounding the integration debate demands attending to many different problems, ideals, and constraints concurrently — they are found to inter-relate in intriguing and important ways.

Notes

(1) A government report in 1972 described educational provision for the visually impaired as follows:

> '. . . there are in England and Wales 18 special schools for the blind, 19 for the partially sighted and two for the blind and partially sighted together . . . All the schools for the blind and five schools for the partially sighted are boarding schools (though in a few cases children who live nearby may attend as day pupils). All schools except two of the selective schools for the blind provide for both boys and girls.'

> 'There are also 3 establishments for the further education and training of blind adolescents, also run by voluntary bodies, . . . there are no such establishments for the partially sighted. In addition to the special schools for the visually handicapped, there are 9 schools for delicate or physically handicapped children which also have a partially sighted unit and 9 special classes for partially sighted children in 8 ordinary schools. There is also an unknown number of visually handicapped children in hospitals for the mentally handicapped and in the new special schools (previously junior training centres); as well as a further unknown number of children suffering from visual defects not all of which are so severe as to merit placement in a special school or class who are being educated in ordinary schools.'

Maintained by	Nursery & Infants			Primary			All-Age			Secondary			Totals			
	B	PS	B/PS	B	PS	B/PS	B	PS	B/PS	B	PS	B/PS	B	PS	B/PS	
LEAs	—	—	—	1	1	—	1	15*	1	—	—	—	2	16	1	19
Voluntary organiza-tions+	6‡	—	—	3	—	—	2	3	1	5†	—	—	16	3	1	20
Totals	6	—	—	4	1	—	3	18	2	5	—	—	18	19	2	39
	6			5			23			5			39			

* One of these schools has a partially selective intake at the secondary stage.
+ To distinguish them from schools maintained by local education authorities, special schools managed by voluntary organizations are known as non-maintained schools.
‡ These Sunshine Home schools normally take children up to seven years old.
† Three of these schools are selective.

DEPARTMENT OF EDUCATION AND SCIENCE (1972). *The Education of the Visually Handicapped*. (Vernon Report). London: HMSO.

(2) The ideas in this paragraph were influenced by a helpful informal discussion with Iain Davidson and others in the Pre-School Blind Children Project, Department of Special Education, Ontario Institute for Studies in Education, Toronto, in 1975.

(3) Mr John Fish, HM Staff Inspector for Special Education in a paper entitled 'The New Frontiers' presented at an International Conference 'Special Education 75 — The New Frontiers', University of Kent, 28th July — 1st August 1975.

(4) Research proposal presented to the NFER Board of Management in December 1973.

(5) The research team was appointed after the project had been approved and funded. The detailed design and specific objectives were left for us to develop after our appointment.

(6) We do not generally include in the main text discussion of detailed methodological questions. In Appendices 1 and 2 will be found a general treatment of illuminative research and also a review of the methods applied in the present study.

(7) See Appendix 3 for a list of organizations contacted, and schools visited.

(8) Phase one, the 'design phase', lasted from September to December 1974; phase two, the 'fieldwork phase', covered the period from January to September 1975; and phase three, the 'reporting phase', lasted from October 1975 to February 1976. See Appendix 2 for a detailed discussion of the organization of the study.

(9) See Appendix 2.

(10) Though this may seem unusually inclusive, a number of exclusion principles were also established. For instance, we did not try to relate the integration movement for the visually impaired to parallel developments throughout special education. Also, we are not writing about British developments for an international audience, nor specifically are we writing with academic social scientists in mind. To have incorporated other target groups would have extended the study and changed fundamentally the character and scope of the report in a way that might have been detrimental to its main function: i.e. to illuminate policies and practices for those directly involved with issues concerning integration of the visually impaired in England and Wales.

(11) DEPARTMENT OF EDUCATION AND SCIENCE (1974). *Integrating Handicapped Children*. London: HMSO.

(12) E.g. see STAKE, R.E. (1973). 'Measuring what learners learn (with a special look at performance contracting)'. In: HOUSE, E. (Ed) *School Evaluation*. Berkeley: McCutchan.

(13) For a critique of this model of evaluation, see HAMILTON, D.F., JENKINS, D., *et al*. (1977). *Beyond the Numbers Game: a Reader in Educational Evaluation*. London: Macmillan and Berkeley: McCutchan.

Chapter Two

Visual Impairment: Facts and Figures

This chapter singles out certain points for brief discussion. Readers closely concerned with educating blind and partially sighted children are unlikely to find here much that they do not already know. Outside this group, however, one finds zones of ignorance that are sometimes sizeable. It is surprising how little is known factually, in the general population, about impairment of vision and, inside education, how children in need are identified and how special needs are catered for. There are erroneous assumptions, and procedures and details not known.

First, for instance, it is not always appreciated that there are numerous different causes of seriously defective vision:[1] among young children, visual impairment is usually due to a congenital or hereditary abnormality or anomaly of the eye that is often irremediable.[2] Examples include congenital cataracts, diseases of the retina or of the optic nerve, and albinism. Causes of loss of vision in later years are different: for those losing their sight in middle-age, a disorder known as diabetic retinopathy is a major cause, as are optic atrophy and myopic chorioretinal atrophy; for the elderly, degenerative conditions are often the cause of visual deterioration, especially macular degeneration; glaucoma and cataract also become increasingly more prevalent.

Disorders of the eyes have a variety of causes, and they lead to different effects on what people can see. Partially sighted children, in particular, may be misleadingly regarded as a uniform group when, in fact, they are strikingly different one from another: a child with 'tunnel vision' has a restricted field of vision, an albino is oversensitive to light. Medically speaking, the two have little in common and in the classroom their problems are not the same; they require different visual aids. Moreover, two children with similar defects can still differ — one child may use his or her remaining or 'residual' vision better than the other. In some conditions there can be day-to-day variations.[3]

A second misplaced but common assumption held in the lay, sighted world is that the condition known as blindness involves no sight whatsoever. In a study made of those being registered as blind from 1963 to 1968,[4] total blindness, without even perception of light, was the exception — affecting only five per cent of the group. Just over 10 per cent were 'almost totally blind' — i.e. not perceiving form — but they had perception of light. Well over half of those registered (53.7 per cent males and 55.7 per cent females) had 'some degree of useful vision'. The study argued that 'the blind population taken as a whole is largely one afflicted with grossly defective vision rather than with blindness in the full sense of the term'.

A third assumption is of a different kind: that because visual impairment is a state that is identifiable and medically known about, national statistics of incidence must be straightforward to compile. The assumption is not warranted. Registration (discussed in Chapter Three) of an individual as blind or partially sighted is not obligatory and many partially sighted children, in particular, are not registered. If a child has another handicap as well, he or she may be included in a different category for statistical purposes. In addition, there is the usual difficulty that statistical information collected for one purpose is rarely quite suitable for another.

Nevertheless, a number of conclusions can be confidently drawn. It is not always realized that, relatively speaking, the visually impaired represent a small group of children in special need. Using figures supplied to the Department of Education and Science by local authorities in England and Wales, one finds that the visually impaired constitute a mere 2.30 per cent of the total number of handicapped children receiving or awaiting educational provision as at January 1974 (0.77 per cent blind and 1.53 per cent partially sighted).[5] Visually impaired children do not all go to special schools for the blind or partially sighted. For example, of 1833[6] *registered* blind in England and Wales, aged between five and 15 in 1974, only 908 attended a special school for the blind; the rest were distributed between other special schools (mainly for the retarded), hospitals, training centres, or were at home.[7] Of 2515 *registered* partially sighted children, 13.4 per cent attend other special schools and 29.8 per cent are in ordinary schools.[8]

The overall general incidence of visual impairment remains broadly constant although there has been a steady decline in the proportion of blind children since 1967, with a marked increase since then in the proportion of partially sighted children receiving or requiring special education.[9] This is thought to reflect a shift of emphasis — as the Vernon Committee[10] explained: 'Since the partially sighted / blind borderline is not fixed rigidly, there may be a tendency to assess as partially sighted for educational purposes increasing numbers of children who might in the past have been assessed as blind.'

The numbers of visually impaired children may not be rising, but the proportion of those with additional handicaps undoubtedly is. A sizeable proportion of visually impaired children have additional handicaps: for example, of 1833 *registered* blind in England and Wales, 43.3 per cent had some additional handicap.[11] The proportional increase in the multiply handicapped is generally attributed to advances in paediatrics — 'such advances have led to a steady increase in the number of survivors among babies formerly doomed by prematurity, intra-uterine infections, embryopathies of varied origin, by perinatal disturbances, and by genetic abnormalities. With so many complex issues, the reduced infantile morality has inevitably brought unforeseen problems and challenges', not least 'disturbances with their distressingly widespread complications (that) illustrate once more that blindness in childhood is now often an aspect of a generalized disorder'.[12]

Discovering visual problems

We have referred to the difficulty of obtaining a comprehensive statistical picture. The problem is more serious still: a sizeable number of children with visual defects may not show up in official statistics at all because their problem has not been detected. They remain undetected until — said one official — "one trips over them and sees they are under-achieving". A number of times we heard reference to 'an iceberg', those already known to have some defect of vision constituting its visible tip. The conviction, on the part of many, is that there exists a large number of school-age children who have received no ophthalmological or other specialist attention but who have defects of vision that interfere with effective school functioning, serious enough in some cases to be defined as partial sight.[13]

There are several pieces of evidence that support this contention. The Optical Information Council, screening a thousand children between six and 15 years (using a Mobile Screening Unit) found that over 20 per cent needed to be referred i.e. 'advised to have a detailed eye examination'. The main types of 'faulty sight' were monocular vision, short-sight and muscular imbalance (a tendency to squint). They concluded that as many as 2,975,000 school-age children (in the UK) may be in need of complete sight tests and that 'it seems plain that the present methods of sight testing at schools need alteration and, at the very least, vision screening should be urgently considered . . . '.[14]

Other evidence for the iceberg comes from experience in Manchester. Shawgrove School for the Partially Sighted transfers some of its pupils to local schools[15] and then provides a peripatetic service for them. At the same time, the peripatetic teachers make contact with other pupils in the authority who are referred to them by the school health service as having a visual problem. They also obtain names from local opticians. In the first five years of the scheme's existence a particular pattern has repeated itself: the peripatetic teachers arrive at a school to discuss any difficulties, educational or visual, that pupils referred to them may be having; then they find they are asked, while there, to advise on other children noticed to be experiencing difficulty. If the peripatetic teacher suspects vision deterioration, the child is referred to the school health service for investigation and treatment. There is therefore a two-way communication between the peripatetic service and the school health service, each referring pupils to the other. In all, some 680 children, who were found to need attention, have been brought to the attention of the peripatetic service in this way. Their visual problems cover the whole spectrum, from straightforward refractive errors, e.g. short-sightedness (myopia), long-sightedness (hypermetropia), squints, and astigmatism − all sometimes requiring correction by glasses − to more serious problems requiring specialist attention from educational and social services. This discovery of children with a visual problem, who have not been classified as in need of educational support because of it, is a phenomenon echoed by special education advisers nationwide.

There is an increasing acknowledgement that improved screening is required.[16] Although simple vision tests are already carried out as part of the routine medical examination on entering infant school, they may not identify all visual problems: they may not detect a restricted visual field; and even near vision is not always tested. Also, some children miss these health checks through absence from school − perhaps children who most need them. Most authorities have further medical examinations at intervals and these routinely include testing of vision;[17] but it seems from the Manchester experience that some still slip through the net. Undetected problems may lead to pupils being mistakenly thought of as backward. Children, quite literally, might not be able to 'see' how to do an aptitude test.

Of course, more serious defects are picked up much earlier. An ophthalmologist reported that most blind infants are seen by consultant ophthalmologists between four and six months. Less immediately obvious conditions emerge later, picked up by parents noticing that their child is having difficulty. Parents draw the attention of their general practitioner to the problem, who may then refer the child for an examination. The ophthalmologist reported that referrals came usually from general practitioners or from child health clinics. However, this still leaves a number of conditions that do not become apparent until the child begins attending school and new demands are placed on sight. Some children can cope with the large print of the earliest books but then run into difficulty when they graduate to smaller print and to fractions in mathematics. The population of known visually impaired children in a single age cohort is therefore one that accumulates: first come the most extreme and obvious visual defects and subsequently those with less severe conditions are added to it.

Placement in schools

Finally, in this chapter, we shall refer to what happens after a child has been recognized as having a visual impairment. The procedures and stages involved are not always clear to teachers and officials, let alone to parents. That local authority practices differ markedly in detail adds to the confusion.[18]

Early decisions about the most appropriate form of education are hazardous. Medically speaking, both diagnosis and prognosis of visual impairment present difficulties.[19] The recently established screening service in Liverpool, operating from a community base, is exploring ways of combining medical and educational advice at the pre-school stage for severely visually impaired children. Its basic concerns are with comprehensive, multi-disciplinary assessment of two-and-a-half to four-year-old children, and in defining present and future educational needs. However, a service of this kind is distinctly unusual.[20]

Local education authorities are responsible ultimately for deciding what kind of schooling children with visual impairment should receive. In the past, authorities have relied almost exclusively on the recommendation of an ophthalmologist. This pattern is changing, particularly since the Vernon Committee reported. Steps have been taken to increase the involvement of other professionals who may be able to advise on the child's 'total needs'. New Special Education (SE) forms – at the time of writing still only in limited use – reflect the official expectation that a different kind of evaluation is required before placement decisions can be made: one couched in educational as well as ophthalmological terms. On the new forms, a child's head teacher and an educational psychologist contribute reports which are considered together with a medical report. The SE forms are supposed to be for all children of school age regarded as having special needs.

Recommended by the Vernon Committee[21] were small round table conferences of the school medical officer, the special education adviser, a representative from the school psychological service, and other relevant parties that may be called upon. These conferences are not yet in general practice. Multi-disciplinary assessment reflects an increasing disinclination both to regard the statutory handicaps as fixed categories, and also to consider a child's condition the exclusive province of a single professional group: 'The need for multi-disciplinary team assessment is vital, particularly when one considers the high proportion of visually handicapped children who have additional health problems, and when the contribution each member of the team can make to help the child achieve his full potential is recognized'.[22]

The trend towards multi-disciplinary assessment for educational purposes is a reflection of the many forces at work in society, as well as in medical and educational thinking, that reflect changes towards those suffering a sensory loss or a physical or intellectual limitation. It is now emphasized that defective vision is not a sufficient basis for making definitive-seeming categorizations of an individual's total state. It is, therefore, perhaps an appropriate time to suggest the use of different, and more suitable terminology. The most common general term or label for those designated blind or partially sighted is 'visually handicapped'. We favour a different term, 'visual impairment', for the reason that an individual may not necessarily be handicapped — held back or put at a social disadvantage — simply because he or she has little vision. A term such as 'visual defect' we discard for being somewhat too encompassing, although it again puts correct emphasis on the state of vision itself rather than on the conjectured consequences implied by 'handicap'.[23]

To be concerned about the choice of terms is not to be pedantic. The connotations or associations of a particular label can reinforce stereotypes and condition thinking. In 1934 the change to calling children 'partially sighted' who were formerly known as 'partially blind' was more than a switch of label — it reflected, and further encouraged, a commitment to using sight rather than 'saving it'.

Notes

(1) Good accounts of the causes and incidence of blindness are to be found in SORSBY, A. (1966). *The Incidence and Causes of Blindness in England and Wales, 1948—62*, 14. London: HMSO. SORSBY, A. (1972). *The Incidence and Causes of Blindness in England and Wales, 1963—68*, 128. London: HMSO.

(2) Some visual defects cannot be remedied but it is sometimes possible that operative treatment may help to improve vision, e.g. discission (or needling) or removing of cataracts.

(3) One special school head teacher went so far as to say that some children seemed to be "blind one day and partially sighted the next".

(4) SORSBY, A. (1972) *op. cit.*

(5) **Total number of handicapped children awaiting places in special schools: receiving education in special schools; independent schools, special classes and units; or boarded in homes as at January 1974: England and Wales**

Category	
Full-time school population	9,560,015
Blind	1,274
Partially Sighted	2,539
Deaf	4,023
Partially Hearing	5,172
Physically Handicapped	13,953
Delicate	7,425
Maladjusted	17,547
Educationally sub-normal — medium	80,045
Educationally sub-normal — severe	30,614
Epilepsy	1,254
Special Defects	1,401
Autism	593
Total number of handicapped children	165,840

For further details, see DEPARTMENT OF EDUCATION AND SCIENCE (1974). *Statistics of Education*. Volume 1, Schools. London: HMSO.

(6) This figure, which refers only to the registered blind, aged between five and 15 years comes from the *Department of Health and Social Security, Local Authority Social Services Statistics, England and Wales Summaries* containing information about *Registration of Blind Persons and Partially Sighted Persons at 31 March 1974*. This figure is larger than the blind school population. It includes, for example, some registered blind children whose main handicap(s) may dictate placement in another kind of school.

(7) **Distribution of children aged 5—15, registered as blind, attending different types of special schools as at 31 March, 1974: England and Wales**

	Male			Female			Total
	Blind only	With Additional Handicap	Total	Blind only	With Additional Handicap	Total	
Attending special schools for the blind.	411	90	501	326	81	407	908
Attending other special schools.	82	63	145	65	53	118	263
Not at school but receiving home tuition.	22	19	41	14	8	22	63
Not at school and not receiving tuition, residing at home or elsewhere.	39	85	124	29	61	90	214
In hospitals for the mentally ill or mentally handicapped.	25	125	150	15	95	110	260
In training centres.	6	65	71	8	43	51	122
Total	585	447	1032	457	341	798	1830

NB. Three pupils of the 1833 (see text) are not accounted for by this table. Data taken from *Department of Health and Social Security, Local Authority Social Services Statistics*, (1974), *ibid.*

(8) **Distribution of children aged 5—15, registered as partially sighted, attending different types of schools as at 31 March, 1974: England and Wales**

	Male	Female	Total
Attending special schools for the partially sighted.	787	437	1224
Attending other special schools.	211	127	338
Attending ordinary schools.	459	290	749
Receiving home tuition.	21	15	36
Others	97	71	168
Total	1575	940	2515

Data taken from *Department of Health and Social Security, Local Authority Social Services Statistics* (1974), *ibid.*

(9) DEPARTMENT OF EDUCATION AND SCIENCE (1972). *The Education of the Visually Handicapped*. (Vernon Report). London: HMSO.

(10) In October 1968, a committee, under the chairmanship of Professor M.D. Vernon, was appointed by the then Secretary of State for Education, 'to consider the organization of education services for the blind and the partially sighted and to make recommendations'. The Committee reported in 1972: 'Our main endeavour has been, on the one hand, to ensure that the special requirements of both the blind and the partially sighted are met; and, on the other hand, to break down outmoded barriers where they exist . . . Our recommendations are designed to extend the opportunities open to visually handicapped children and to enable them to lead richer and fuller lives'. (DEPARTMENT OF EDUCATION AND SCIENCE (1972), *ibid.*). The Report, while describing existing educational provision for the visually impaired, made many recommendations for improvement in the following areas: the planning of educational services, medical services for children up to school leaving age, provision for children under five, organization of schools, school curriculum and teaching aids, further education, higher education, vocational guidance, the training of teachers and residential child care staff, and further research.

(11) **Young blind persons registered at 31 March 1974 who have additional handicap: England and Wales**

	Male	Female	Total
		age 5 — 15	
Additional Handicap			
Mentally ill only	10	6	16
Mentally handicapped only	179	114	293
Physically handicapped only	92	81	173
Deaf without speech only	9	12	21
Deaf with speech only	7	6	13
Hard of hearing only	9	1	10
Mentally ill and other physical, sensory or speech handicaps	12	15	27
Mentally handicapped and other physical, sensory or speech handicaps	117	95	212
Physically handicapped and other sensory or speech handicaps	16	13	29
All persons with additional handicap: *Total*	451	343	794

This table represents the 43.3 per cent of registered blind with additional handicaps only. Data taken from *Department of Health and Social Security, Local Authority Social Services Statistics*, (1974), *op. cit.*

(12) SORSBY, A. (1972), *op. cit.*

(13) This issue was stressed at a one-day conference for special school head teachers organized by the research team in May, 1975.

(14) OPTICAL INFORMATION COUNCIL (1970). *The Eyes of the British*, Section 3, Children and Elderly. These figures should be treated with caution — there is little information given about how the sample was chosen.

(15) For further details, see Chapter Eight.

(16) Efforts to improve screening and assessment procedures of pre-school children are on the increase; almost all Area Health Authorities now have developmental screening programmes for pre-school children. Vision screening forms part of these programmes and 'suspects' are referred for further examination and treatment.

(17) The vast majority of LEAs test the visual acuity for distance of all children within their first year at school. In about 12 per cent of LEAs, annual reviews are undertaken of every child from 5—16 years; others vary from almost yearly to two or three yearly review. Colour vision is tested in all but

a handful of LEAs, usually between ages 10—12 years (see FINE, S.R. (1973). 'Subnormal vision in school children'. In: WOLFFE, M. (Ed) *The Problems of the Visually Handicapped. Transactions of a Symposium held at the University of Aston in Birmingham in May 1972.* University of Birmingham: Department of Ophthalmic Optics).

(18) One special school head reported that he had to deal with 17 different LEAs and none operated in precisely the same way. For example, when children were being referred to his school by an LEA, he could have anything from "complete documentation to a telephone call". The contact might be made by one of several different local authority officials.

(19) To define accurately the nature and likely future pattern of a visual defect may necessitate a long process of testing, lasting up to one and a half days, and some of it painful. Such detailed diagnoses are usually put off if the child is young — especially if no major change is anticipated within two or three years and if the child has been 'managing' to date. An ophthalmologist made the point that there was no use in knowing the prognosis for age 50 when the child was aged 10.

(20) The Liverpool screening service, founded in 1975, is based on two hypotheses: first, that visually impaired infants are not identified early enough and, second, that their developmental needs have not been appraised sufficiently accurately in the past. It is a peripatetic, multi-disciplinary service, based upon the Family, Child and Educational Advisory Centre: its function is to assess severely visually impaired infants at the earliest age. It is not a clinical centre and they insist on all children who come for assessment having been investigated ophthalmologically beforehand. They work with severely handicapped children and encourage referrals from medical personnel working from the community centre and from opticians — but not, as yet, from general practitioners. The team consists of a psychologist, an ophthalmic paediatrician, an RNIB educational adviser, an LEA peripatetic advisory teacher, a psychiatric social worker, and a clinical medical officer with experience in the field of visual impairment, and they can call on a consultant ophthalmologist as and when required. The community base is purpose-built. There are two fully equipped rooms for visual and hearing assessment. Among their concerns are (i) family and parental worries (e.g. What does visual handicap mean? What educational consequences are there and what options?); (ii) developmental management within the home; and (iii) issues such as educational placement, welfare benefits, etc. The team has rapidly discovered that since they began, a demand has emerged. Currently they face a number of dilemmas — the most acute of which is whether to extend the service (still in its infancy) to include multiply handicapped pre-school children.

(21) Once children have been identified as having a visual impairment, the Vernon Committee recommends that they should 'then be referred for combined ophthalmological/educational assessment to a regional assessment team including an ophthalmologist with particular skill and an interest in children, an educational psychologist and a teacher of the visually handicapped' (DEPARTMENT OF EDUCATION AND SCIENCE (1972) *op. cit.*).

(22) FINE, S.R. (1975). 'Registration and Notification', *Child Care, Health and Development*, 1, 5, September/October.

(23) Barraga is also concerned about terminology in use. She thinks a 'realistic term (for blindness) would be "low vision" since this more nearly emphasises true characteristics and indicates the presence of some vision'. She would favour, instead of 'partially sighted', the term 'visually limited'. (BARRAGA, N.C. (1975). 'Visually Impaired Children — Development and Learning', *Eyepiece*, 1, 4.)

Chapter Three

Vision Testing, Vision Use, and Registration

In this chapter we introduce some other basic points about vision loss — particularly with regard to its assessment. We begin with the standard tests for visual acuity and discuss their limitations for decisions concerning schooling. Then we spell out some of the new thinking about how, when some vision remains, its efficiency can be improved by training or by the use of more powerful optical aids than were available in the past.

Acuity tests

The most commonly used tests for distance vision are the 'Snellen Test Charts'. These display rows of letters or symbols arranged in descending order of size. The sizes of each row of letters are based on what a normal eye could read if hypothetically the letters were placed at particular distances: thus the largest letter is of a size that could be read by a normal eye if placed at 60 metres distance. The next row of somewhat smaller letters could be read at 36 metres and subsequent rows of progressively smaller letters at shorter and shorter distances (24, 18, 22, 6, 5, 4 metres). A man being tested stands six metres from the chart. If, say, he can read only the first and largest letter, it means he can read at six metres what someone with normal vision could read at 60 metres: his visual acuity for distance is expressed as 6/60. If he can read down to the smaller letters, say in the '18 metre' row, his acuity would be recorded as 6/18. Normal vision is 6/6. Severe vision loss may require the person to move nearer the chart, to a distance of three metres. If he can still only read the largest letter the acuity is given as 3/60 (a level of acuity used in the UK for identifying someone as legally blind). For young children there are special tests which do not depend upon an ability to read.[1]

A test for near vision (the N print test) uses cards of different sizes of print, viewed in good light and held by the person being tested at any distance he or she likes.[2] The person reads, starting with the largest print, and works down to the smallest he or she can read. The cards are numbered so that the designation N12 means that the person can read type size print N12.[3] A full ophthalmological examination will also include tests of the person's field of vision. For all the tests, each eye is tested separately and with glasses worn, if prescribed.

What has at once to be appreciated, in considering the usefulness of these tests, is that they do not in fact give an accurate indication of an individual's actual ability to read, move around independently, or cope with daily life. One of the persistent complaints made by those concerned with educating the visually impaired is that decisions about school placement have in the past been based primarily on an ophthalmological assessment;[4] the educators complain that ophthalmologists do not see children at work or play but rely almost entirely on the acuity test measurements;[5] and these·are inadequate predictors of how effectively children can function, how well they can "use the sight that they have".

There is enormous individual variation. An ophthalmologist explained how he had seen two individuals at about the same time who had identical acuity measurements; one "behaved like a blind person", required help, moved about cautiously, did not recognize people. The other, by contrast, behaved like a sighted person, walked without assistance of any kind, and could recognize people.

Phenomena such as these have come to be more widely acknowledged. It is now almost commonplace to argue that appraisal of vision, especially for educational purposes, should be based as much on real life kinds of tests as on traditional acuity measures.[6] Reliance on medical assessments of vision has proved insufficient in making educational decisions. One prominent educator, discussing the problem of deciding whether a child with very limited vision should use print or braille, opposed the idea that one should turn automatically to an ophthalmologist for guidance: "The decision ought to be based on trying both mediums with the child in the classroom, not on acuity with print indicated by a vision chart."

A head teacher of a special school was similarly sceptical about the validity of formal measures alone for making educational judgments. "Tests", he said, "are given under optimum conditions ... it's variable ... the child may be a bit off that day." He wondered sometimes if, anyway, the children were not "foxing them — these kids know Snellen off by heart". He described how he relied on his own judgments as well as on the test records: "I take them to the window and I say 'what can you see?'" When they reply that they can see "grass" or "trees", he questions them — "grass? That's all over the place; trees? Well, there are bound to be trees"; there is a marked tendency, he thought, for children with limited vision to guess and to make out that they see more than they do.

An obvious difficulty in appraising functional vision, whether in this relatively crude fashion or in more systematic ways, is in codifying and quantifying it with anything approaching the precision of the Snellen chart.

There have been critiques of the usefulness of acuity tests from the research community as well. Barraga, for instance, suggests that several assumptions held about visually impaired children are incorrect: '(a) what a person sees will be determined by the extent of their impairment . . ., (b) that visual acuity tells us how much a person can see . . . and (c) that visually handicapped children should be protected from eye strain'.[7] Such fallacies are widespread. She argues that, from an educational point of view, measures of acuity are insufficient indicators of a child's ability to see: equally important, if not more so, are 'visual functioning . . . how a child uses whatever vision he has in all his activities'; and also 'visual capacity . . . the potential of the child for learning to use his vision in the most meaningful and effective way. Capacity cannot be measured nor can it be observed'.[8]

In another paper, Barraga quotes Faye (1970): 'Visual acuity measurements (distance) have little or no relation to how well the child may be able to use his vision for learning (at near point)'; and also Bateman and Wetherall (1967): 'There is no relationship between measured acuity at either distance or near, and efficiency in reading among visually impaired children.'[9] Such statements have an authoritative ring. They remind us — as do also the teacher's experiences mentioned above — that visual impairment is a complicated phenomenon, and certainly one not straightforwardly related to sensory loss, measured on a single dimension.

Making better use of residual vision

That an individual can make more — or less — use of his or her remaining (or residual) vision is an idea that has recently been increasingly emphasized. A number of experimental schemes and training programmes designed, almost literally, to teach a child to see, have been developed in the USA[10] and in Denmark. Trials have also been going on in Britain.[11]

Perhaps the most notable work has been done in the USA by Dr Natalia Barraga. 'In recent years', she has written,

'studies, both medical and educational, have indicated that spontaneous visual learning does not occur always when there is impairment in the structure and functioning of the eyes. Because children learn so much about their world and the people and objects within it just by looking, when there are limitations in sharpness and clarity of what is seen at any distance, the child picks up much less just by looking. Guidance, assessment, and constant supervision in visual activities will help such children to discover things they might not see by themselves, recognize objects that are blurred, and develop more accurate estimates of visual space'.[12]

A practical approach developed by Barraga typically includes the following procedures: 'The first step in visual perception development is that of stimulation . . . (next) attention should be directed . . . towards the discrimination and recognition of all basic geometric forms, from large to small, from very unlike to very similar'. These steps would be followed by tasks of sorting and grouping. Further activities, for example, noting likenesses, matching forms, ordering, identifying missing portions of forms, integrating discrete elements of forms follow next. 'The developmental approach', writes Barraga, '. . . enables the child . . . to develop a visual frame of reference' and also, 'to determine for himself how efficient he can be visually'.[13]

Results of these programmes have sometimes been dramatic: children with extremely limited vision, who would automatically in the past have been considered braille users, have been taught to read print. In a similar programme at Refsnaesschool in Denmark, a girl in the eighth grade of school, who had always used braille, was able to read as quickly in print as she could in braille after only 35 lessons of 45 minutes each. She had sight in one eye only, with an acuity of 2/60. She was thought exceptional in the rapidity of her progress. But many children of reasonable intelligence are considered eligible candidates, and take on average 40—50 lessons to reach a similar level of competence.

The devising of programmes to improve the use of residual vision by perceptual training, represents a significant development. There is a parallel and complementary major change in progress: the establishment of low vision clinics designed to prescribe and provide powerful visual aids for visually impaired persons. A variety of different devices are employed: telescopes that can be attached to spectacle frames, hand-held monoculars and binoculars, illuminated magnifiers, and clip-on lenses. In Britain there are several clinics regularly providing these, the main one at Moorfields Eye Hospital.[14] In the USA they are gradually increasing in number, but at least one-third of the states still have no low vision clinics at all. Technically speaking, these clinics are doing nothing that could not have been done before: as one American ophthalmologist remarked, there was, in optical terms, "nothing significant since Galileo invented the telescope". What is new is a different medical and public attitude: instead of saying to a patient with deteriorating vision (as might have been said in the past) "there is nothing we can do for you", the attitude now was "but maybe you can read and keep your job" (consultant ophthalmologist).

Clinics can give many examples of patients who have been able — using their low vision aids — to continue careers that would otherwise have had to be abandoned; they continue to function as 'sighted' persons instead of being forced to regard themselves as 'blind'. Many children (and this is of direct relevance to integration) are able to see the blackboard with aids, and to be print rather than braille-users.[15] The opinion of the American ophthalmologist interviewed was that the single most important factor in encouraging integration of the visually impaired, at least in Massachusetts, was "the utilisation of low vision aids to keep people in school". He explained how "Johnny might have vision of 20/400 . . . (he needs) a low vision evaluation which discovers 'sure it's 20/400'; however, with low vision aids he has 20/40, so he can go into the ordinary class. If he is 20/400 he'll have to function as a blind person".

Those in low vision clinics often feel they are up against an entrenched notion — medically unfounded — that people with limited vision can "use up their vision, straining their eyes — use it all up". This used to be the medical view as well, even 50 years ago. Partially sighted children were then sent to 'sight saving schools'. The opposite view now obtains: injured limbs need to be exercised and strengthened; much the same is held for vision. There may even be "reduction of vision with disuse" (ophthalmologist).

The significance of these twin revolutions — training programmes for using residual vision, and the provision of aids that were not available in the past — is that they both reflect a more 'robust' and less 'protective' stance towards visual impairment. This change of attitude is one that is separable from that favouring increased educational integration, but naturally it can be held to reinforce it. The days of special schools for the blind actively forbidding children with some small amount of vision from making use of it are not long past, but they are unlikely ever to return. The trend is jointly towards making more of individual capacities and towards assimilating into normal society those with conditions that would have isolated them in the past. Low vision aids and programmes for increasing visual efficiency will not in themselves accomplish these widely endorsed goals. Almost inevitably, however, they are major contributory developments.

Registration

Although many children may not be registered as blind or partially sighted while they are young, at some point they may be. The categories 'blind' and 'partially sighted' are statutory categories of handicap. In the past, the pattern was that a child with a certain visual acuity measurement would be certified by an ophthalmologist as either blind or partially sighted, registered as such by the local authority, and would then be automatically regarded as eligible for a special school of the appropriate type. Today, for educational purposes, the distinction increasingly used is that between 'braille users' and 'print users'.

Registration of the handicapped is voluntary in England and Wales (unlike Denmark, where it is compulsory), and is usually carried out in order to secure benefits.[16] There are different Department of Health and Social Security registers for blind and partially sighted persons and statutory definitions for inclusion on one or other of them. The examining ophthalmologist, on Form BD8 (the form used for certification and registration)[17] has to answer 'Yes' or 'No' to the question 'Do you consider the person "so blind as to be unable to perform any work for which eyesight is essential"?' If the answer is 'Yes' the person is certified as blind. If the answer is 'No', there is another question: 'If the person is not at present "so blind as to be unable to perform any work for which eyesight is essential" do you consider that the person is substantially and permanently handicapped by defective vision caused by congenital defect, or illness, or injury?' If the answer to this second question is 'Yes', the person is certified 'partially sighted'. It is stated categorically that the 'principal condition to be considered (in deciding between 'Yes' and 'No') is the visual acuity'. But the ophthalmologist is given some degree of interpretive latitude by taking the patient's field of vision into consideration.[18] The importance of visual field was emphasized by an ophthalmologist: "a patient may be able to read the whole chart (Snellen), but not be able to get out of the room". He described his working policy as follows: "If it appears that the (partially sighted) patient needs help . . . if he or she is no longer managing . . . I will register that person if he needs special facilities . . . I will register anyone blind, however, who is entitled to it".

Registration is the responsibility of the local authority. However, the patient's approval (or that of his or her parents) is a prerequisite. Registration is important from a legal point of view: there are certain social security and other benefits available to the blind. If a child is to go to a school for the blind, he or she must usually first be certified as educationally blind though not necessarily registered. The Royal National Institute for the Blind charges reduced prices on a number of aids for those who are registered blind and often voluntary societies demand evidence of registration before offering assistance. There is less urgency in being registered as partially sighted in that the scope of benefits is less. However those who are so registered also become eligible for special vocational training, for help in finding jobs, and for certain social security benefits.

In conclusion — raising a different point — a word about the partially sighted as a distinct group: traditionally, they have received less public notice than the blind, and societies and associations formed for supporting the blind have a longer history than those for the partially sighted. As a result, the blind population may have received disproportionate amounts of attention relative to those with partial sight. The severity of the latter group's problems may have been under-acknowledged. This report differs in that it concentrates more on the partially sighted than on the blind. This is not a deliberate attempt to redress the balance: it is simply because many of the examples of integration discussed relate predominantly to the partially sighted. More partially sighted than blind children are integrated in ordinary school settings. For our purposes they are therefore a critically important group.

Notes

(1) For example, for illiterate infants and very young children, there is the STYCAR test of vision (SHERIDAN, MARY D. (1973). *Stycar Vision Test*. NFER.). This is a simple letter-matching test of visual acuity. The PANDA test, also designed by Dr Sheridan, but for more severely handicapped young children, is based on the same principle as the STYCAR test. Also for children who cannot read, there exist Snellen charts based on symbols instead of letters. Crude visual function in infants can also be assessed by electrical means using an electroretinogram.

(2) Another well known test of near vision is the Jaegar Test — a test for reading, in which lines of reading matter are printed in a series of type sizes, often written J 1, J 2, etc.

(3) Newspaper print size is usually N8.

(4) For educational purposes, the blind are defined (according to the 1944 Education Act) as 'pupils who have no sight or whose sight is or is likely to become so defective that they require education by methods not involving the use of sight'. The partially sighted are defined as 'pupils who by reason of defective vision cannot follow the ordinary curriculum without detriment to their sight or to their educational development, but can be educated by special methods involving the use of sight'.

(5) Ophthalmologists would repudiate this suggestion — most are guided by the patient's (or parents') opinion of their ability to cope. These opinion(s) would be combined with visual acuity measures before any recommendations about school placement were made.

(6) The Vernon Committee devoted much attention to the improvement of assessment procedures. See DEPARTMENT OF EDUCATION AND SCIENCE (1972). *The Education of the Visually Handicapped*. (Vernon Report). London: HMSO.

(7) BARRAGA, N.C. (1974a). 'Children with impaired but useful vision — medical and psychological issues', *Proceedings of the Australia and New Zealand Association of Teachers of the Visually Handicapped*. Conference, January, 1974.

(8) BARRAGA, N.C. (1974a). *ibid.*

(9) BARRAGA, N.C. (1975). 'Visually impaired children — development and learning', *Eyepiece*, 1, 4.

(10) For more details, see (a) BARRAGA, N.C. (1964). *Increased Visual Behaviour in Low Vision Children*. New York: American Foundation for the Blind, Research Series 13., (b) BARRAGA, N.C. (1970). *Teachers' Guide for Development of Visual Learning Abilities and Utilisation of Low Vision*. Louisville: American Printing House for the Blind., (c) BARRAGA, N.C. (1974a) *op. cit.*, (d) BARRAGA, N.C. (1974b). 'Perceptual development in visually handicapped children — a practical approach', *Proceedings of the Australia and New Zealand Association of Teachers of the Visually Handicapped*. Conference, January 1974.

(11) The Schools Council is currently funding a project on 'Visual Perception Training of Blind and Partially Sighted 5—11 Year Olds' at the University of Birmingham, under the leadership of Miss E. Chapman and Dr M. Tobin. In addition, research on the use of residual vision is described in TOBIN, M.J. (1972a). 'A study in the improvement of visual efficiency in children registered as blind', *The New Beacon*, 56, 659.

(12) BARRAGA, N.C. (1975) *op. cit.*

(13) BARRAGA, N.C. (1974b) *op. cit.*

(14) In addition, the Disabled Living Foundation in London has a permanent exhibition of aids for the handicapped, including low vision aids for the visually impaired.

(15) Two recent studies conducted by ophthalmic opticians at Moorfields Eye Hospital have pointed to the difference that low vision aids can make to the type of educational experiences visually impaired pupils can enjoy. They conclude:

> 'Many visually handicapped children, particularly those with relatively stable visual prognoses and classified as 'partially sighted' rather than 'blind', may continue to make satisfactory progress within the normal educational system in the presence of certain conditions: 1. The school must be sympathetic. 2. The child (and parents) must be well motivated. 3. There must be a comprehensive ophthalmic service (including the supply and maintenance of aids) readily available.'

GOULD, E. and SILVER, J. (1974). 'The education of children using low vision aids', *Transactions of the Ophthalmological Societies of the United Kingdom*, **XCIV**, 1. See also, SILVER, J. and GOULD, E. (1976). 'A study of some factors concerned in the schooling of visually handicapped children', *Child Care, Health and Development*, 2, 3.

(16) For details of benefits available for the registered blind and partially sighted, see BBC. (1973). *In Touch, Aids and Services for Blind and Partially Sighted People*. BBC: Kent.

(17) Form BD8 is currently being revised. The Vernon Committee made recommendations as follows: first, that the Form BD8 itself should be filled in at the age of 16, with the recommendations regarding education being deleted; that, new sections 'requesting information on near vision . . . and on visual field defects' should be included. The committee further suggested that for children of a younger age a new form ("Notification of Visual Handicap (NVH)") should be devised that requested information about '(a) personal details, (b) means of referral to the ophthalmologist, (c) history of the visual defect, (d) estimation of the visual acuity, for distance in Snellen or Snellen equivalents, for near vision if possible in Times Roman or equivalents, (e) estimation of the visual field with details of vertical or lateral defects, (f) definitive or presumptive diagnosis'. DEPARTMENT OF EDUCATION AND SCIENCE (1972). *op. cit.*

(18) Thus, 'in general a person with visual acuity below 3 / 60 Snellen may be regarded as blind'. However, if his visual acuity is between 3 / 60 but less than 6 / 60 Snellen, he 'may be regarded as blind if the field of vision is considerably contracted but should not be regarded as blind if the visual defect is of long standing and is unaccompanied by any material contraction of the field of vision'. It is stated that a person with a visual acuity of 6 / 60 Snellen or better 'should ordinarily not be regarded as blind', but again there is a small proviso: if the 'field of vision is markedly contracted in the greater part of its extent, and particularly if the contraction is in the lower part of the field' then the individual may be designated 'blind'. A similar kind of specification exists for deciding that someone is 'partially sighted'.

Part Two

Form and Practice

We begin this section of the book with a brief historical resumé of educational provision for the visually impaired. To understand current patterns it helps to appreciate their evolution. Chapter Four discusses integration as it was practised in an earlier educational era and places present developments within a wider chronological context.

Chapter Five introduces the various common and basic kinds of scheme, singling out for discussion certain critical differences between them. We point to the variation in both ideology and practice that are embodied in different approaches to organizing integration.

Chapters Six to Nine then introduce a number of particular schemes, both at home and abroad, that we were able to observe at first hand. These chapters are abbreviated accounts of the schemes. They are deliberately skeletal: the bare bones of their workings, organization, history, special claims and working difficulties. None of these schemes has been the subject of a detailed study and, arguably, a systematic review of individual schemes is long overdue. However, it was not part of our project to undertake comprehensive evaluations of specific programmes and practices, but rather to examine and report on the whole movement towards integrating blind and partially sighted children in ordinary schools. What we include, therefore, are mainly descriptive summaries and a certain amount of interpretative and critical comment. What is intended is that the reader should find here a useful annotated compendium.

Chapter Four

A Historical Perspective

Our study was not conceived in historical terms and what follows is only a brief review of what would certainly merit greater attention. Integration had an earlier life: the present movement is a re-birth of sorts. This is how it came about.

By the end of the 18th century there were four residential schools for the blind — in Liverpool, Bristol, Edinburgh, and London, and others followed in the 19th. The schools for the blind did not, however, cater for all blind children; their selectivity provided the momentum for a movement to educate other blind children in schools for the sighted.

Alexander Barnhill, writing in 1875, argued that more of the population of blind children should be educated; and that to achieve this would probably mean their attending ordinary schools:

> 'Much difficulty or expense has usually stood in the way of the admission of blind children into institutions, and many have been entirely neglected . . . Sufficient indication already appears that the country will not tolerate the education of 50% in institutions, and leave the remainder to grow up uncared for . . . Teaching blind children with the sighted has not been advocated for the purpose of withdrawing children from institutions, but to overtake those not being educated, and to give any one an opportunity of having his child taught at home. Which may be the better education need not be inquired into at present . . . The great matter is to get a good education for all'.[1]

Barnhill, in Glasgow, was one of the leaders of what was obviously a strong movement in favour of educating the blind in sighted schools. The report, in 1889, of the Royal Commission on the Blind, Deaf and Dumb, showed clearly the extent of integration at that time:

> 'The school boards at Bradford, Cardiff, Sunderland, and Glasgow

have undertaken the education of the blind within their district, and 61 children in all are under instruction in these towns, 28 being educated in different schools in Glasgow alone. In most cases the children follow the ordinary time-table with their seeing companions, and associate with them both in school-time and play-time, Bradford and Sunderland being the only exceptions to this. On the occasion of (a visit) to Glasgow, the school board and their teachers expressed themselves as satisfied with the success of the experiment of educating the blind with the seeing in the board schools.

In London the blind children usually attend the ordinary day schools, and share as far as possible in the instruction there given; but they also on specified days, receive special instruction at centres, of which there are 18 . . . The children are examined with the other scholars at the annual government examinations of the ordinary day schools which they attend.'[2]

The 1889 Royal Commission report also revealed the serious state of education for the blind: approximately half of those trained in institutions 'were contributing nothing to their livelihood. Judged by the industrial success of their pupils the institutions had unmistakably failed'.[3] However, the Commission made no proposal for extending education for the blind in sighted schools, despite its expressing the view (described by the Vernon Committee as 'very enlightened') that 'free intercourse with the seeing gives courage and self-reliance to the blind, and a healthy stimulus which enables them to compete more successfully with the seeing in after-life than those who have been brought up altogether in Blind institutions'.[4]

What the Royal Commission did recommend, however, was compulsory education for blind children. This was enacted in the Elementary Education (Blind and Deaf Children) Act 1893: ' . . . the fact of a child being blind or deaf shall not of itself . . . be a reasonable excuse for not causing the child to attend school . . . '. The Act also enjoined 'school authorities . . . to enable blind and deaf children resident in their district . . . to obtain such education in some school for the time being certified by the Education Department as suitable for providing such education'.[5]

The principal way in which education authorities discharged these obligations was through paying of fees to existing voluntary schools. These schools — the antecedents of some of the non-maintained special schools of today — therefore expanded and improved. And since the pressure for integration in the 1870s and 1880s had to do with obtaining education for those without it — rather than with displacing the special schools — these schools emerged as the norm, a trend further reinforced by the new procedure under which schools 'suitable' for teaching the blind had to be officially certified.

There were other trends in the same period that did not favour integration — notably the triumph of braille. Though long over, it is worth examining further what has become known as the 'War of the Types': its military history is remarkably contemporary.

The early ideas of Barnhill, that blind children should go to schools for the sighted, was linked to the idea that they should not learn a type that bore no resemblance to the shapes used in ordinary print: they should not, in other words, learn braille, because it could lead to separation: the sighted could not read it or teach it without being specially trained. On the other side, Abbé Carton, writing in 1838, expressed the argument for raised print (the basic alternative to braille).

'The largest number of blind is found amongst the poor, and the greatest misfortune of the blind consists in their isolation. All our efforts should tend towards bringing them near to ourselves, and to make their education as like our own as possible, and to begin this education as quickly as may be, and not to think that a special institution is needed for teaching them to read. If the characters in their books are those which we teach to other children, ordinary schools will be able to admit from their infancy these unfortunate beings who have been hitherto kept afar off under a false pretext; and their misfortune will lie less heavily upon them, their intellect will be developed and the advantages they will derive from their stay in special establishments will be in harmony with what they will have learnt before entering them.'[6]

As we know, of course, the Dot triumphed — in a War of the Types that was vehement and vituperative. That it did so was due to the discovery that it was easier for the blind to learn and to use braille than other tactile types that were currently being advocated, all of which were based on adapting roman shapes (good for visual but not tactile discrimination). Although the blind pupil might learn to read in a less 'ordinary' way, his or her eventual performance (in reading) was rendered superior by the 'special' nature of the medium used. Armitage (1886) explains this:

'It has often been urged that the blind ought to employ the same character as the seeing in order to receive assistance when reading. This argument might be of some weight if no simpler character existed: but where the choice lies between a character to read which the blind man requires assistance and one which is so simple that he can read it himself, there ought to be no doubt as to the choice. Another common, but equally fallacious, argument is that by adopting a different character from that used by the seeing there is danger of the isolation of the blind being increased; this is not feared by those who it is intended to benefit. A man is isolated by everything which renders the acquisition of knowledge difficult and tedious and his isolation is diminished by everything which facilitates his power of self-education. The best type for him to use is evidently that which he can read most fluently and most correctly; therefore, in the great majority of cases, it will *not* be the roman character.'[7]

We have dwelt on this issue not only because the displacement of the early integration schemes was stimulated by the adoption of a reading medium requiring special instruction; but also because we find here, in different form and scale, an argument similar to one in the present day in favour of special schooling: that it may be less 'natural' to go to a special school but the final outcome (independence in society and a satisfying life as an adult) justifies its non-usual nature.

The consolidation of the special schools continued, with legislation in 1920 (Blind Persons Act)[8] and 1921 (Education Act)[9] confirming these as normal practice. In 1936, a joint committee of the College of Teachers of the Blind and the Royal National Institute for the Blind reported on the education for the blind in Britain. Their report demonstrates how taken for granted separate education for the visually impaired had become by that time:

'... it should be stated that there are certain serious administrative problems that would have to be faced if the education of blind children in schools for the seeing were attempted in this country ... The same difficulties were encountered by the Committee on Partially Sighted Children, when they framed the recommendation that where possible partially sighted children should be educated in special classes in the ordinary schools, but in the case of the blind the difficulties are increased fourfold; for there is only one blind child to approximately 3,500 sighted children, whereas the proportion of partially sighted children is one to 1,000.'[10]

Nevertheless, the 1936 report also showed that the idea of educating the visually impaired with sighted children had not altogether withered, and that there were lively disagreements.

'... If, however, the education of the blind with the sighted were intrinsically desirable, an effort to overcome administrative difficulties would have to be made. What, then, are the educational advantages claimed for the system? They may be summed up under two heads:

1. The advantage of the blind child remaining in his home environment.
2. The social and educational advantages of the blind child being brought into contact with fully sighted children in the ordinary Elementary Schools.

The first argument is essentially one in favour of the Day School over the Residential School. It is, moreover, an argument which can be used by both sides. The advantages of a satisfactory home environment are obvious, as they provide elevating and stimulating factors in a child's life. On the other hand, bad home conditions, due to poverty and neglect, or over-indulgence and ignorance, will have an even greater effect on the young blind child than on the young sighted child. With regard to the second argument, the Committee fully appreciate the view that there are certain broad social advantages attaching to the system of educating blind children in ordinary Elementary Schools. We are agreed that the socializing force and normality of the ordinary school would be a great benefit to blind children, but in our view this benefit would be offset by certain serious objections ... Our witnesses were not in agreement with the claim that competition with other children is likely to stimulate blind children to greater endeavour, or to engender the feeling of equality of the blind child with his sighted fellows. They are of the opinion that the sense of being different from the sighted will be accentuated, and that he is likely therefore to develop an "inferiority complex" ... We think that the advantages of the system of educating blind children in ordinary schools are outweighed by the disadvantages. We are of the opinion that the education of blind children, particularly of young blind children, is of too specialized a character to permit of its being treated as an appendage to the scheme of education in the ordinary elementary school.'[11]

However, the Committee left the door slightly ajar:

'In forming this conclusion, however, it should be understood that the Committee has in mind the blind child of average attainments. The conclusion must not be construed as definitely closing against the gifted blind child all other avenues than the present type of school for the blind. Different considerations arise with the child suitable for secondary and University education.'

The Committee also acknowledged one danger inherent in special schooling:

'The strength of the position of those who advocate the education of the blind child side by side with the seeing is emphasized by the danger of "segregation" and "institutionalism". Though many teachers today are alive to these dangers, we feel that much more might be done in our schools to overcome the inevitable disadvantages of segregation . . . '

Special schools for the partially sighted developed much later than those for the blind: until the end of the 19th century partially sighted children attended either schools for the blind or ordinary schools where they were taught (with what skill or sensitivity one can only guess at) alongside sighted pupils on the same lines. In 1934 the Board of Education[12] recommended that partially sighted children should no longer go to schools for the blind, and that 'when possible, partially sighted children should be educated in classes forming an integral part of elementary schools'; when this was not possible they should attend residential schools that should be 'set apart for partially sighted children'. After the Second World War, and the Regulations[13] following the 1944 Education Act that differentiated the partially sighted as a separate category of handicapped pupils, four special residential schools for the partially sighted were set up. Little progress was made in establishing special classes in ordinary schools, the numbers not being sufficient.

The next major development in thinking about educational arrangements for the visually impaired was the Report of the Committee of Enquiry on the Education of the Visually Handicapped, published in 1972, to which we have already drawn attention. This discussed at some length the arguments for and against increased integrated provision. It could not be said to come down firmly in favour of integration, nor firmly against it. It provided, for instance, an extract from evidence by a former HM Inspector that was cautious:

' " . . . the majority of teachers do not know the special techniques, methods, equipment etc. required . . . When experiments of this kind are made, especially in the case of blind children, care must be taken to see that the conditions in the ordinary school are suitable as far as premises, organisations etc. are concerned; that the school is one which welcomes the exceptional child; that the staff involved are prepared to accept help and advice. The child, too, must be carefully selected. It is most likely to work with an intelligent, competent, independent child w.. has already learnt self-management and the basic skills of reading and writing braille" '.[14]

The Committee spoke of integration's 'dangers as well as its merits': 'It can lead to a demand that handicapped children should be given exactly the same educational treatment as other children; and we realize that it is impossible for visually handicapped children to progress satisfactorily in a sighted school unless they are given special facilities'. At the same time, the members of the Committee were 'deeply impressed by the argument that, if visually handicapped children are to be fitted through their education to live in a world with sighted people, the best way for them to acquire the necessary ability and confidence is to mix as freely as possible with sighted children during their school days'.

They reviewed some of the American literature on the supposed effects of integration, (a literature marked by its confused conclusions and the difficulty in generalizing from it)[15]; reported, in some detail, the Tapton Mount scheme of 'open education' (discussed in Chapter Six); heard evidence about a scheme of integrating blind children in ordinary schools that had survived until the 1930s in Glasgow; pointed out that many other countries still had residential schools; and concluded that 'before any firm judgments can be made about the extent to which integrated education is possible . . . we believe that further systematic experimentation, with education both in ordinary and special classes, is desirable . . . '.

Following publication of the Vernon report there was extensive and lively discussion of its findings and recommendations among those directly concerned with educating the visually impaired in England and Wales. Disappointment has been widely expressed that little governmental or local action seems to have followed it. In the ensuing debate specifically to do with integration, a major contribution was provided in some extended comments from the Association of Blind and Partially Sighted Teachers and Students (ABAPSTAS) and the National Federation of the Blind (NFB), in which, along with much else, an elaborate countrywide scheme of 'supported integration' in ordinary schools was proposed. 'Integrating' schools would be ones where,

' . . . though the great majority of the pupils are unhandicapped sighted children, provision is also made for the education of a group of visually handicapped pupils, who receive a considerable part of their education as members of the ordinary, predominantly sighted classes, but who enjoy there the support of, and also receive some part of their education in, a unit for visually handicapped established within the school . . . '[16]

Many more visually handicapped children would thus be able to live at home.

These proposals, advanced in a fairly outspoken manner, provoked strong resistance, which in turn led to further advocacy. It is not our intention here to try to summarize the arguments stemming from the Vernon Report and this major critique of it. To do so would lead us too far from our own independent examination of integration at work. However, the issues raised will certainly recur in later chapters and we shall draw on both documents.

In conclusion, what is highlighted by this foray into the past is that the move to integrate is of long-standing – indeed, more blind children were in ordinary schools in 1889 than there are now. Also clear is that contrasting forms of schooling have provoked, through the years, a series of important although basically similar arguments centring on the question: 'What kind of schooling benefits the visually impaired child the most?' The predominance of special schooling can be seen as having arisen through a combination of influences – not least the invention, in the late 19th century, of braille and its adoption as the basic educational medium for the blind. The early advocacy of ordinary schooling for the visually impaired was superseded, and the early examples of integration consigned to oblivion.

Notes

(1) BARNHILL, A. (1875). *A New Era in the Education of Blind Children.* Glasgow: Glass and Co.

(2) REPORT OF THE ROYAL COMMISSION ON THE BLIND, DEAF AND DUMB (1889). In: RITCHIE, J.M. (1930). *Concerning the Blind*. Edinburgh: Oliver and Boyd. This quotation, however, should be treated with caution. In 1889, payment was by results and teachers may not have bothered to teach children who were more difficult to educate because they might not earn a grant. In 1889, the school leaving age was 10 years and children of three or four were often encouraged to go to school. So while an appreciable number of quite severely handicapped children may have attended ordinary schools and thus been integrated, evidence that they actually achieved anything is tenuous. The only alternative to such schooling was often no schooling and perhaps only in this sense was ordinary education considered satisfactory. The main driving force in the late 19th century was to ensure that all blind children received at least some education. None of the advocates of ordinary schooling was opposed to special schooling.

(3) RITCHIE, J.M. (1930) *ibid.*

(4) This quotation draws attention to the disadvantages of the then special institutions and not specifically to the advantages of ordinary schooling for the blind. Had there been clear evidence at the time that education of the

handicapped was better in ordinary schools than in special schools, the latter would never have grown as they did.

(5) ELEMENTARY EDUCATION (BLIND AND DEAF CHILDREN) ACT (1893). London: HMSO.

(6) ABBÉ CARTON (1838). In: RITCHIE, J.M. (1930) *op. cit.*

(7) ARMITAGE, T.R. (1886). *The Education and Employment of the Blind.* London: British and Foreign Blind Association.

(8) BLIND PERSONS ACT (1920). London: HMSO.

(9) EDUCATION ACT (1921). London: HMSO.

(10) COLLEGE OF TEACHERS OF THE BLIND AND THE ROYAL NATIONAL INSTITUTE FOR THE BLIND (1936). *The Education of the Blind: A Survey.* London: Arnold.

(11) COLLEGE OF TEACHERS OF THE BLIND AND THE ROYAL NATIONAL INSTITUTE FOR THE BLIND (1936) *ibid.*

(12) BOARD OF EDUCATION (1934). *Report of the Committee on Partially Sighted Children.* London: HMSO. In 1931, the Board of Education appointed a Committee under the chairmanship of Dr R.H. Crowley 'to enquire into and report upon the medical, educational and social aspects of the problems affecting partially blind children'. The Committee's report was published in 1934.

(13) HANDICAPPED PUPILS SCHOOL HEALTH SERVICE REGULATIONS S.I. (1945). No. 1076. London: HMSO.

(14) DEPARTMENT OF EDUCATION AND SCIENCE (1972). *The Education of the Visually Handicapped*, (Vernon Report). London: HMSO.

(15) For example, McGuinness, in a study of 97 totally blind pupils aged 8–10 years who were integrated either in resource room or itinerant teacher programmes, or who were attending a day special school found that: (a) braille reading skills could be taught as effectively in integrated settings as in a special school; (b) 'integrated settings result in greater independence and social maturity than the special school setting'; (c) that integrated pupils were more likely to have sighted friends. (McGUINNESS, R.M. (1970). 'A descriptive study of blind children educated in the itinerant teacher, resource room, and special school settings', *American Foundation for the Blind, Research Bulletin*, 20.) Havill, in a study of 63 integrated visually impaired children, each matched with a sighted child, concluded that 'the visually handicapped subjects were of lower socioeconomic status and thus less well accepted than their normally seeing classmates, but that above average achievement and itinerant service were factors which had a positive effect on status'. (HAVILL, S.J. (1970). 'The sociometric status of visually handicapped students in public school classes', *American Foundation for the Blind, Research Bulletin*, 20.) Since the publication of the Vernon Report, one very important contribution to research on integration has been published. Schindele, as part of an exhaustive study, tested 36 visually

impaired pupils integrated in resource or itinerant programmes, who were matched with a visually impaired group in residential special schooling, and with a sighted control group of equivalent size. He found no significant difference in the social adjustment of visually impaired and sighted pupils, nor between visually impaired pupils in different kinds of schools, nor between the samples of partially sighted, severely visually impaired, and totally blind pupils. Likewise there were no differences between males and females and between 'resource' and 'itinerant' integration programmes. He was able to show a slight connection between social adjustment and intelligence for children who were visually impaired and integrated: the more intelligent were more socially adjusted. This connection was not evident in children who attended residential schools. He also found a little evidence to suggest that children from higher socioeconomic backgrounds in residential schools were likely to have 'low social adjustment' (SCHINDELE, R. (1974). 'The social adjustment of visually handicapped children in different educational settings', *American Foundation for the Blind, Research Bulletin*, 28.)

(16) NATIONAL FEDERATION OF THE BLIND AND THE ASSOCIATION OF BLIND AND PARTIALLY SIGHTED TEACHERS AND STUDENTS (1973). *Educational Provision for the Visually Handicapped: Comments on the 'Vernon Report'*. London: The Association.

Chapter Five

Varieties of Integration

'Integrated' is perhaps one of the most over-used and worn out words of our time. Aside from integrated personalities and integrated communities, schools have integrated days and integrated (inter-disciplinary) curricula. As a term it has acquired certain overtones — it tends to be surrounded by a positive aura. Whatever is integrated is not disjointed, not segregated, not unnecessarily fragmented; customarily, whatever is integrated is coherent, unified and together — and by implication, good. It would be good perhaps to be rid of the term in the context of special education — the favourable aura around the word itself does little to assist in unravelling the complexities of alternative patterns of schooling. It helps to polarize attitudes and oversimplify issues. Unfortunately, there is no alternative, more neutral term: 'mainstreaming' is used in the USA, but this could easily lead, according to one official, to special schools being caricatured in time as 'backwaters'. We do not see the need to import an American term: we use 'integration', but are mindful of its hazards.

Integration, in the field of special education, serves several purposes: it is a slogan and a battle cry; it is an educational goal; a social movement in progress; and a loose, summary description of various educational procedures — ranging from occasional functions where visually impaired and sighted children are brought together for social mixing, to the intended complete assimilation of visually impaired pupils into a sighted teaching milieu.

The current debate about integration raises fundamental questions about the aims of education. It proceeds in parallel with a wider debate about the value of comprehensive schooling, raising the issue of selective, separate education versus equality of provision for identifiable groups. It goes beyond education: what is involved is a wider question of the treatment of minority groups, and societal attitudes towards assimilating them into open society. As a head teacher of a school for the blind explained, it was a trend in society generally to involve the handicapped person in the community; a similar concern was evident in other fields: "Unmarried mothers, young criminals, the physically disabled" were all thought to benefit from being drawn into the community. The 1959 Mental Health Act[1], for instance, effected a transformation in the treatment of the psychiatrically ill, returning many who had formerly been hospitalized to their local communities.

Like so many educational debates, the controversy surrounding integration has political and ideological components: it is often emotive. One of the most outspoken critics of special schools for the blind spoke directly about this: "It's a political issue, and every political issue, by its very nature, is emotional — people's interests are involved; if (we) had not felt emotional the current debate wouldn't exist". Others, usually those in favour of retaining special schools, preferred a less highly charged discussion.

Our own aim is neither to decide nor dampen the debate but to move beyond it, to look at the wider framework that contains it. However, we can contribute the following two observations about the debate itself. First, similarly fierce controversies have taken place elsewhere — for example, in the United States between five and 10 years ago, when the issue of integration for the visually impaired was hotly debated. Now the argument has subsided: integration is widely accepted, and in the light of this, many special schools have redefined their aims and operations. There is general acceptance of the idea of 'options' — that children with visual impairment may take a variety of educational routes, according to their need. One American, firmly convinced of the value of integration for the visually impaired child, was nevertheless adamant that special schools should remain as an alternative. The second observation is that discussions about integration are currently proceeding apace in several other European countries, notably West Germany, Austria, and Sweden: in other words, it is not a local British dispute.

Integration, as a descriptive term used in talking about kinds of schooling, is elusive and imprecise. There is a lack of uniformity in its use, and evidence of confused thinking. For instance, according to some people, visually impaired children attending their local ordinary schools are, by definition, integrated: i.e. they are not attending special schools. However, if these same children spend most of their time in a special class, or a unit attached to the school, many people would argue that they are not 'properly integrated'. Others insist that *bona fide* integration is when visually impaired children take part in ordinary lessons alongside sighted pupils. Even then, a minority would still require evidence that these children were fully accepted by their sighted peers, were not isolated in either a social or an academic sense, and that they felt an identity with their class, before accepting that they were genuinely integrated. This suggests that integration is an ideal: it is like equality — something that may never be attained to a degree that is beyond further challenge.

Differences between schemes

No one single scheme qualifies as *the* paradigm of integration. When we use the term we are speaking of a number of different organizational formats which share elements of a common philosophy — and often that is about all they share. Given the variation in the criteria used to assess what constitutes integration, it is hardly surprising that the various schemes we examined — all laying claim to be legitimate exemplars — were often quite dissimilar from one another.

All this might imply that schemes or styles of integration are somewhat haphazard. However, the variation is not altogether disorderly. A comprehensive and detailed classification of schemes might become rather involved, but there are certain dimensions along which schemes arrange themselves.

The first major dimension has to do with deployment of resources — financial, technical, and human. A unit, for blind or for partially sighted children, attached to an ordinary school, represents one common kind of integration scheme. It represents a concentration of resources in one place. Pupils are usually gathered from a sizeable catchment area, live at home, and travel daily to the unit where the resources (teachers, braille or large print books, low vision aids, typewriters, etc.) are assembled.

In terms of resource management, units may make eminent sense, although they require a sufficiently large group of children with broadly similar needs in order to be viable. However, children provided for in this way will, by definition, be associating with others of a similar kind — at least according to the public definition of partial sight or blindness; there is therefore the possibility of limited interaction with sighted children.[2] In addition, although a handicap may be common to a number of children, the consequences of that handicap are likely to vary from child to child, so that grouping them may make less sense in practice than it does on paper.

A unit of this basic type has a certain activity level, and this may also influence the degree of interaction between handicapped pupils and non-handicapped peers. A certain tension can be identified: the more active a unit tends to be, the more may the children it caters for be treated in ways other than 'ordinary'; conversely, if a unit is not particularly active, it may not be justifying its existence. If it plays a large part in teaching visually impaired children, it means that these children spend less time in ordinary classrooms; on the other hand, if it plays too small a role it does not justify its cost. Certain units we visited were highly active for individual children at times when they needed individualized attention, specialized resources, or temporary withdrawal into a less demanding environment, but otherwise stayed out of day-to-day teaching activity and responsibility. This is in contrast to the more usual kinds of unit found in England and Wales, that tend to retain certain children as 'their' pupils.

The opposite end of the 'resources dimension' is where both resources and children are distributed rather than centralized. Pupils in this form of integration attend a local school — not necessarily the neighbourhood school — and specialized resources are literally brought round to them by a peripatetic teacher.[3] Under this system, pupils have far more restricted access to resources, whether human or technical. Balanced against this, however, is that usually they do not have to travel far to school, have their school friends for out-of-school friends as well, and are not in any sense institutionally separated. They are likely to be based in a sighted class, spending most of the school day as full members of that class, being withdrawn only for specified purposes — for example, typewriting lessons or extra reading practice.

This, then, is a major dimension or division of schemes: it pertains to whether pupils travel to a particular centre with its concentration of resources and teaching expertise; or whether resources are distributed across a number of schools, in which case there will be fewer of them for each individual school. In some ways, it is analogous to the contrast between shopping from the van which comes round twice a week, or going to the high street store. As in provision of educational support and services, there are advantages and disadvantages in both.

However, there are other classificatory dimensions too. Schemes, for instance, differ in the emphasis they accord to 'social' and 'academic' goals. All schemes may claim to weigh both these elements highly within a child's total school experience; but in fact there are marked discrepancies in the ways different schemes have been constituted and are run — their philosophies in action. The desirability of social mixing, for example, is more likely to be emphasized when an individual scheme moves away from being explicitly academic. If a child studies 'higher status' subjects (e.g. mathematics, English) in the unit, and 'lower status' subjects (e.g. music, home economics) with sighted peers, it is clear that integration is probably regarded as desirable — but in non-academic ways. In its most extreme form, the non-academic view of integration is evident when pupils take part only in such activities as assembly and dance.

A third dimension of difference concerns the child's sense of identification with the school or sighted pupils with whom he or she is integrated, together with a sense of responsibility or 'ownership' that the staff involved feel toward the child. Both these factors are closely related to the actual working policy pursued. If a child is attached to a unit but has some lessons with sighted pupils in the main school, does he or she feel a member of that class? To what school entity does he or she belong? Who is ultimately responsible for him or her, the unit teacher or the teacher of the sighted class? The various arrangements we studied differed greatly in this respect: most units operated as a child's 'home base', although some were only visited for equipment such as low vision aids or for specific individualized teaching. Where two separate schools are involved — as in integration from a day special school — the questions of membership and responsibility become even more complicated.

These dimensions of difference are not the only candidates, but we fix on them as three of the most basic. As we briefly examine the various integration schemes, we shall see how each relates to these dimensions and to others yet to be introduced.

Notes

(1) MENTAL HEALTH ACT (1959). London: HMSO.

(2) The limited opportunity for interaction with sighted and non-handicapped children was a common criticism of special school campuses — a minority form of educational provision for the visually impaired which we have decided against discussing in detail. There are three campuses in England and Wales which include a school for the visually impaired alongside other special schools. The basic rationale of such an arrangement is that it allows for sharing of facilities and staff, and provision of a range of experiences greater than any one school could offer by itself. The underlying ideology is one of encouraging contact with sighted pupils even if these pupils are handicapped in different ways. The Vernon Committee recommended further experiments with campus provision '. . . in order to meet regional needs, in the grouping of several children with different handicaps on campus sites, sharing a full range of educational and medical resources, with ordinary schools adjoining'. (DEPARTMENT OF EDUCATION AND SCIENCE (1972). *The Education of the Visually Handicapped*, (Vernon Report). London: HMSO.) At present, there exists limited contact with ordinary schools and for this reason we have not included campuses as an example of integration.

(3) In America, what we call here 'peripatetic integration', is referred to as 'itinerant integration'.

Chapter Six

Three Schemes for Integrating the Blind

Most of the schemes of integration discussed in Part II involve the partially sighted. In England and Wales, there exist only two schemes specifically designed to integrate blind children. Both are based on special residential schools, St Vincent's in Liverpool and Tapton Mount in Sheffield. The two schemes have involved only a small number of carefully selected secondary-aged blind children, all except one, braille users.[1] Pupils are attached to the special school, which serves as a base and a central resource bank, but they attend a local school for the sighted on a full-time basis.

Both experiments were regarded as revolutionary at their inception. They received only muted official support – introducing and keeping them going relied heavily upon the efforts of firmly committed individuals whose names still remain closely linked with the schemes. They have widely been referred to as experiments in 'open education' and we use the same term here.

Open education was prompted by observation of experiments overseas, particularly in the USA. It seems appropriate, therefore, to include in this chapter a note about a particularly well-established scheme in the USA, where integration of the blind has existed for some time and is no longer considered unusual.

Open education – outline of two schemes[2]

First, we briefly discuss the two British schemes separately, before considering the characteristics they share in common. St Vincent's is an all-age, Roman Catholic residential school for both blind and partially sighted pupils,[3] with a national catchment area.

The rationale for introducing open education in Liverpool was that a small number of pupils should have the opportunity of following a full GCE O-level curriculum,[4] St Vincent's itself only offering CSE. During the day, therefore, the open education pupils attend two single-sex, Roman Catholic grammar schools, both located within walking distance of the special school. St Vincent's continues as the pupils' residential base until their fifth year, after which they are boarded out locally.

Following the receipt of formal approval by the Department of Education and Science and the clarification of the administrative arrangements, the St Vincent's scheme began in 1961 when the first pupil entered the fourth year of the boys' grammar school. This late entry was unusual. Normally, subsequent children have entered the first year, (although aged 12+, having completed an extra year in the primary department at St Vincent's[5]). The first girl began at the girls' grammar school in 1962. Altogether, a total of 12 pupils have been involved.[6]

Contact between St Vincent's and the local grammar schools is not extensive. A counsellor, based at St Vincent's and only visiting the grammar schools by rare invitation, supervises and assists pupils with their homework every evening, offering tuition to supplement day-time lessons where necessary, reads extracts of books not in braille, consults reference books, and transcribes print into braille or arranges for transcription.

Pupils' friends come from both schools, although their St Vincent's friends leave the special school at the end of the fifth year; thereafter the pupils' affiliation tends to be more with the host grammar school. The problems of identification referred to in Chapter Five are apparent in this scheme. After attending the grammar school for the whole day, the pupils return to St Vincent's for a specified period of homework every evening and thus re-enter the special school milieu. There, they are set apart from their peers, not only because they have their own "grammar school room" for study — "no one else was allowed in there apart from ourselves and our tutor" — but also because homework time does not coincide exactly with that of the St Vincent's pupils. This sense of 'split identity' was frequently remarked upon by the ex-pupils: "We used to come home in the evenings and we were the *grammar school* children. We had some kind of rank . . . You did tend to think you were better than other people". Keeping up friendships with sighted peers was also hampered by this arrangement — at least, until the sixth form when pupils were boarded out — as they could only meet such friends at weekends.

Some of the open education pupils admitted to conflicting loyalties, faced as they were with two schools, one their 'surrogate home' which, in turn, was different from their parental home: "It got a bit confusing at times . . . in the sixth form, it got even more complicated . . . You've got one set of rules at St Vincent's, a set at the grammar school, a set at your lodgings, a set at home . . . you can't please four sets of people at once".

Turning now to the Tapton Mount scheme, we find a broadly similar experiment to integrate blind pupils. The scheme in Sheffield was launched in 1969, some time later than the one at St Vincent's. Tapton Mount is a local authority residential primary school for the blind.[7] Open education, however, involves secondary-aged pupils; it is a scheme for Tapton Mount's school leavers. To date, nine pupils have been involved. The host sighted school is, in this case, a coeducational comprehensive school, one-and-a-half miles away. Pupils attend the comprehensive school daily, returning in the evening to their residential base — a hostel attached to Tapton Mount school.

The underlying rationale in setting up the Sheffield scheme again included an academic component: it was hoped that pupils who were potentially "university material" could be catered for in an integrated setting. The scheme also placed particular emphasis on social aspects of integration: "total segregation is wrong . . . children are living a shut up life, shut away from the good and evil influences that other children have . . . we should teach them to be independent . . . (if they) have to go out at 17+, why shouldn't they go out earlier?" (originator of the Tapton Mount Scheme).

Unlike the Liverpool scheme, there is very close collaboration between the two schools in Sheffield. Specifically, two teachers from Tapton Mount have been designated 'resource teachers' to the pupils taking part in the scheme. They operate in both schools, running a small resource centre in a temporary prefabricated building on the comprehensive school campus. This provides storage for equipment, facilities for typing, brailling, tape recording, and serves as a quiet workroom for both resource staff and pupils. A thermoforming machine is also available. The resource teachers make maps, thermoform diagrams, braille texts, and record teaching material. They are also responsible for liaising between different agencies, e.g. examination boards, the RNIB, external readers and volunteer braillists. Occasionally they assist in the classroom at Tapton Comprehensive, though they have no formal teaching responsibilities there. They also have residential duties in the hostel at Tapton Mount.

The two open education schemes share much in common. Certain understandings were established when the schemes were set up. Thus, in both cases, the receiving schools accepted open education on a "goodwill basis", teachers "assured that they would not be expected to alter methods of approach to their work"; integrated pupils would be well prepared, and the special schools would be responsible for their out of school time. Emphasis was placed on resources: "supportive services are the key to it all . . . attempts at integration by (simply) shoving a child into a school are doomed to failure". The extra staff (counsellors in Liverpool, resource teachers in Sheffield) were appointed.

In advance of setting up the schemes there was much else to do: brailling of necessary books, locating volunteer readers, transcribers and helpers, setting up facilities for thermoforming, providing equipment, storage space, and living accommodation. At Tapton Mount, braille book production alone made use of some 30 volunteers (housewives, prisoners, and members of charitable clubs) — "if you are going to admit (blind) children into a comprehensive and expect them to do research work using reference books, then you must realize that ordinary (i.e. sighted) children have ten times as many books as blind children" (originator of the scheme). The preparations began well before the first pupil's transfer, and further resources have been added since. In both cases, the host schools were described as suitable because they were "relatively traditional" in curriculum terms: the problems of brailling would be far greater with a resource-based teaching programme.

The curriculum offered to integrated pupils was as near to that of the sighted pupils as possible. Those interested and able to join in games and craft subjects did so; academically no subjects were prescribed.[8]

In the classroom, pupils used cassette recorders and Perkins braillers for note-taking. They were provided with braille copies of texts, prepared in advance, which were often complemented by recorded extracts on tapes. Two sets of bulky books and heavy equipment were supplied — one set stored at each location. Material for particular lessons could be transcribed and thermoformed or recorded at short notice as both schools had the necessary equipment. Homework was usually typed, although subjects like maths needed to be done in braille and were 'written over' by the resource teachers. Teachers at the ordinary schools helped by verbalizing more material or, if appropriate, by drawing larger than normal diagrams on the blackboard; sighted peers assisted by reading notes off the board and by partnering the blind child for science experiments.

At the inception of the schemes, the introduction of blind children into the ordinary school prompted a tendency for both teachers and sighted pupils to overcompensate. Teachers at the ordinary school confirmed that they were self-conscious of their behaviour (particularly in subjects which relied heavily on visual material) and the visually impaired pupils felt themselves to be over-indulged and marked out as special. As the novelty of the schemes wore off, teachers became more confident and were prepared deliberately to gloss over difficulties; for example, they became less concerned about discussing poetry based on visual simile, symbolism and metaphor.

The visually impaired pupils themselves were anxious to be as independent as possible but ready to accept assistance where necessary, for example, with geometry, light and colour experiments in science, and mapwork in geography. Such problems were partly overcome with the help of the resource teachers or counsellors who transcribed maps and graphs into tactile form, made models, and adapted 'light' into auditory sensations where possible.

What is striking about both open education schemes is that they are highly selective. The choice of pupils has rested largely with the two special school head teachers. Likely candidates are identified early in the junior school, and in their final junior year, extra preparatory tuition is given in typing, braille and mobility. In both schemes, selection is rigorous. Pupils must display most, if not all, of the following: emotional and social maturity ("They must have no chips about their handicap"), "absolute mobility" (they were not to be viewed as "physical cripples"), an equable personality, expertise in braille and typing, and — in the words of one head teacher — be "physically acceptable". Most of all, candidates had to demonstrate high academic potential. No candidate from St Vincent's suffered from an additional handicap. Three of the Tapton Mount pupils had useful residual vision, but as the then head explained: "this was not a reason for selecting them, but was coincidental to their satisfying the other criteria".

The selection criteria have rarely been relaxed: the innovators wanted to demonstrate that integration was both viable and desirable, and individual failures would have cast doubt on the schemes themselves. The originator of the Sheffield scheme remarked that he "was under the microscope, I could not afford to fail — for myself or for the sake of the children". This cautiousness, in choosing for integration only those children whose success is reasonably well assured, has continued. A lack of "suitable candidates" recently has led to declining numbers of children in the two schemes.

Several past pupils queried what they saw as rigidity in selection, although they all agreed that integration was not suitable for every blind child. Often they thought that non-academic criteria for selecting candidates were the most significant in determining whether integration was successful or not. Here are some of their remarks:

"In a sense, an intelligent blind person will make it anyway . . . it is the middle ground — the blind child who can get a couple of O-levels or three CSEs . . . who is the person who needs integration . . . and needs it most."

"For open education, (you have to be) a hard worker, friendly and conform to what they (the sighted) do."

"If you ignore the academic side, they (i.e. candidates for open education) . . . have got to have the will to mix and get independent . . . they don't want to have a chip on their shoulders . . . or feel sorry for themselves."

"(For integration) . . . you've got to be adjusted in that you've got to be used to mixing with people."

Almost without exception, pupils thought that their "psychological make-up" had enabled them to derive benefits from integration. Essential characteristics were thought to include "an ability to adjust", an acceptance that one had "to play the game by other people's rules", and a capacity to "see the normal world and to accept it as it is" — in effect, "a coming to terms with ordinary society".

Both teachers and pupils agreed that the integrated pupils were well accepted by both peers and teachers in the ordinary schools. Pupils from Tapton Mount were described as "totally absorbed" in an atmosphere of "continuing acceptance of the scheme by the staff of the comprehensive" (Head of Tapton Mount). The head of St Vincent's felt that "the sighted people reacted to them (the blind pupils) as people". The pupils themselves agreed: "Once the kids in the school realized I was a normal functioning individual who knew far more dirty jokes than they did, would give cheek to the teacher, would stick with the lads when it mattered, wouldn't snitch, then what difference could it make to them that I was blind? . . . It was satisfying to know that you could make friends and your sight didn't matter". A current pupil remarked, "I love coming here (i.e. to the sighted school) because I am no longer special . . . The teachers' attitudes are very healthy".

Open education has involved children atypical of the blind population as a whole. Yet it is frequently described in terms of its being 'an experiment' from which a lot might be learned of a more general use. Others consider that all it can prove is that integration of this nature can work because it involves children "who will make it anyway". What this raises explicitly is the possibility of relaxing selection criteria and seeing whether open education could work with a less highly selected group. It should be recognized, however, that anything but a highly cautious approach in the early years might have been irresponsible: as one person involved put it — "Educational experiments involve tinkering with other people's lives".

Proposals to extend open education — other than by selecting a broader group for the present schemes — include extending the experiment to other special schools; using more and different host schools with the present special schools; and involving younger children. However, all proposals have to be weighed against the need for sizeable amounts of support (both technical and human) that are required to sustain it successfully. The importance of such resources was repeatedly acknowledged, not least by some of the pupils: "One ought to emphasize that the 'backup' services for integrated education are enormous . . . absolutely huge . . . I couldn't have done integrated education without a massive amount of work behind the scenes, especially braille transcription . . . ."

Finally, while the open education schemes may have explicitly adhered to academic goals, social benefits were those most frequently commended by ex-pupils: "I think the major thing gained was independence . . . getting on with people, being tolerant of people who do not understand the situation", said one. Another added, "Socially, I think I had the greatest gain because it helped me realize exactly the sort of environment that I will be mixing in with in everyday life". All the pupils interviewed felt they had succeeded in integration, had lost nothing through attending a sighted school, and all were grateful for the invaluable experience they had gained. Many commented as well on the ease with which they had been able to approach further education or employment as a result of familiarity with the demands of the "sighted world".

Braille Resource Program, Medford, Massachusetts[9]

Both the schemes described above were based on ideas gained in the United States. An opportunity presented itself to study an American example of integration for blind pupils. It is included — despite the fact that only a very limited study could be made of it — because it represents an example of 'total' integration of blind pupils. In both the Sheffield and Liverpool experiments the special schools retained an important function.

At Kennedy School in Medford, Massachusetts, a resource programme specifically designed for braille users was set up in 1957: its main aim being to serve integrated blind pupils from kindergarten to Grade 8 (the end of junior high school). At the time of our visit in autumn 1975, 10 blind pupils were attached to the centre, only one of whom came from Medford itself.[10] The other nine came from neighbouring areas, all within 40—45 minutes drive from the school.[11] The child's home town pays for a taxi service as well as meeting tuition fees. Often a town finds it more economic to make use of the Medford centre than to pay for a special teacher for only one or two blind children.

The braille resource centre is a room set aside at the Kennedy Elementary School. It is staffed by one full-time teacher (with previous experience at a special school for the blind), who is responsible for the programme. The resource teacher has several responsibilities: teaching braille reading and writing (using the Perkins brailler, and the slate and stylus); the use of the abacus adapted for the blind; typewriting and handwriting (so that each pupil is able to write his or her name). In addition to tuition in these basic skills, the resource teacher also provides training in reading with the Optacon — an electronic reading device that converts printed images into direct tactual representations which can be felt by the fingertip. The resource teacher — having attended a training programme in its use — had carried out a pilot experiment teaching six children to use it. She was enthusiastic about its potential as an alternative learning medium to braille. Certainly, at Medford, the Optacon was in daily use and some of the children observed were able to read with facility.[12]

Pupils attached to the resource programme also receive mobility and general self-care training (table manners, general posture, help in eradicating 'blindisms') from an itinerant mobility officer who works in the resource centre for three days a week. 'These skills include techniques of daily living as well as specific travel training. The blind pupil is thus encouraged to travel independently in the area of the school and in his own community.'[13] These activities, in the Sheffield and Liverpool schemes, are the responsibility of the *special* schools.

The resource teacher at Medford is responsible for providing and keeping braille books, all of which match printed texts used in the ordinary school;[14] and for ensuring that all necessary equipment is located at the centre. The brailling of printed tests, selected sections of texts and teaching materials is done on the premises by the resource teacher, as is the 'translating' of pupils' brailled homework into print before it is returned to the class teacher for marking. General counselling also forms part of the resource teacher's role: she is not only responsible for supervising the blind children, but also for liaising with the school counsellor and parents.

Of the 10 pupils attached to the centre, four of the older ones attend the junior high school adjoining Kennedy Elementary School, in which the other six are located. After leaving the programme — at age 13–14 years — pupils go on to their local high schools. With the help of the school counsellor, they are responsible for obtaining books and equipment. By then they are deemed fully capable of functioning without resource staff.

The pupils in the junior high school receive much less attention from the resource centre than do the younger pupils: the resource teacher remains available to deal with specific problems, but does not offer instruction. While the elementary school pupils attend the centre more often, they spend 80 per cent of the school day in the ordinary classroom: "The blind pupils are fully integrated into their grade with sighted pupils . . . (they) come to the resource room only for part of the day, usually for an hour or less, for special instruction . . . The blind pupils are thus part of the school as a whole, not a segregated unit" (resource teacher). In the classroom, the integrated blind child has a special desk, equipped with a Perkins brailler, a bookcase of braille books and a typewriter.

The times when a blind child leaves the sighted classroom for individual tuition in the resource centre rest with the class teacher. The children are not automatically removed from lessons dependent upon high visual content, e.g. art. In fact, they are often given complementary work to do, for instance, modelling, which both teachers and pupils are reluctant to sacrifice. Normal lessons are pursued, therefore, as far as possible together with sighted peers. For science, "we tend to pair them off" with a sighted partner, who is mainly responsible for carrying out the laboratory experiments while the blind child takes notes and observes. Blind pupils join in sporting activities whenever possible; the only difficulty is that they "cannot play in organized sport": instead, they act as score keepers and cheer leaders and thus "feel included".

The "full acceptance" of the programme by the school staff was seen as one of the main reasons for its becoming firmly established. The resource teacher is one of the ordinary school staff and, perhaps significantly, has been there since the inception of the programme: 'Teachers welcome the blind pupils into the classroom as part of their regular class. There is close rapport between the resource teacher and other members of the faculty'.[15]

Neither the open education schemes nor the Medford programme have been thoroughly evaluated. However, in the view of those responsible for and involved in all these schemes, each has proved very successful: pupils have been seen to derive both academic and social advantages. All three schemes, however, have highlighted the extensive support necessary for braille users integrated into ordinary schools. In these cases, provision is concentrated in a centre which caters for a small group of similarly handicapped pupils: but the units are considered more as 'resource' not 'teaching' centres, though some teaching goes on there. The visually impaired children spend a great deal of time with their sighted peers.

The obvious difference between the three schemes lies in the nature of their clientele: the rigid selection of pupils for open education almost by definition ensures the schemes' success. The Medford programme takes more risks by accepting a wider spectrum of blind pupils. Its survival for so long — unlike other American units and arrangements — suggests that it might be possible for the open education schemes to be more open without necessary calamity.

Notes

(1) The only current pupil in the St Vincent's scheme is partially sighted. He is the first who has not been blind.

(2) One researcher spent a week at both St Vincent's School, Liverpool and Tapton Mount School, Sheffield, during November and December 1974. At both schools, a total of 28 staff and pupils were interviewed; group discussions were held and lessons observed. Visits were also made to the 'host' ordinary schools and the head teachers were interviewed. Ex-pupils from both St Vincent's (N = 10) and Tapton Mount (N = 4) who had attended ordinary schools were also interviewed at length.

(3) There are only two special schools in England and Wales which officially cater for both blind and partially sighted pupils: St Vincent's, and Bridgend School in Wales.

(4) In the event, some pupils stayed on to take GCE A-level examinations.

(5) It is standard practice for blind pupils to complete an extra year at primary level.

(6) No transfers took place in 1965, 1967, 1969, 1972, or 1974.

(7) Tapton Mount School caters for pupils up to the age of 12 years.

(8) The range of O-level subjects taken and passed by open education pupils confirms that there was no particular restriction of their curriculum: English language, English literature, history, French, Latin, Spanish, Russian, German, maths, physics, chemistry, biology, geography, music, general science, nutrition, and cookery.

(9) In November 1975, one of the team visited the Braille Resource Program in Medford, Massachusetts, USA. During his one-day visit he interviewed the teacher in charge of the programme, and the itinerant mobility teacher. He observed children at work in the resource room and in the ordinary classroom and watched mobility training in action. Further discussion about the programme was held with Dr Gerald Friedman at Boston University Low Vision Clinic. We are indebted to Ms Lynn Fraleigh, the teacher in charge of the programme, for her help in this part of the research.

(10) The resource programme exists to 'service not only Medford but also any surrounding communities which might wish to avail themselves of the special services offered to blind children who must learn braille and related skills' (Official hand-out).

(11) State legislation forbids that a child should have to travel more than one hour to school.

(12) A thorough evaluation of the Optacon in England has been conducted by Tobin and James. They were less optimistic about its value and usefulness. The research showed, however, that the more successful Optacon readers were younger than the blind population as a whole, had 'learned braille at an earlier age, and obtained superior scores on the touch, memory and braille

reading tests'. They found no significant correlation between Optacon reading ability and intelligence. (TOBIN, M.J. and JAMES, W.R.K. (1974). 'Evaluating the Optacon: general reflections on reading machines for the blind', *AFB Research Bulletin*, 28, October.) These results were broadly confirmed in the 'practical field trials' at Medford, albeit under less controlled conditions. The six pupils were braille readers with little or no vision; their IQs varied from 95 to 160 and they were aged between six and 11. Some of the pupils already knew the shape of print letters. Optacon training took half an hour a day for the first year at least, and regular practice, both at home and in the resource room, was encouraged. The resource teacher claimed that pupils were "enormously excited and very highly motivated at the thought of learning to read in print". The results had been encouraging: a six-year-old was reading print as quickly as braille, having spent the same amount of time learning both mediums. The experiment suggested, first, that pupils found no problem in transferring from contracted braille to uncontracted print; second, that training as early as possible was advisable; third, that there was nothing to suggest that success with the Optacon was related to IQ; fourth, those who read braille fastest were also most rapid with the Optacon. Optacons are increasingly in evidence in the USA, in Scandinavia, and elsewhere. Their use in Britain is still limited, not least because of their cost (around $3000).

(13) Official hand-out produced by the Kennedy Elementary School.

(14) Braille books are obtained from a central braille library which has a nationwide information network; anyone who brailles a book notifies a central agency so that when a particular book is required, it is thermoformed, with the school paying for postage. If a book does not exist, The National Braille Press in Boston will produce it on request.

(15) Official hand-out (*op. cit.*).

Chapter Seven

Unit and 'Special School Based' Integration

We look now at two versions of integration for the partially sighted. Each entails a scheme that draws on centralized resources (see Chapter Five). The first example, that of partially sighted units (PSUs), is fairly orthodox — there are a number of PSUs of relatively long-standing in England and Wales. The second example — a scheme run by Joseph Clarke School for the partially sighted in conjunction with a neighbouring comprehensive school — is probably unique: to our knowledge, it is the only school-based scheme of integration practised from a day special school.

Unit based integration[1]

Units for the partially sighted (PSUs) represent a minority form of educational provision. In 1974, there were eight units or special classes in seven ordinary schools catering for 86 children in all.[2] The number of children educated in this way seems to be increasing.[3] Seven special classes are attached to primary or middle schools; there is only one secondary unit.

A PSU is usually a classroom within, or adjacent to, an ordinary school that caters for partially sighted pupils for part of the school day. The actual time that such children spend in the unit varies considerably from school to school. In most cases it was determined by the child's age, educational ability, emotional and social maturity, and whether there were additional handicaps. In one instance, children from the unit joined their sighted peers only for less academic activities such as worship, music, and dance. However, the policy of most units was for pupils to take an increasingly greater proportion of their lessons in ordinary classes as they progressed up the school, so that by their final year, the unit would be visited for specific help or technical resources, only if necessary.

Staff and head teachers interviewed were widely in agreement: a policy of gradual assimilation was a more realistic way of achieving eventual total integration — whether at secondary level or in later life — than was immediate and total immersion. One unit teacher spoke for many in commenting, "I don't think these children would make the academic progress they are making without the unit". The sort of child with whom her unit dealt would be unlikely to contend happily with a complete transfer to an ordinary class, at least at the middle junior stage: 'They do tend to be slower . . . they have an inability to concentrate for very long on anything . . . they need individualized attention", was a typical assessment. On the other hand — and here one sees how unit provision has a 'halfway house' type of function — complete integration remained the goal held by teachers for most partially sighted children; it was widely described as essential that they should compete with their sighted peers on the latter's terms; academic proficiency should not be judged solely by the standards of the unit.

None of the units we visited had rigorous conditions of entry: children of varying ability qualified; they were usually registered as partially sighted; some had additional handicaps, although not of sufficient severity to require special school placement. Admission was often the outcome of a referral from the school medical service, but sometimes had been determined at a multi-disciplinary case conference (of a kind similar to those discussed in Chapter Two). Early admission to units was regarded as particularly beneficial: it reduced the possibility of a child acquiring a label such as 'backward', 'lazy', or 'a misbehaver', when in fact his or her problems were primarily visual but were not recognized as such. However, in the case of very young children, admission was as much based on speculation about how the child would cope as it was on the visual defect *per se*.

Each unit visited was staffed by a teacher and an aide. The presence of an aide made it possible for one adult always to be available to help younger children with general mobility, in the playground, with particular academic tasks, or to assist in the ordinary classroom.

Units usually are presented as integral parts of the parent school, not tacked onto the periphery; but in practice there is a tendency — or danger — of a unit developing a separate existence with effectively no contact between partially sighted pupils and their sighted peers, or between unit staff and their counterparts in the main school. One special school head teacher commented on this: "Units are a bit vulnerable. If they are very self-contained, pupils are more isolated than in a special school". Others, even more sceptical, warned of their becoming "precious little places": pupils could be retained within their walls far too easily, so that what in theory was integration became, in reality, little more than "child minding".[4] The more widely approved model was when a unit was genuinely an integral part of a school while retaining some separate specialist identity — rather like, say, a French or science department.

Among units visited, there was variation in the amount of contact. Thus, one unit was relatively self-enclosed; in a second, both staff and pupils from the unit spent every afternoon in ordinary classrooms — this seen as ensuring that the unit did not become isolating or over-protective. In a third instance, team teaching was encouraged, involving both unit teacher and other teaching staff; this was justified on the grounds that it kept the unit teacher in contact with normal child development, while giving other teachers practical experience with handicapped children. The unit teacher was enthusiastic: "Dealing entirely with the partially sighted was a bit stultifying . . . there is so little measurable progress . . . I thought it would be better for me . . . to have more variety, take ordinary lessons, and get some feedback, and that this would benefit the children too".

Certain difficulties and structural problems with this form of provision were identified. First, at least two teachers in charge of units had had little specialist training. Second, units catered for a small number of pupils — rarely less than seven, generally no more than 12 — and covered a wide age range. This meant that an individual child was unlikely to have more than one companion of the same age in the unit. Third, there was a tendency for younger children to ask older pupils for help, thus disrupting their work. Finally, a probable disadvantage for units at the secondary level would be that a single teacher would have to cover the full subject range.

Other potential problems included the following: (i) Unit teachers often felt protective towards their already hard pressed colleagues: they were regarded as having enough pupils to contend with already, without being asked to take an additional responsibility for children with visual difficulties. (ii) Fitting unit pupils into an ordinary class for part of the day, when that class did not work to a fixed timetable, often presented difficulties. (iii) It was equally a problem to arrange for individual children to join in ongoing project activities on a temporary and often irregular basis.

In all cases, it seemed, the 'success' — of both integrated pupils and of the unit itself — was measured chiefly in terms of the social mixing achieved and the social competence developed. Thus, one unit teacher remarked approvingly: "They're now completely accepted — even in the playground. Originally, they were seen as a bit odd . . . ". Another teacher, echoing others' views, remarked that "it keeps them like ordinary kids to be among ordinary kids . . . but they definitely need special attention . . . ".

This concentration on the social realm is not to imply that academic aspects were ignored. It might be considered as one measure of their success, as a form of provision, that few pupils from units we visited had been known to require transfer to special schools. In the few instances where such moves had been made, deteriorating vision was invariably the cause. The vast majority had either gone on to attend local secondary schools, or alternatively, a secondary level unit of some kind.

An argument forcefully advanced in favour of this form of provision is that units can provide the same level of individual care as special schools, with the added bonus of doing so within the sighted community. However, simply on the grounds of resources, it is debatable whether this is possible. It was a striking feature of the units we visited that they were far from being well equipped; and there often seemed little encouragement for pupils to use the few low vision aids that were available.

Of course, there is more to individual care than technical aids, and a unit may be able to provide a supportive milieu reminiscent of the special school. Thus, one unit was described as "a perfect example of an integrated unit" by an HMI in special education: he reported that there was ready cooperation between the respective staffs; partially sighted pupils were not "molly-coddled"; both teacher and pupils spent at least half the school day outside the unit; the unit itself was simply a small private room offering certain specialized facilities; partially sighted pupils were confident enough to ask the assistance of any member of staff; and parents were fully aware of the scheme, and could visit whenever they liked to see at first hand what happened there.

One of the main issues associated with this type of scheme was introduced in Chapter Five: to which entity does the child feel affiliated — the ordinary class or the unit? And who, on the part of staff, has a sense of personal responsibility or 'ownership' of the pupil? The answer seemed to be that the majority of pupils, who spent a good part of the day within a unit, looked upon it as their base and as a source of identity. In turn, unit staff were seen to accept full responsibility for these children. This state of affairs was often implicitly acknowledged in exchanges between unit staff and teachers of ordinary classes when a visually impaired child was the subject of a dispute or query.

Examples of different kinds of unit scheme were described in Chapter Six, where integration of blind pupils was discussed. Both the braille resource programme at Medford and the open education scheme at Sheffield involved units. In both cases, the reader will remember that pupils used a resource room as a centre where specialist attention and facilities were always available. Other than that, they were full members of regular classes. The closest we came to finding anything similar for partially sighted children was in the unit described by the HMI in such enthusiastic terms.[5]

Special school as a 'home base'[6]

Here we discuss a scheme of integration which to our knowledge is unique. It operates from the Joseph Clarke school in London, a day special school for the partially sighted. As a scheme it was planned well in advance, with the approval of the Inner London Education Authority. The special school was deliberately relocated in 1971 to a site already occupied by an ordinary school, the intention being to encourage interaction between sighted and partially sighted pupils. The current scheme of integration was inaugurated in 1972. Although our study of the scheme spread over four months, it represents only a 'snapshot in time' in a rapidly evolving programme.

The basic plan of the scheme is that all the Joseph Clarke school pupils aged 14 years or over are transferred to the adjacent senior high school for some part of their school day.[7] In theory, pupils spend a considerable part of the school day on the premises of the comprehensive school; in practice, except for a few, they are present only when timetabled for specific lessons.

The head of the special school explained why it was only a partial and not a complete transfer to the high school — why pupils retained their membership in the special school: 'If any of them didn't need extra assistance then we would have total transfer, but they all need our help". He pointed out two reasons for the cautious approach. First, the intake of the Joseph Clarke school had in the past been "creamed" of the more academically able partially sighted pupils; and, second, the senior high school was characterized by large classes, a high staff turnover, and examination pressures which demanded that pupils be "shot through" CSE and O-level in a mere five terms.[8]

In outlining the scheme's rationale the head teacher commented, "I am pro-integration, but with a safety net. I'm all for kids mainstreaming, but it can't be done without increased back-up facilities". The image of 'safety net' seems to fit: compared to the school they are transferring to, the special school is altogether safer: it is smaller, it treats the partially sighted as a majority rather than minority concern, and it enjoys greater stability (e.g. less turnover of staff).

The Joseph Clarke staff appeared equally well disposed towards integration, both as a concept and a working policy: the scheme, they said, gave partially sighted pupils a chance to learn both to "cope with society", and also to have increased access to academic options. Integration was not "pursued for the sake of exams alone . . . (it) is intended to teach them to cope . . . (it) is for social competence".

Pupils acquired "the ability to handle themselves in an environment that isn't doing anything to help them", and a chance to "appraise themselves against ordinary kids in ordinary situations and adjust realistically". The head teacher believed that his pupils wanted to mix with normal children — rather than with those having similar or other severe problems. And he was convinced, too, that all his pupils should get the chance to win back their confidence within the working environment of a school for the sighted: over 75 per cent of his pupils had arrived at Joseph Clarke as "rejects from ordinary schools".

The special school continued to serve as a 'home base' for integrated pupils: no special resources were provided for them within the comprehensive. The special school could make good certain weaknesses in the comprehensive. For example, at the time of our study, there was an acute shortage of maths teachers at the high school. Effectively, this meant that only those most proficient at mathematics could be given examination opportunities. Under such circumstances, the comprehensive's primary responsibility was seen to be to its own registered pupils. 'Back-up' from the special school was then found to be essential.

Other kinds of back-up included the provision of tapes, worksheets, large print books, typewriters, and low vision aids; the possibility of doing certain practical or vocational subjects (e.g. typewriting, woodwork) within the special school; and follow up lessons to complement those taken at the comprehensive: "They can hold their own (with sighted peers) given the support we provide", claimed one Joseph Clarke teacher.

One of the features of this scheme is that the Joseph Clarke school appears to have made great efforts to ensure that the comprehensive school is minimally disrupted. No request was made to the school to modify teaching practices or materials in order to facilitate integration — "no corners are to be bent". One of the primary aims was for "partially sighted pupils to acquire a working understanding of their own limitations and to adjust accordingly". A Joseph Clarke teacher remarked: "It's not their teachers' responsibility for ensuring that our kids speak up and assert themselves . . . That's what our kids are there for".

However, there is a second reason why the special school did not request any changes: integration, they realized, had been "imposed" on the high school — "rather than come from them . . . Make too many demands and we'll be rejected". This led to a deliberately "passive approach" adopted by the special school, "making sure . . . we grow into the system". However, this raises an important question: whether it is possible, indeed realistic, to implement any scheme of integration without asking the host school to make at least minor concessions.

An unanticipated consequence of this policy of 'no bending of corners' may well have been that integrated pupils did not receive enough attention at the ordinary school. There were some indications of this being the case. The head teacher of the host comprehensive, for example, appeared to take it for granted that providing the Joseph Clarke pupils with the opportunity for integration was almost sufficient in itself: "We've aimed at making as few special arrangements as possible. That way they can go about as normally as possible". Again, this strikes one superficially as an appropriate reaction when organizing an integration scheme. However, one consequence (in the words of a teacher in the comprehensive school) might be that integration tended "to act as an informal activity on the fringe of the formal organization".

Those in the special school did not seem unduly worried by this. Realistically, they pointed out that 13 partially sighted children absorbed into a population of over 2,000 comprehensive pupils over a three year period inevitably represented a minority interest: it would take time for the scheme to evolve until it became "part of their way of life". However — and perhaps slightly paradoxically — Joseph Clarke teachers were also critical of the lack of enthusiasm shown by many of their counterparts in the comprehensive: "The scheme needs their teachers being more aware of the problems our kids face, together with a willingness to take responsibility".

At the time of our study, staff contacts between the two schools had been limited. This was despite a strong conviction in the special school that the scheme's "organization has to be understood by both sides, and by the kids involved".[9] Effective inter-staff communication had been hampered by difficulty in finding the time for serious interaction. Even more, there had been a tendency for each group of staff to suggest that the scheme's problems were the other's responsibility. Thus, Joseph Clarke staff commented on the tendency of the high school "to let the scheme ride"; they referred to the lack of "a nucleus of dedicated teachers . . . who could take these kids year after year" and develop a working expertise; they remarked on the lack of relevant experience among the staff of the comprehensive; and the general impersonality of the much larger school.

In turn, the comprehensive staff — while sometimes critical of the basic decision to put "the facilities of the school at the disposal of other people" — seemed more concerned that they had not been encouraged to develop a commitment toward partially sighted pupils, nor did they feel they had been given the opportunity to do so. Several even complained that the special school head "doesn't make enough demands. He feels we're doing him a favour". One head of department openly admitted, "there's very little effort being made on our side. If they were in some way a part of this school (we would show) far more enthusiasm and commitment. At present it's unreal, it's like they're always visitors". This last remark was mirrored in comments from the integrated pupils themselves: "You feel as if you don't belong there . . . it's not your school . . . you feel as if their pupils have got priority".

If the above comments refer to certain difficulties with the scheme, it should also be remembered that there are a number of practical constraints in organizing any inter-school scheme. For instance, in this case, the school day of the two schools differed slightly because partially sighted pupils had to travel daily from a wider area; this meant they missed part of the first and last lessons at the comprehensive school, if they were timetabled for them. The school terms were also slightly different. Further, integrated pupils were obliged to return to the special school for lunch, thus missing out on a singular opportunity for establishing social contacts.

Academically speaking, the partially sighted pupils were regarded by the comprehensive staff as slower — because of their visual defect[10] — and thus tended to be placed in the less academic subject bands. Here the classroom climate was not always conducive to academic work, and integrated pupils often found themselves "in with a load of loud kids" (in the words of a member of the comprehensive staff). Several of the comprehensive teachers pointed out that the behaviour of sighted pupils was the "make or break point" in how, finally, integrated pupils got on: it determined how much specific attention they could be given.

Interestingly, this issue of school placement also presented the integrated pupils with a problem of adaptation: should they identify with their sighted peers by engaging in classroom 'messing' activities, or distance themselves further by seeking to work hard in a context where academic application was not always the norm? Classroom observation — backed up by reports from staff — suggested that they chose the latter: "(They) work like mad . . . all trying to prove . . . they're as good as sighted pupils and that they have certain things to offer". For some integrated pupils, placing them in higher bands — where the atmosphere was quieter — might have overcome this disadvantage.

We next turn to the question of pupils' school identification. The partially sighted went from the special school — where they were important, where staff were as much friends and confidants as teachers — to the comprehensive school, where they were virtually unknowns, or "perpetual visitors" in the earlier teacher's words. Furthermore, they did not live in the neighbourhood served by the high school, and having to travel considerable distances meant they were inevitably estranged from most, if not all, of the out-of-school activities at the comprehensive. In the light of these various constraints, it is not perhaps surprising that the integrated pupils were spoken of as follows:

"They see themselves as attending this (special) school and going to the comprehensive occasionally". Social relationships were inevitably rendered difficult. However, the integrated children made remarks such as, "We go over there for the lessons, not to talk", which suggested they had no high expectations of making friends in the comprehensive. In this respect, it may not have helped that usually they were paired — there were two from Joseph Clarke in a class, so that they rarely had a strong impetus to be outgoing. However, among those integrated were some who resented any presumption that they were incapable of interacting with sighted peers, had they wanted to: "We mix with our friends alright at night, and they haven't got anything wrong with their eyes. Just because we've got bad eyes they think we can only have other divvies[11] for friends . . . We aren't monsters you know".

Most of the integrated pupils expressed a measure of antipathy towards their peers in the comprehensive school. For instance, two of the more extrovert partially sighted girls considered sighted pupils were "horrible to us; the girls don't talk to you or else they ask nosey questions, and the boys make rude comments". Others reinforced this; stating that sighted pupils tended to "treat you as if you're halfway round the twist — their kids think this school (Joseph Clarke) is a nut-house". Additionally, the likelihood of their merging into the comprehensive scene was hardly encouraged by teachers there making the occasional thoughtless comments such as, "Speak up, these two can't see", and "Stop messing around: I've got enough problems as it is with these two blind kids". The following common reaction — expressed here in the words of one partially sighted boy — is hardly surprising: "I'd rather people didn't know about my sight, then they'd accept me as I am. As it is now, we're always on show".

By way of summing up, the special school head teacher was confident that integration had brought both social and academic benefits. It was socially beneficial in that integrating pupils were "maturing faster" — they were more "socially composed" than they would have been had they remained full time at the Joseph Clarke school. Integration, he considered, was more than a matter of simply making friends: "If these pupils are learning the social lore without actually taking part, then it's not altogether a bad thing". However, it may be that little learning can be achieved without fuller active participation. As one comprehensive teacher remarked, "Being honest, I rarely notice them. They're so scared that they try to be as inconspicuous as possible". Academically speaking, the Joseph Clarke head pointed to the fact that integrated pupils were obtaining CSE passes in a wider range of subjects than would have been possible had they remained at the special school. He hoped that they would begin taking O-levels in the near future.[12]

In conclusion, the same issues of allegiance, identity and responsibility, which were discussed at the end of the section on units, emerge as pertinent here. It seems clear that pupils integrated in the comprehensive felt no particular sense of membership there, nor did the senior high school feel they were ultimately responsible. Another similarity between units for the partially sighted and the Joseph Clarke scheme is structural: in many respects, the special school can be thought of as an expanded unit for those who are integrated; units and the special school both serve as a central store of teacher expertise, technical facilities, and academic resources. However, drawing a parallel with unit provision is not meant to belittle the special school: it clearly has a much greater educational and resource capacity than any existing unit for partially sighted children in England and Wales.

Notes

(1) Our comments are based on visits to four partially sighted units: one was for infants only (aged 4½–7 years); two catered for the full primary age range (5–11 years); and the fourth was a double unit, separately serving children aged 5–8 years and 8–12 years. During these visits, carried out by different members of the research team, working singly or in pairs, a total of 13 staff from both units and host schools were interviewed, classroom activities observed, and conversations held with older pupils.

(2) THE NATIONAL ASSOCIATION FOR THE EDUCATION OF THE PARTIALLY SIGHTED (1974). *List of Schools and Classes engaged in work with Partially Sighted Children.* London: The Partially Sighted Society.

(3) In October 1975 a spokesman for the DES estimated that on the basis of the latest returns, 104 children were receiving education in a unit.

(4) Several critics pointed out that those children who were heavily dependent upon units would be better off in a special school where a broader curriculum, wider range of activities, larger peer group, and fewer daily reminders of their 'handicapped' status would be evident.

(5) This was, however, a unit for infants only.

(6) The school was first visited in Autumn 1974 as part of the opening phase of the research. On that occasion, discussion was very general, ranging across many different aspects of the education of the visually impaired. A further six visits were subsequently made. The initial intention was to study the school as a special school, and accordingly, the head teacher and the seven full-time staff were interviewed. Discussion was very open at first, but a specific orientation soon emerged – notably, the perceived importance of the integration scheme – and later, interviews became more structured. During this period, five lessons were also observed and 10 older pupils interviewed, both individually and in a group. Later visits concentrated on integration 'in action'. The head teacher of the special school arranged the

researcher's entry into the comprehensive school. The head teacher of the comprehensive school, in turn, set up interviews with teachers from various departments, nine of whom were subsequently interviewed. Observation of lessons attended by partially sighted pupils was also carried out. This mini-project concluded with a clarification and feedback session with the head teacher of the special school.

(7) The only exceptions are pupils with severe additional handicaps — perhaps some physical disfigurement, or an inadequate command of the English language. However, we understand that in the present school year (1975—76), for the first time, an emotionally disturbed boy is being maintained in the scheme, being given a high level of support. The virtual lack of selectivity represents a significant aspect of the Joseph Clarke scheme and marks it out as very different from, say, the open education schemes described in Chapter Six.

(8) Entry to the senior high school, for all pupils, was at 14+.

(9) A member of the Joseph Clarke staff was recently appointed to act part-time as 'link man' or liaison officer between the schools. He spends six periods a week performing this duty. It is indicative of the scheme's continuing to evolve that plans exist for him to spend, in the following year, half his time at the comprehensive — not specifically with integrating pupils.

(10) Research undertaken by Lansdown (1973) found that in a matched group, rate of work was the *only* difference between partially sighted and sighted pupils. (LANSDOWN, R. (1973). A study of the effect of severe visual handicap on the development of some aspects of visual perception and their relationship to reading and spelling in children in special schools for the partially sighted. Unpublished PhD thesis, NE London Polytechnic.)

(11) A term used by partially sighted adolescents to differentiate others like themselves from the non-handicapped.

(12) This has come about — by the time of producing this report — with the first partially sighted sixth formers attending the comprehensive.

Chapter Eight

Individual Integration with Peripatetic Support

The individual integration of visually impaired children in ordinary schools is perhaps easier and less expensive to organize and instigate than founding a unit or resource centre of the kinds discussed in the previous chapters. Nevertheless, it is clearly the form of integration that is most vulnerable to being done 'on the cheap' or of being poorly organized. As discussed in Chapter Five, it is an approach to integration in which support and resources are distributed rather than centralized, with a visiting, peripatetic, or itinerant resource adviser or teacher regularly visiting children who are individually placed in ordinary schools.

In England and Wales, organized integration of this kind is on the increase. Several local authorities have appointed peripatetic advisory teachers to organize and supervise the education of visually impaired children in primary and secondary schools.[1] Outside of these authorities, an unknown number of partially sighted children — whose impaired vision may or may not have been recognized — have somehow found their way into ordinary schools in both state and private sectors. In the present chapter we do not discuss these children: although they are experiencing integration, they are not part of any formalized scheme.

Instead, we discuss two forms of peripatetic integration that we investigated. The first scheme relates to the work of one advisory teacher, whose work routine and professional philosophy we investigated at some length. Although widely considered to be especially dynamic and effective, there is no reason to believe that she is markedly non-typical among her professional group — either in the work she does, or in the arrangement she sets up and administers. Contact with her counterparts in other LEAs confirms this assessment. The second itinerant scheme described is a more elaborate service developed by a team of peripatetic advisory teachers in Manchester, operating from a day special school for the partially sighted.

Peripatetic advisory teaching[2]

The individual advisory teacher whom we observed was appointed in 1972. The local education authority was particularly prompt in taking up one of the recommendations of the Vernon Report, namely, that 'a peripatetic teacher, working in association with staff carrying out other forms of counselling and with the regional assessment team, might have particular responsibility for carrying out counselling about educational provision and ways of promoting cognitive development'.[3]

The Vernon Committee recommendation was specifically for advising at the pre-school level. The scheme described here is an extension, fulfilling a much wider need. This advisory teacher's responsibility was for the general welfare and educational provision of all visually impaired individuals from pre-school through to further education.

The advisory teacher had a great deal of leeway in interpreting the nature and policy of her work. This was naturally influenced by her wider professional views. She had pronounced ideas about integration: for her, partially sighted or blind children could not be thought about collectively — "I prefer to think of them as individuals with a little educational problem". She thought they had "a right to be educated in the ordinary school" and given the necessary support. She also believed strongly that except in the severest cases of visual defect, "it is not visual impairment *per se* which creates educational difficulties", but impaired vision together with the attitudes and expectations of those surrounding the child towards his or her handicap. She argued that it was more 'normal' for children to live at home, and felt that ordinary schools could provide both a thorough educational and social experience. Integration should be achieved as young as possible: "If they are to pass through the ordinary school system it is imperative that they begin in it". Her principal concern was to minimize the sense of 'difference' partially sighted children often experienced: "wherever differences exist we highlight them, and I think this is wrong".

Since her appointment, the advisory teacher had only had to determine the educational placement of partially sighted children; the need for her to place an educationally blind child had not yet arisen. However, she did not regard blind children as incapable of being integrated. She recently wrote that she hoped 'some brave parents of totally blind children (will) have confidence in me and my methods'.[4] The major difference, she thought, would be that a blind child would more likely be integrated into a school where some form of unit already existed.

Placement decisions concerning partially sighted children in the local authority rested mainly with this advisory teacher, although parents had the ultimate right to veto any decision reached. She drew on her extensive experience in special education in making these judgments. She studied medical reports and family circumstances, and consulted with educational psychologists, ophthalmologists, and social workers. Factors she took into account included: the age of the child; the nature and severity of the visual loss; whether there were additional handicaps; and the parents' views on keeping the child at home as opposed to his or her attending a residential special school. She emphasized the importance of ensuring that everyone involved was kept informed, and that she herself got to know each child personally. She aimed to make certain that the child was not isolated, over-protected, or made too special; and that parents were encouraged to allow the child to be as independent as possible.

In most cases, the partially sighted pupils under her jurisdiction were placed in carefully chosen ordinary schools on an individual basis, and attended for the whole day. Others – perhaps more physically fragile, or those with reading and writing problems – were placed in schools containing some kind of unit. There were no units for the partially sighted within the authority but use was made of units for the partially hearing or for children with learning difficulties. The advisory teacher justified this on the grounds that such placement allowed for individualized attention from a specialist teacher – even though the specialism was not visual impairment: "If I feel a child might benefit from individual attention then I'll make sure he gets it; I don't care where it comes from . . . the important thing, if a person is qualified as a teacher, is to know the age group". Those children with severe additional handicaps usually go to special schools or may be categorized according to these other handicaps.

Once a child had been placed in a school, the peripatetic teacher offered practical assistance by advising teachers and arranging extra tuition for the child. For example, for infants she aimed to give one hour per day individual tuition, falling off to two hours per week by the end of primary education if good progress in the basic skills of reading and writing had been made. She explained: "I have this theory that a child requires individual attention to read and write. The visually handicapped are no exception, they just need more attention. If they can master these areas then they will be on a more equal pegging with other children, and much that would later be a problem falls into place". She regarded this degree of attention in the early years as essential if integration was to continue into later years: "The child's standing on these two criteria at the end of junior school will determine whether he can cope in an ordinary (secondary) school or whether he needs a specially selected senior school".[5]

For older children who were in ordinary schools, she aimed to make monthly visits — more frequently if necessary. She maintained contact with every child and regularly reviewed his or her progress. Before a pupil transferred to a new school, she contacted the school in preparation for the child's admission. She also took both child and parents for at least one advance visit and arranged opportunities for discussion with school staff.

As her title suggests, she had advisory as well as teaching responsibilities. These she took very seriously. She considered there was an urgent need to explain to teachers what the integrated child's difficulties were, or could be: "Visual handicap needn't be a monumental problem. The predominant attitude of teachers is a concern, a worry that they are not doing enough for the child". Promoting good understanding of the child's potential problems helped to overcome teachers' apprehensions and misunderstandings: "It's a matter of getting teachers to have the confidence to retain the child in the school situation". It was also imperative that all staff knew of the presence of a partially sighted child in the school, "so as to achieve consistency in handling him". If all staff were informed, then when difficulties arose in the classroom, teachers were less likely to respond to the label 'partially sighted' as if the vision impairment was automatically the cause. However, a serious possible weakness of a peripatetic scheme such as this is that staff turnover can cause havoc, upsetting both local arrangements and the contacts made between the advisory teacher and school staff.

The advisory teacher also distributed resources: "Whenever I go into a school I take with me a variety of resource material plus some low vision aids which I let the child try out. If any prove useful then the child is given them". She was "delighted when low vision aids have been provided for pupils by hospitals", but noted that children did not always find them useful within the actual classroom context. Other advice was tendered: for example, the importance of suitable lighting conditions and where the child needed to sit in order to maximize vision.

Finally, her other functions included: (a) organizing voluntary in-service training courses for teachers — in some instances she had taught braille to a teacher so that an integrated child with a poor medical prognosis could receive some degree of preparation for a possible future of blindness; and (b) liaising between parents and educational authorities, to "try and convince parents that we're giving their children special treatment within the ordinary school setting".

Clearly, an itinerant or peripatetic scheme of this kind rests heavily on the work of advisory teachers — in this instance there was only one for the whole authority.[6] She consulted, of course, with other professionals — e.g. special education advisers, head teachers, educational psychologists — but this did not diminish the workload. She hoped eventually to disperse her activity by disseminating sufficient information and expertise to enable a network of informed people to be built up. This could also ensure the continuation of the system were she to depart: otherwise, the criticism that this scheme of integration is heavily 'person-dependent' is a fully justified one. It is probably fair to say, as one researcher on visual impairment wrote, that 'at its best this system is undoubtedly very good; at its worst it is appalling'.[7] Only by institutionalizing the practice, involving a variety of people, and reducing the onus on single individuals, can this potential danger be defused.

A peripatetic team approach to integration[8]

Operating from the home base of Shawgrove School, Manchester, a day school for the partially sighted, nine peripatetic advisory teachers work as a team "to cater for the needs of the visually handicapped child capable of integration" (head teacher). All concerned have had some previous experience of teaching visually or otherwise handicapped children.

This 'peripatetic service' began in 1970. The original intention was to perform a "domiciliary role" — teaching and caring for the occasional visually impaired child attending ordinary school who was considered "in need" of some extra attention. In the event — as described in Chapter Two — a considerable number of children in Manchester have been identified as being in need. Indeed, over a five year period, the peripatetic team has worked with about 680 children. The majority of these have been children suspected by the school health service or by school personnel of having a visual problem of some kind, and therefore reported to the team. The team undertakes basic vision screening, referring children to ophthalmic specialists if necessary.

The peripatetic team is responsible for assessing the effect of a child's visual impairment on school attainment; for providing help with social or behavioural problems, for seeking information on difficulties stemming from the environment of the home, helping head teachers and teachers by giving basic information and practical advice, and undertaking teaching duties if required — mainly one-to-one or small group tuition. This is in addition to general counselling, advising and liaising with staff and parents, and distributing low vision aids on permanent loan. They place great emphasis on perceptual development and on making maximum use of residual vision.

The team supports pupils who were formerly at Shawgrove School and are now in various local schools, as well as maintaining contact with the much larger group of pupils already referred to. At the time of our study, no less than 140 children were being visited weekly by a member of the team; a further 50 were being seen monthly, and another 25 at least termly. The remainder of the current case load are visited annually. For those pupils who receive regular support, the head of the peripatetic service and the team member responsible for the individual, review his or her progress in the light of the assistance provided. On this basis decisions are made as to what kind of provision should be arranged for the following year.

The practice of integrating or re-integrating former Shawgrove pupils is an interesting feature of this scheme. The intention is to place the pupil in an ordinary school for at least a few months before he or she reaches school leaving age. Even though the most severe cases might not be integrated prior to leaving Shawgrove School, it was claimed that "there is every impetus for entering them into further education where, during their first months, they will be covered by the peripatetic service". This practice stemmed from the belief that the handicapped child's search for employment would be eased if his or her education was completed in an ordinary rather than a special school. Care was taken "to match the right school and the right child". Points borne in mind when placing a pupil included the following: socioeconomic factors; home background; the degree of social adjustment that the individual exhibited; educational progress to date; presence of any physical problems; and the physical layout of the receiving school. Many of these are similar to those considered in the itinerant scheme of integration described above.

This particular version of itinerant integration overcomes many of the problems that the single peripatetic teacher might face. One of its prime assets is its flexibility. A child can receive intensive short term support — for example, tutorial sessions three times a week — or, if necessary, even be temporarily withdrawn into the special school: "If children are failing and the peris (peripatetic teachers) can't hold them, they may be recommended to come into (the school) for varying periods of time". This means that the special school and the peripatetic service, between them, can cater for the full range of handicap — except perhaps the most severe cases, or the multi-handicapped. In addition, the peripatetic service makes use of the special school's services and facilities — its specialist teachers and equipment, and its medical and ophthalmological contacts. A further advantage is that team members can be supportive toward one another, while their diverse range of backgrounds gives a greater opportunity for matching a team member with the most appropriate background for the individual child's needs.

A number of questions can be raised about this scheme. Because the service exists, does it create a demand artificially in order to justify its existence? And is it justifiable to offer extra support to children with visual problems that are perhaps not sufficiently severe to be seriously handicapping, when the same resources might be diverted to helping children with more severe forms of handicap?

Integration of the kind described in this chapter clearly depends, to a large extent, on the experience, energy and personal skills of the staff involved. The number of peripatetic advisory teachers employed seems also important: under-staffing could detract from the quality of service provided.

We have described two types of peripatetic scheme, one of which aptly demonstrates that integration and special schooling need not be mutually exclusive. The scheme in Manchester is a good example of a special school serving as both a focal point and a fundamental part of an integration programme — such an arrangement is still unusual in England and Wales but is widely practised in Scandinavia. We go on to discuss integration in Denmark and Sweden in the next chapter.

Notes

(1) In addition, the RNIB has its own specialist team of advisers, seven in all.

(2) In the opening phase of the research, we were told of supposed merits and disadvantages of integration with peripatetic support. It was chosen as a specific sub-theme. We heard of a local authority which was among the first in the country to employ a peripatetic advisory teacher, and arranged an introductory, semi-structured interview with this person. Emphasis was placed on the theoretical aspects of her work, her professional beliefs and the constraints facing her. It seemed a logical development to examine how theory related to practice, and two full days were subsequently spent accompanying the teacher on her visits to children, families and schools within the local authority. During this period of observation, the researcher kept a low profile: the aim was to observe and listen to a series of interactions between the advisory teacher, children, teachers, medical representatives, and others. A further development was to conduct case histories of individual children who were the responsibility of the advisory teacher. Ten children were chosen for detailed study, and more is written about the methods used in the introduction to Part IV of this book.

(3) DEPARTMENT OF EDUCATION AND SCIENCE (1972). *The Education of the Visually Handicapped*. (Vernon Report) London: HMSO.

(4) In a letter to the research team. In essence, this entails providing extra tuitition in the early years of schooling.

(5) These were referred to earlier. They are usually ordinary schools that have some form of unit (e.g. for the partially hearing) attached to them.

(6) At the time of our investigation, this scheme of integration had only been

operational for about 18 months.   We understand a second advisory teacher has now been appointed. The success of the system is clearly dependent upon sufficient expertise, and the local authority frequently reviews the situation.

(7) In a letter to the research team.

(8) Awareness of the peripatetic service operating in Manchester came much later. Two of the research team spent a day at Shawgrove School, the 'home base' of the peripatetic service. In the morning, a group discussion was held involving the head teacher, one of the peripatetic team, representatives from Manchester's special education department, and the headmaster of an adjoining primary school into which older juniors from Shawgrove are integrated for part of each day. In the afternoon, we spoke at length with the head teacher of Shawgrove School, and later with the head of the peripatetic team.

Chapter Nine

Integration in Scandinavia

For the final chapter of Part II, we turn to two examples of integration abroad, in Denmark and Sweden. In both countries, integration of the visually impaired is organized on a national basis and is characterized by close cooperation between the special school(s) and those engaged in supervising and / or teaching integrated blind children. What is distinctive in both Denmark and Sweden is that they have national systems of integration rather than piecemeal implementation of different schemes. Cultural contexts make this possible: there is more centralization of special education in Scandinavia generally, and responsibility for ordinary and special education is not divided between the public and private sector. By contrast, English education suffers from — or enjoys, according to your point of view — a great variety of local policies, programmes, practices and initiatives. It would therefore be misleading to suggest that the Danish system of integration, for instance, could be replicated here, but it may offer some useful insights and guidelines.

The Danish system of integration[1]

This system was inspired by the American experience, although it meshes comfortably with recent educational thinking in Denmark. Back in the 1950s, Danish mainstream education had stringent streaming by ability. The 1960s saw the advent of comprehensive schooling and mixed ability teaching. The integration of children who were other than 'normal' into ordinary schools was regarded simply as an extension of the same principle. The decision to integrate was unambiguously political and, as elsewhere, was accompanied by heated debate. Parental pressure ultimately swung the balance in favour of instituting integration.

Today in Denmark, there are basically three options for the schooling of the visually impaired child:[2] (a) 'to remain in normal classes with extra coaching and suitable aids; (b) to attend a special class in an ordinary school or, if necessary, one of the primary (for pupils aged 7—14) education centres for severely handicapped children; (c) to enter a special school or, in case of need, a special boarding school'.[3] These options are listed in the order in which they are generally recommended: 'the most important factor . . . is that it (special education) should interfere as little as possible with the pupil's normal schooling'.[4]

For those visually impaired children in Denmark who cannot be integrated at all, there are two special schools. One is predominantly a primary school (ages 7—14), at Kalundborg; the other, a secondary school (ages 14—18), *cum* further training and vocational centre, in Copenhagen. There is little separate provision for the partially sighted, save one small private school shortly expected to close.

Both basic systems of integration (discussed in Chapter Five) are employed in Denmark — one involving placement in an ordinary class backed by itinerant assistance; the second involving units, or 'centre classes'. This latter form of provision is for those handicapped children with additional problems — mental, emotional or social — and includes those 'who would previously have been directed to one of the state institutions, and those with a considerable handicap who (would be) unable to derive sufficient benefit from education in a normal class'.[5] Each county has a network of such centre classes, which are located in ordinary schools. Children suffering from similar handicaps are grouped together. Thus, a centre class for the visually impaired exists exclusively to provide special help for the more severely handicapped who need not be sent to a special school. We see here, then, the 'classical' unit approach to integration. Centre classes are well-equipped, regularly visited by medical officers, and staffed by trained teachers. Every effort is made to encourage pupils to attend activities within the ordinary school wherever possible.

Turning now to the itinerant — and more highly favoured — form of integration one finds, first, that there are 100—150 blind children of school age[6] in Denmark of whom some 50 per cent qualify for individual placement in ordinary schools; second, that there are also about 450 partially sighted children, of whom some 95 per cent are individually integrated; third, that individually integrated pupils include all those deemed "normally gifted" and whose "home conditions are reasonably good"; fourth, that decisions about placement are made by the local school psychological team;[7] and fifth, that individually integrated children are supported by an itinerant teacher or 'educational counsellor', each of Denmark's 14 counties having such a counsellor specifically for the visually impaired.

Not unnaturally, the support offered to an individually integrated blind child is more extensive than that offered to a partially sighted child. In the case of a pupil who has been diagnosed as blind and assessed as eligible for integrated education, a certain procedure is set in motion. Staff at a local ordinary school are approached and asked whether they are willing to accept the pupil. If approval is received, the class teacher who will be assuming responsibility for the blind child is encouraged to attend a two- to three-day course at one of the special schools; (in Denmark, a single teacher continues with the same class from age seven to 14 years). Only one blind child is placed in each ordinary school. The educational counsellor's job is then to ensure that the child receives the necessary materials, and that teachers, psychologists, parents, and pupil receive sufficient advice and equipment. Each blind child is provided with two sets of the necessary materials: two Perkins braillers, two typewriters, two tape-recorders, and two copies of the necessary textbooks; one set is kept in school, the other at home. The educational counsellor also offers extra tuition and help in 'handicap compensating techniques', mobility and social training, wherever necessary. The counsellor is also responsible for instructing and advising the local teacher, and for paying regular visits to the blind child both at home and at school.

Besides catering for the percentage of pupils who cannot be placed in centre classes or be individually integrated, the two special schools for the blind have a crucial supporting role in the national system of integration. Effectively, they operate as multi-purpose service centres — responsible for preparing equipment, undertaking research on teaching materials, and for carrying out educational, psychological and personality testing; they give courses for teachers (specialist and non-specialist); they counsel parents and provide 'parental courses'; and they offer 'booster courses' during the summer vacation for integrated pupils.

Three of these functions are worth reporting in more detail as they reflect the close cooperation between special schools and those involved in integration. First, short courses of two or three days for teachers in ordinary schools are seen as an essential component of the nationwide integration plan. Attitudes of teachers in mainstream schools are considered crucial: whether the integrated child thrives or not is thought to depend largely on the ordinary teacher's energy and effort. While not all teachers attend them, the majority do, and they are widely held to be invaluable. A teacher will typically receive instruction in basic braille, be shown how to use a Perkins brailler, and learn about the conditions of impaired vision. After this initial course, teachers are encouraged to attend periodic refresher courses if they can be released from school.[8]

A second special school activity is their sponsorship of courses for parents, their integrated blind children, and their educational counsellors. These courses, held once a year, last two to three days. Their primary aim is social — to enable parents to meet others in similar situations. The course programme concentrates on teaching parents how they can best help their children, what new developments have occurred in medical and educational research, and what teaching methods are being used in schools. Such courses have only been in existence for four years but are deemed to be very beneficial to parents.

Third, there are summer vacation courses, arranged by the special schools, for integrated pupils from around the country. These provide a chance for the special school teachers and educational counsellors to observe the blind child in a different context and to decide whether he or she needs extra assistance. They enable the integrated children to meet others with visual impairment and to realize that they are not alone — an opportunity they might not otherwise have. The summer school was described as a summer camp for the pupils, with fun as the first priority.

It is acknowledged that not all visually impaired children manage successfully in integrated settings. If there is doubt about a pupil's progress, the initial move is to make a team assessment on the spot. If the 'failure' can be compensated for by more tuition or assistance, this is then arranged; if necessary, the integrated child may be sent to a special school for extra tuition and observation — such sessions vary in length from one month to one year. Alternatively, the child can be moved to another local school if this is considered beneficial. What is characteristic of the Danish system is its flexibility — it allows for easy transfer between integrated and special forms of schooling.

Finally, in the opinion of those involved, integrated education in Denmark has had a profound effect upon blind children: blind mannerisms and social adjustment problems have been fewer: 'We have learned that a visual handicap, no matter how severe, can be compensated for through materials, educational support, (and) cooperation between the persons involved, so that the child can be taught in a local school where he belongs and live as normal a life as possible'.[9]

The Swedish system of integration[10]

The Swedish system is "less developed" than the Danish in that it involves fewer pupils and is constrained by geographical factors. In the mid-1950s, slow and cautious integration of blind children was inaugurated. It was restricted to certain blind pupils who had completed the first eight of their ten years of compulsory schooling in a special school (Tomteboda School in Stockholm), and whose parents supported them in their desire to spend their last two years of schooling in mainstream education. A government commission, examining educational provision for the blind and deaf, reported in 1965 that the integration scheme as it had been set up from Tomteboda School should become *the* model system for integration; and that many more children should be integrated in their last two years of schooling.[11] Since 1965, between 60 and 70 per cent of Tomteboda School pupils (all of them educationally blind) have completed their schooling in an integrated setting, arranged on an individual basis with peripatetic support.

The scheme for integrating blind pupils works as follows. After seven or eight years of compulsory schooling at Tomteboda, the head teacher confers with both the parents and the pupil about the prospect of going to a local school. Once agreed, the local school is contacted, an order is made out for books and materials the child will require, and from then on the pupil's education effectively becomes the responsibility of an itinerant teacher, who liaises with the local school and visits the school with the incoming pupil to meet prospective classmates in advance.

On the technical side, availability of braille material and educational aids was considered essential. All the necessary materials are provided by Tomteboda School. Book production has expanded rapidly but is still considered inadequate. To some people this signified insufficient planning for integration; resources, both human and technical, have always been scarce; there have been difficulties with delivery of books, and an insufficient number of itinerant teachers. It was widely felt, among those interviewed, that unless there were more resources, the present system of integration could not, and should not, be allowed to develop further.

Although, in theory, all blind children aged 15 are eligible, some selection criteria do operate. It is considered important that the child should have a good intellect, but this is not the most important criterion; nor does "physical appearance hinder integration". Instead, greater emphasis is placed on social status and social background; whether prospective candidates can make friends, are able to cope with living at home, whether their parents can cope, and whether teachers in the school are prepared to deal with them. It is widely felt that pupils who are to be integrated must learn to help themselves and have a "positive orientation". The "passive child" is not thought to have much hope of succeeding.

Although few people call this system "real integration" — because it occurs so late in a child's school career — it is nevertheless considered more radical than the other type of integration currently practised in Sweden — namely, "class (unit) integration". This latter type is mainly for the partially sighted.

Special classes for the partially sighted were established in the three largest Swedish cities (Malmo, Gothenborg, and Stockholm) in the early

1960s. Currently these cater for some 60—70 pupils in all.[12] There is strikingly little enthusiasm for these classes, partly because grouping the partially sighted together is thought to "slow down the tempo of learning". Before these classes were set up, there was no special provision for the partially sighted. The remainder of the partially sighted school population (about 500—700) are to be found in ordinary schools, receiving little or no specialist support.

Itinerant teachers for the blind and partially sighted have recently been amalgamated. There are now 10 itinerant teachers, regionally based (two in each of the five counties), and affiliated to Tomteboda School. Their responsibility is to support Sweden's entire visually impaired school population. Not surprisingly, they are judged to be overworked; many partially sighted pupils are lucky to receive more than one or two visits in the course of their entire school career.

It is widely hoped, among those directly concerned with the integration of the blind in Sweden, that it will continue to expand and that in time younger children will be integrated. The main questions — aside from the general one of attracting sufficient financial support — seem to centre around how best to advise parents, and how to explain thoroughly to all concerned their different roles in an integrated system. It is thought essential that parents should continue to have the opportunity of choosing which type of provision they want their children to have.

In conclusion, one can note parallels between the Swedish and Danish systems of integration although their aims and practices are different. In Denmark, the goal is one of immediate and complete integration with special schooling provided only if it is shown to be really necessary. In Sweden, the philosophy is more cautious with integration confined to older pupils, who are judged to be more skilled and better able to command the respect of their peers. What the two systems have in common is their centralized organization. As in Denmark, the director and staff of the Swedish special school and the itinerant teachers meet several times a year to discuss problems. Again, as in Denmark, Sweden's special schools provide materials and offer special educational provision when necessary.

Notes

(1) In August 1975, one of the research team visited Denmark for one week. Several different organizations and schools were visited (see Appendix 3). Much of the data on the Danish system of integration was collected with the help of the senior educational counsellor for the visually impaired and representatives of the Ministry of Education who arranged for visits to schools where blind children were integrated. Several teachers and itinerant

counsellors were interviewed, and discussions conducted. Both the special schools for the visually impaired in Denmark were visited and in-depth interviews held with principals, teachers psychologists, educational counsellors, social workers, care staff, researchers and administrators. The language barrier prevented any lengthy conversations with pupils, although one or two older students at the Royal National Institute for the Blind in Copenhagen were briefly interviewed.

(2) The definitions of blindness and partial sight are the same in Scandinavia as in England.

(3) JORGENSEN, I. SKOV (Ed) (1970). *Special Education in Denmark, Handicapped Children in Danish Primary Schools*. Copenhagen: Det Danske Selskab.

(4) JORGENSEN, I. SKOV (1970). *ibid*.

(5) JORGENSEN, I. SKOV (1970). *ibid*.

(6) School age in Denmark is between 6—7 and 16—17 (ten grades of compulsory schooling).

(7) A borough with 5000 pupils will have a psychological team consisting of: 1 chief school psychologist, 2 educational psychologists, 2 clinical psychologists, 1 social worker (all full-time) plus the following part-time teachers / advisers: 1 counsellor each for the speech / hearing impaired, the mentally retarded, backward readers, the emotionally and socially handicapped, and the backward school leaver, 1—3 counsellors for special classes and 1 psychiatric adviser.

(8) The Royal Danish School of Educational Studies offers an annual training course, usually lasting a week, which is more 'academic' in content than the in-service courses at the special schools (but is designed to complement the latter). These week-long courses concentrate on the theoretical aspects of teaching the visually impaired and are usually restricted to one topic per course. They usually result in a report, later disseminated to all teachers who are responsible for the visually impaired.

(9) LINDAU, HANNE (1975). 'Special Education in Denmark and integration of visually handicapped children in normal classes in the public school', *Child Care, Health and Development*, 1, 5.

(10) A member of the research team spent one week in Sweden observing integration there. Visits were made to Tomteboda School in Stockholm, and extensive discussions were held with the principal and the director of the resource centre at the school which serves integrated pupils. Representatives of the Swedish Association of the Blind were interviewed, as was the coordinator of the teacher training programmes for intending teachers of the visually impaired. Researchers at the University of Uppsala were visited and interviewed. It also proved possible to interview one of the educational counsellors and to visit one of the special classes for the blind in Gothenborg. Lessons were observed and teachers interviewed at length. Again language barriers made it difficult to interview pupils.

(11) The commission's underlying philosophy was that all blind pupils should receive a thorough grounding at the special school before integration was attempted. This had not been the original intention of the instigators of the Tomteboda experiment: they had started with older pupils only in order to demonstrate the viability of integration; their intention had been to extend it eventually to younger pupils.

(12) A partially sighted child who lives outside the three cities does not usually have access to a special class.

Part Three

The Search for the Normal

Chapter Ten

Agreements and Disagreements

In Part III of the book we examine the arguments, philosophies, and supposed effects of integration; the contrasts between ordinary and special schooling for the visually impaired school child; the underlying hopes, doubts, intentions, questions, and likely effects of different systems. We have spoken of a debate about integration but have yet to outline the arguments assembled on either side. They are many in number and diverse in form. The book taken as a whole is designed to illuminate them and put them into perspective. What is offered in this first chapter of Part III is a short guided tour of the principal landmarks.

We find that the debate has several major themes. We select three of the most contentious and important: one to do with the residential nature of schools for the blind; another with academic standards and expectations; and a third that relates to the 'search for normality'.

The first area of disagreement, about boarding education, is perhaps the most straightforward. Schools for the blind are residential;[1] some have a system of weekly boarding, where the child travels home every weekend, but this is not universal. Schools for the partially sighted are predominantly day schools. One of the chief arguments for extending integrated provision is that it is wrong to take children away from home, especially young blind children.[2] If anything, the argument goes, children with special problems need more parental support not less. The argument against this is that, harsh though it may sound, not all parents are capable of looking after a child with severe visual impairment, nor do they always want to. A special school head teacher, speaking of the general desirability of weekly boarding, thought that parents might "enjoy the child at the weekend" but were relieved that "there is a gap of five days".

A special education adviser, willing to place children with visual impairment in ordinary schools, made another point: she thought that integration had become a 'hurrah word' because it allowed the child to remain within the family unit, as if this were automatically 'a good'. She explained her position: "I'm all for keeping kids at home as long as everything is OK, but mums aren't trained to bring up abnormal children: home isn't necessarily the best place . . . My principal concern is what is best for the child and best for mum".

Those favouring more integration reply, in the words of one spokesman, that: "The majority of parents genuinely would not want their children to go away if they felt there was a viable alternative — they like having their kids about, they *even* like having blind kids about".

All are agreed that a handicapped child is likely to impose strain and difficulty on a family, and that not all home contexts are suitable. The special education adviser (quoted earlier) thought that, "some children are not able to be helped by their parents until their parents have been helped to deal with their children". One proponent of integration went so far as to suggest that integration would lead to "a better education for parents". An integration scheme in Medford, Massachusetts (see Chapter Six) involving blind pupils living at home, did not leave this parental education to chance. They had introduced parental counselling on which they put a high premium. There is a growing demand for parental counselling of some kind in this country.[3]

There are many other strands of argument about residentialism; we are forced to be selective. One point to realize is that residential schools, as we said, are mainly for the blind — partially sighted pupils more often live at home and travel daily to a day special school. In this case, there are difficulties — that affect specialized units too — with pupils having extensive daily travel; also, their school and home friends do not overlap. Both of these consequences can detract greatly from the naturalness of their total home experience. Of course, on the other side, residential special schooling also creates friendship problems. Critics argue that pupils' friends are drawn exclusively from others similarly handicapped; and that they have little chance in school holidays of making friends with sighted children in their home environment.

Let us turn next to the thorny question of academic standards — the second dispute we examine. It is widely agreed that children with low or limited vision are often at stages of academic development behind those of the normally sighted.[4] The dispute is whether this is inevitable — a function of the added difficulties in reading and studying for those with low vision, and of the general reduction of external stimulation that the visually impaired child experiences; or — alternatively — whether it reflects poorer quality education on the part of special schools. Some educators we spoke to could not "believe that people, because they are blind, have to be that far behind". Others, with experience of teaching a large spectrum of children with differing abilities, degrees of visual impairment, and combinations of additional handicaps, disagreed. They argued that special schooling, far from being inferior, was superior – it could give more individual attention, staff were specially trained, curriculum options were wide, and there were specialized technical facilities. This area of dispute is exceedingly difficult to unravel, let alone adequately to summarize and adjudicate.

Where there seems a significant measure of agreement is that both in the special schools and outside there is concern about the 'non-grammar' special schools: inadvertently they may have come to expect lower standards, have a reduced "educational ambition" and as "small schools with routinized set-ups" they may "encourage a working down to a certain average". Arguably, a move to greater integration could introduce stimulation and competition.

Those sceptical of the value of any wholesale swing towards integration also expressed fears of an academic kind. Visually impaired children, they thought, placed individually within ordinary schools, might be overchallenged or underchallenged; they could be teased, fussed over, ignored, left behind, or misunderstood. While it would be stimulating for some, for others it would be a disaster. Much would depend on the goodwill and involvement of individual teachers,[5] who often have no specialist training and who lack experience with handicapped pupils. One critic of integration pointed out that planning often stopped with getting the handicapped child into the ordinary school: "Just putting a child into a sighted class is inadequate; the school, teachers, and the class structure must all be fitted to the individual child" (special school teacher). Integration on an individual basis *might* be appropriate for intelligent, extrovert, confident pupils, with no additional handicaps. But this excludes a sizeable proportion of pupils with defective vision, in fact possibly (according to one's definitions) a majority.

There were profound worries, on the part of those opposed to integration, about the level of support. One head teacher of a partially sighted school – whose worry was "that children will be pawns of an ideal" thought that, "It's no good a peripatetic going around and giving an hour a week and saying that's adequate support – it's ludicrous". The ordinary class teacher would also have to be "a super teacher – they can barely deal with their ordinary kids".

The final argument, in this brief selective overview of the debate, is a more far-reaching one. In favour of more integration these views are advanced: first, since on leaving school, the boy or girl with a visual impairment will have to contend with working and living in a world geared to the sighted, adaptation to it should begin as early as possible; second, that special residential schools embody and reinforce a 'handicapped sub-culture' that is inward - (towards 'the world of the blind') rather than outward-looking (towards the 'world of the sighted') and which socializes pupils into regarding themselves as handicapped persons. As one proponent of integration explained: "Children who have been taught that they are blind are often incapable of doing things". Another agreed: "To grow up in (that) particular environment until you are 18+ must do a lot to close a lot of options . . . it deprives people of the feeling of mixing with sighted people".

The argument the other way is that all are agreed that those with an impairment of vision should not be excluded from normal society. But the greatest assurance that, as adults, they will live as near normal lives as possible is that they should receive a first-rate educational preparation, and that this is the first and most urgent priority. In short, there is a shared aim of producing 'normal members of society'. Where opinions differ is in how this goal can best be attained. Let us examine this more closely.

Producing normal members of society refers basically to preparing the visually impaired person for eventual entry into 'the sighted world'. At the time of entry, they should have sufficient independence and initiative to fend for themselves. For a minority, some continued support may be necessary, like a community of similarly handicapped people or a sheltered workshop. But the goal is maximum independence in everyday life for as many as possible. Those advocating or practising education that is integrated argue that being in the ordinary education system is already being part of the sighted world: there is no need to negotiate 'entry' at a future point, as there is when a child leaves special schooling. It is held to be "more realistic" and "more natural" to give the child with limited or low vision the opportunity "to measure himself alongside sighted peers and then adjust realistically". As one blind person further explained: "What we have in common with the sighted is much more extensive than that which distinguishes us".

Those favouring the retention of special schooling argue differently. The visually impaired child is best prepared, they say, by learning certain specialist techniques and skills — in what must necessarily be a somewhat artificial and modified environment — before "coming out into the real world". They argue that it is unnatural and wrong to place a person with a disability in the same educational race as those without disability, without making allowances and without providing specialized preparatory help. One special school head teacher who favoured integration at sixth-form level, commented: "I believe you give them the expertise, the equipment and facilities, and *then* you integrate".

This reflects one of the most basic of educational dilemmas, almost a conundrum — i.e. is it better to learn to swim in the deep end straightaway, or to go through exercises in a planned, progressive sequence at the shallow end? There is no clear 'answer': it is an inherent pedagogic tension, a balance to be sought, a case of where to draw the line.

We shall encounter many examples of this archetypal deep end / shallow end dilemma. It turns up in strikingly different guises. Take a simple example — a purpose-built school for pupils with visual impairment, with architectural guides for easier mobility and no steps or sharp corners. It provides a 'shallow end' physical environment. But then — it could be argued — it is also a 'less natural' environment than a school built without the visually impaired specifically in mind, a usual type of school replete with the customary architectural irregularities and unpredictables. Here, a visually impaired child would have to face, get used to, and master a 'deep end' kind of environment. The dilemma is, therefore, whether a purpose-built school is solving a short-term and essentially organizational problem at the expense of a longer-term educational goal; or — alternatively — whether the removal of unnecessary strain in the short term serves to help the child with visual impairment to match the sighted child's attainment sooner and more effectively.

The basic thrust of many pro-integration arguments comes from a wish for 'normality'. In the words of one exponent:

> "We are committed to the basic idea that blind people should be in a situation where any opportunity there is for developing natural and constant relations with their sighted peers should be taken advantage of . . . Integration is more likely to be a stretching out of horizons. Socially, being educated together with sighted boys and girls would be liberating . . . Integrated education is an attempt to assert and contribute to the right of the blind to be right in the life of the community."

No-one in special education would probably disagree with these views in principle: what is questioned is the extent to which they are realizable. Those who question whether the severely visually impaired can be integrated into ordinary schools question and worry about the practicalities more than the philosophy. There is a general cautiousness that 'things could move too far' and that the special help that a group of people sharing a disability have enjoyed in the past will no longer be provided to the same degree. The kind of cautiousness expressed is simply but dramatically portrayed in some remarks by Sorsby (1972), writing in a more general context and specifically about the blind:

'Coming to terms with blindness is a bitter experience and this is not made any easier by evasions or circumlocutions. To accept blindness and all its consequences is the first step in adjusting oneself. It cannot, for instance, help the parents of a blind child if attempts are made to gloss over the child's blindness when it is essential to educate and train the child to a life of irremediable blindness. The realities of the situation are the blindness, the blind school, and the blind occupation; and there is a substantial danger for blind children no less than for blind adults that their needs will receive less attention if illusory advantages are being pursued.'[6]

These views already, four years later, sound unfashionable. But they represent many of the views privately held, if not publicly expressed, by those in special schools. Today, however, opinion has swung further towards integration: more people now argue that the greater illusion is to believe that one can give the visually impaired child the ability to cope with ordinary life through attendance at a school that is special and far from ordinary. The pendulum of opinion, however, could well swing back.

The various points summarized above are some of the more basic arguments. The task we have set ourselves is to comprehend the ideology, practical questions, types of organizational thinking, and results of integration, not to tot up marks or votes for and against it.

Notes

(1) Where pupils live within easy reach of the school, they may attend as day pupils.

(2) Blind children can be sent to special residential schools from the age of five. Provision for younger children is available in one of the six Sunshine Homes run by the Royal National Institute for the Blind, but this is usually restricted to blind children who suffer from severe additional physiological or social handicaps.

(3) The Vernon Committee recommended that:

> 'Every family of a visually handicapped child under the age of 5 should have access to a team who can meet their different needs for counselling. To this end, local authorities should be responsible for securing an adequate number of staff with the requisite training and experience to provide, for parents of young visually handicapped children in their area, psychological support and advice about the day-to-day handling of their children. These staff should work in close association with the teachers or educational psychologists who would carry out educational counselling and with the regional assessment

team, which should co-ordinate their work.'

DEPARTMENT OF EDUCATION AND SCIENCE (1972). *The Education of the Visually Handicapped*. (Vernon Report). London: HMSO.

(4) In a review of recent research on this subject, Tobin writes:

'The implications of some of the studies . . . on such topics as concept formation, perceptual skills, and time required to process incoming data, are such as to suggest that the blind pupil would lag behind his sighted peer in terms of academic achievement in the conventional school subjects. To compensate for these handicaps, a variety of procedures have been adopted, including the extension of schooling, additional time allowances in public examinations, and better pupil / teacher ratios. Little direct comparison between blind and sighted has been made . . . nor is there much evidence of the effects on achievement of different methods of teaching blind pupils.'

(TOBIN, M.J. (1971a). 'Report on overseas research', *Teacher of the Blind*, **LIX**, 3.) In a later review, Tobin writes, 'Investigations of the intelligence of partially sighted children have tended to be somewhat inconclusive, but there is no evidence that there are significant differences between them and their normally sighted peers'. (TOBIN, M.J. (1971b). 'Report on overseas research', *Teacher of the Blind*, **LXI**, 4.)

(5) Research into teachers' attitudes is far from encouraging. Tobin (1972) in a study of 80 new graduates and experienced teachers who enrolled on post-graduate certificate in education or advanced diploma courses, found that both groups gave low ratings to blind and partially sighted children in terms of teaching preference and 'knowledge about' visually impaired children. Among experienced teachers, these low ratings were correlated with relative unwillingness to accept such children in the integrated setting. He remarks,

'Integration then, is not going to be solved as a problem merely by handpicking a few able pupils, (and) providing them with the appropriate devices and materials, (and) then extrapolating from these its suitability for a wider cross-section of ability . . . If, as Murphy (1960) puts it "Attitudes in the community . . . can be more crippling than the handicap itself", a basic requirement is a change in the attitudes of the non-specialist teacher.'

TOBIN, M.J. (1972c). 'The attitudes of non-specialist teachers toward visually handicapped pupils', *Teacher of the Blind*, **LX**, 2.

(6) SORSBY, A. (1972). *The Incidence and Causes of Blindness in England and Wales, 1963—68*, 128. London: HMSO.

Chapter Eleven

Integration in the Context of Special Education

The last chapter concluded that discussion about integration has to do with its practicalities: the principles are not so obviously in dispute. Those concerned to preserve the special schools more or less in their present form express doubts about schemes of integration: Can they match the education provided by special schools? Can they marshall enough support, in resources and expertise? Can they understand sufficiently, and cater for, the visual and other problems of the blind or partially sighted child? The rhetoric and idealism behind much integration thinking is difficult to disparage; but what of the detailed mechanics?

We have chosen to approach answering these and similar questions by asking a question of our own: Exactly what are the 'special' components of special schooling? What opportunities and potentialities are available to children in special schools that might be denied them in ordinary schools?

What makes special schools special?

Before identifying any of these components, some words of caution. British experience with integrating blind children is limited to the open education experiments;[1] other schemes in this country have been with the partially sighted. Yet the discussion that follows refers extensively to special schools for the blind as well as those for the partially sighted. Also, there are marked individual differences between special schools so that conclusive generalizations are dangerous; those we advance have to be more tentative.

The claims made for what special schools provide are many. We have selected some of the chief ones and listed them below. We do not pretend to provide exhaustive documentation of the various claims advanced.

i. 'Tailor-made' classroom teaching

Vernon[2] succinctly summarized this advantage of special schooling: '. . . information and learning facilities are available in the form most appropriate for acceptance and assimilation by visually handicapped children'.

Routine in special schools is the adaptation of curriculum materials, teaching aids, laboratory and other equipment; and also changes in approaches to teaching. For example, books are transcribed for braille users; maps and diagrams are converted into raised form for tactile perception, using the thermoform process (taking care to ensure that not too much information for tactile discrimination is included); readings on laboratory apparatus are given brailled stick-on labels; scientific phenomena usually demonstrated by visual means are re-thought so as to use the senses of hearing or touch instead; three-dimensional models — often using straws and pipe cleaners — are devised, particularly for mathematics; and extensive use is made of cassette recorders.

Special schools for the partially sighted, using print as the reading and writing medium, have fewer adaptations of this order to make. But they concern themselves with ensuring that low vision aids, large print texts and easy to read worksheets are available and are used; that lighting is of the right kind and intensity; that visually presented information is adequately understood; and that the pace of work is adjusted according to what each individual can see.

ii. Teaching is individualized

This is one of the primary strengths of special schooling. With differing and sometimes varying degrees of residual vision, there is a specific need for pacing the work rate. Kirk[3] points out that sharing a label such as 'partial sight' is an inadequate basis for devising children's educational programmes: 'Labels might have a conversational use but they are of little value to teachers in developing appropriate programmes'. We have already noted that the same visual condition can affect two children in disparate ways. Also, it has been shown that there is greater diversity in the rate of perceptual development among blind than sighted children.[4] Therefore, to force visually impaired children into normative categories, on the basis of modified IQ or achievement tests, is probably even riskier than with children who are sighted. A need for individualized teaching seems strongly reinforced.

In fact, there is little class teaching of the conventional kind in special schools. Older children especially work to individual timetables at their own speed. A danger in any self-paced régime is, of course, always present: the increased difficulty of knowing whether pupils are really trying and extending themselves. Some senior advisers felt there was a need for visually impaired pupils of secondary age to be encouraged to work harder and more quickly, in spite of their handicap. There was a danger in their falling behind their age group if not.

Individualized attention makes obligatory the favourable teacher/pupil ratios found in special schools. We rarely observed any class with more than 15 pupils, and some had as few as six. The teacher in the special school also needs time to look up references for blind pupils when these do not exist in braille, and also for preparing lesson material such as master copies of diagrams and models for thermoforming. Teachers also have to edit sections of books required by their class and get them brailled.

The less pressurized work rate and the smaller classes also permit each pupil "the chance to experience something for himself" (science teacher); and for extensive contact between staff and pupils. Education is considered in 'round the clock' terms.

iii. Resource centres

Special schools customarily have available a variety of technical aids. These can include: facilities for braille transcription and duplication; enlarging equipment; 'talking books'; cassette recorders and record players; audio calculators; large print books and typewriters; high intensity lamps; modified reading stands; magnifiers and other low vision aids. This is not a complete listing; nor do all schools have identical equipment, nor to the same extent. Those catering for the more academically able — e.g. Worcester College and Exhall Grange — tend to be the better equipped schools.

We were able to confirm the conclusions of the Vernon Committee on the question of resources: 'aids to teaching and learning in schools for the visually handicapped . . . have revealed much ingenuity and effort on the part of individual schools and teachers to meet the particular needs which have arisen, but the overall picture is one of shortage'.[5] Certainly, more aids and equipment could help; but no technology is useful unless it is used, and used imaginatively. What seemed notable, in many schools, was not so much the presence of novel technical aids as the extent to which modifications had been made of standard equipment. Highly sophisticated technical aids for the visually impaired are often advocated as necessary. But this is subject to question.[6] At one school for the partially sighted there is a recently developed resource room.[7] With the exception of closed circuit television, enlarging apparatus, and an induction loop system, everything else could easily be found in a well-equipped ordinary school. Sophisticated and specialized equipment that is very expensive, may not be as necessary for teaching visually impaired children as a greater abundance and more equitable distribution of more straightforward aids, such as cassette recorders: one school for the partially sighted only acquired its second cassette recorder in 1975.

iv. The nature of visual impairment understood

At present, for teachers in schools for the blind, there is a diploma in special education (visually handicapped) at Birmingham University or, alternatively, teachers have to undergo a course of in-service training run by the College of Teachers of the Blind, within three years of taking up a teaching post. Some teachers in schools for the partially sighted have also completed the Birmingham course, but no equivalent special training is yet mandatory.[8] Part of the training relates to disorders of vision. The teacher learns about the various medical conditions, the ways in which sight is affected, and about teaching methods that can be deployed. He or she becomes aware of the developmental consequences of a child's experience when restricted by limited vision. In other words, the teacher has a grounding in a specialized field of study and research; and this is founded on knowledge of visual impairment.

Those outside the special schools appreciate the expertise that they contain. One special school head teacher commented on how often he was telephoned by heads of ordinary schools who had on their roll a pupil who was partially sighted: could he provide the names of publishers of large print books? The head teacher recounted how he would respond by asking the inquirer: "What's the eye problem?" or Does he have an LVA (low vision aid)?"; the caller was often at a loss to reply.

Staff in special schools are closer to the problem. For example, they have contact with medical personnel and they tend to know pupils' medical histories and family backgrounds. They are also concerned about their pupils' use of low vision aids. These are commonplace for partially sighted children, but many users of braille have optical aids as well.[9]

Part of the teacher's task is to get children to use their aids. This is a very real problem: staff at special schools felt that pupils needed constant encouragement to use them.[10] One incentive is to make them widely and more easily available for loan within the school, and to encourage the child to experiment. This is done at Exhall Grange School for the Partially Sighted; the head teacher described aids as "a means to an end, to get my kids to see what I want them to see . . . If a child chooses one he will use it because he chose it". However, this practice and philosophy were criticized in certain medical quarters: choosing low vision aids was a skilled task, it was asserted, and one that needed to be medically handled. The non-medical distribution of low vision aids was described as "dangerous dabbling". On the other hand, not all children attend low vision clinics and prescribed aids may need changing quite frequently: a 'bank' of them in the school thus fulfils a clear need. Whether the medical opposition is a professional 'restrictive practice' or a substantiated and valid ophthalmological warning is unresolved: there were sharp divergences between the views of different groups.

v. A broadly conceived curriculum

Many special school teachers spoke about the breadth of the curriculum offered at their schools. Not only did they match ordinary schools in subjects such as literature or language — relatively straightforward for pupils with impaired vision — but they also taught more problematic subjects as well: e.g. science, handicraft, and physical education.

In addition, special schools offer specialized activities such as mobility training. This needs to be continuous and to be given by specially trained staff. All schools for the blind provide this — some even timetable it — and increasingly, schools for the partially sighted are making similar provision, more particularly for those pupils whose prognosis is not good. Mobility involves more than simply finding one's way about with the help of a long cane: it incorporates posture training, body awareness, spatial concepts, direction seeking, and developing and coordinating the use of other senses. Physical education is an allied component in that it can help build confidence in movement, which is an essential. The elimination of so-called 'blindisms' — mannerisms commonly displayed by the blind[11] — is also important.

Other additions to the curriculum may include typing and self-care activities. And though not formally timetabled, most school staff envisage social training as part of their professional work. They encourage appropriate table manners, seek to coordinate physical gestures, and generally to transmit social rules. In some respects, teaching staff in residential special schools act as surrogate parents, aided by ancillary staff who in many cases form an integral part of the school scene.

vi. Specialist knowledge of career opportunities

This is a common claim of special school staff, but one that is sometimes contested. Without question, job placement for the visually impaired is a hazardous business. An accurate prognosis is what is most required, but not always possible. Decisions on training are particularly difficult when the prognosis is not good and yet current vision is reasonable. In this case, should the individual be encouraged to train for employment that he or she is capable of doing at the moment? Or, alternatively, should the school leaver be edged towards a job that could still be done if vision deteriorated further? Other factors rendering job placement a difficult exercise include the following: school leavers may have unrealistic ideas about their capabilities or about the visual demands of certain jobs; and employers are often ignorant — especially of partial sightedness — or they underestimate what the visually impaired can do.

With regard to job placement, the partially sighted may be worse off than the blind. In many cases, the partially sighted boy or girl needs to try out a particular job before knowing whether he or she can see sufficiently well to perform the specific tasks entailed. For this reason, schools for the partially sighted often seek to organize a week's work experience in advance of leaving. This may cover two or three different jobs. The value of this is illustrated by two examples — both concerning partially sighted girls. One wanted to work as a bank clerk, the other as a nurse: the first was turned down at interview because it was found that she could not read the signatures on cheques; the second was given a week's trial, during which she discovered that she could not see sufficiently well to read a thermometer. She too was rejected. Reading signatures and thermometers are, of course, single tasks among many that go with the jobs: however, they happen to be considered crucial.

What is underlined here is the value of specialized counselling and careers advice, which the special schools claim to provide. For blind pupils, school and RNIB careers officers work in conjunction. Much careers advice is disseminated informally but, in addition, RNIB officers visit schools to discuss potential sources of employment and post-school life generally with individual pupils, parents, school counsellors, and head teachers. For the partially sighted, the head teacher or a deputy may operate as a part-time careers teacher, reinforcing the efforts of specialist careers officers employed by the local authority. Both then liaise with Youth Employment Officers, either locally — in the case of day special schools — or in pupils' home communities, in the case of residential schools.

Special school staff claim they 'know the ropes'; that they have well-established links with the relevant personnel, and a fund of experience to draw upon. Certainly they have close links with further education establishments — notably Hethersett, Queen Alexandra and Royal Normal Colleges, all of which now accept partially sighted as well as blind school leavers[12] — as well as with industrial rehabilitation units. Some special schools organize small-scale conferences covering career choices for final year pupils. They invite speakers from outside and visit establishments that might be potential employers.

This was the general, positive picture. However, we found some evidence from talking with pupils — both past and present — that all was not so straightforward. For instance, several partially sighted young adults complained at how little counselling they had received at school, and how they had subsequently ended up wrongly or unhappily placed in employment. A good many blind pupils also expressed dissatisfaction: there was some feeling of being pressured into particular channels — "Yes, fine, but have you ever thought about telephony?". It led one girl to remark, "My mum said they must get paid for every physiotherapist (they enlist)". Some even suggested that RNIB careers officers had internalized the notion of 'special education for special jobs'. Certainly, pupils were acutely aware of the range of jobs held out as available to them and, more important, of those occupations of which their schools approved and disapproved. There were some comments on the difficulties they faced in trying to break away from established expectations: "You've got to push yourself . . . otherwise they'll push you into an RNIB corner".[13]

At the same time, there was a great deal of discussion in special schools about the need to open new doors careerwise. The difficulty they have is in deciding how, on the one hand, to encourage individual initiative while, on the other hand, maintaining a realistic stance. Sometimes they may veer too far in one direction. One post-school establishment openly admitted influencing their students' job aspirations: " . . . if need be these are modified by what it is realistic for them to do". The danger is that long experience may lead to expectations becoming rather fixed: it is of interest that many adventitiously blinded individuals, for instance, have successfully carried out jobs that are not even considered in special schools.

vii. A supportive milieu

Many of the features of the supportive milieu have already been referred to. The special schools offer understanding, encouragement, practical assistance, technical and medical support, and opportunities to take part in a wide variety of everyday activities. Taken together, these contribute to forming a total milieu — an environment and ethos — geared to the handicapped child's needs.

However, there are other identifiable features not yet mentioned. For instance, the special school is also a supportive milieu for staff: they can learn from each other, particularly from the experience of older colleagues. The special school also functions as a rehabilitation centre for the adventitiously visually impaired — i.e. those whose impaired vision is a result of accident or sudden illness. In general, as one teacher remarked, "we are geared to cope with the difficulties"; while another commented, "Being in a concentrated encounter with blind pupils gives me the opportunity to develop sophisticated ideas for overcoming practical problems".

Finally, residentialism itself is not without its advantages: it may be of benefit to handicapped pupils to spend part of their development as individuals in the company of those similarly afflicted. Certainly they are more likely to assist each other and to obtain mutual encouragement: "Because they know how other girls have coped, they can see where they are getting to" (teacher in a girls' special school). For the child who meets with rejection from the home or whose parents, despite their good intentions, hinder rather than help, the residential school can usefully relieve pressure.

Staff of special schools made numerous other points about the advantages of special schooling. A composite, selective summary is given below:

"Special schools are able to give greater attention to individual development."

"We are better able to help the disturbed and the disruptive."

"We have something more to offer by way of teaching, an unequalled educational opportunity."

"We offer children opportunities to pursue activities they enjoy, and to do so at their own speed."

"We offer the opportunity for the child to try everything."

"A specialist teacher cannot be replaced by a peripatetic."

"The average teacher hasn't a clue about the partially-sighted, they either seem over-worried or else reliant on pragmatic discovery."

viii. Transfers from ordinary to special schools

Head teachers of special schools, particularly those for the partially sighted, emphasized how often they were called upon to take the 'failures' of integration. One remarked upon the increased tendency, compared with a few years ago, to retain the child in ordinary schooling for as long as possible: "Unless a child is failing diabolically, the trend is to keep children in ordinary school".[14] He went on to describe a number of individual cases. The problems children had in ordinary schools were sometimes academic, and sometimes behavioural. He was aware that sometimes local authorities encouraged him to take a seriously disturbed child "using partial sight as the excuse".

Perhaps the best way _ demonstrate this role of the special school is to consider two examples.

First, let us examine the experience of a girl we shall call Sarah. Sarah's parents had evidently "fought" to get their child into the special school. Her mother had told the head teacher (in his words): " 'I've been trying to get my child into a school like yours for some time' ". Sarah had been doing very poorly in the ordinary school she was attending. Her school career was as follows: born 1960; left infants school in 1967; attended a middle school until 1972; went to secondary school from 1972 to 1974; then transferred into the partially sighted school. In 1974 her acuity readings were 6/60 (left eye) and 6/36 (right eye). She suffered from a rare type of macular degeneration and had a history of night epilepsy.

When Sarah transferred to the special school, her school records went with her. There were a number of revealing comments from teachers at her previous ordinary school. Clearly, Sarah's condition had not been taken for granted: 'Sarah needs to be near the blackboard. Her optician prescribed spectacles which she should be able to see with but she still seems to have difficulty'. The report went on: 'She has poor manual control, poor presentation of work. She enjoys reading but she finds difficulty in using books for reference.' The head teacher of the special school drew our attention to some other remarks. Thus, the report on physical education − 'She works well on her own' − suggests an absence of participation in group work. Another comment drawn to our attention was this: 'By working on programmed texts she has kept up her own standard. However, this is *of course* well below that of the rest of the class' (head teacher's emphasis).

The general picture of Sarah that emerges is one of reticence and non-participation. Sarah's IQ was given as 86: she had been in a remedial department of 40 in a year with an intake of 340. She was now in a class of about 12, receiving a great deal of individual attention, being encouraged to work, and her progress was considered satisfactory. She was taking four CSE subjects.

As we shall see in later chapters, there is a crucial role for parents to play. It is clear that without Mrs P's insistence on Sarah's attending a special school, she might not have done so. A report from the Area Health Authority (specifically, the senior medical officer of the Community Health Branch) read as follows:

'Her future is academically bleak . . . Sarah cannot receive the individual attention she requires, and due to her lack of drive she just sits back and is not making any progress. I think she requires special schooling, and as she is now 14 years this is a matter of urgency . . . Mrs P. is a very dominant character and is now getting rather aggressive about Sarah's educational treatment at T. I think she has some justification and feel the answer is a placement in a partially sighted school as soon as possible'.

The head teacher had also established good contact with Sarah's mother, relieved now that Sarah was at a special school. He explained about his contact with parents: "I can have a deep personal relationship with the family because of our size: the parents feel involved in their child's education, they don't feel cut off".

Our second example is of a boy, called here David, born in 1961. He attended an infant school (1966—1968), an ordinary junior school (1968—1970), went to another junior school (1971—1972) and before arriving at the school for the partially sighted in 1974 had been a pupil at a grammar school for two years. He suffered from cataracts and a convergent squint and had a visual acuity of 6/60 in both eyes. He was described as being on the "lower end of the PS category".

As with Sarah, reports from his previous school suggest that staff were uncertain about how to deal with David. It seems that he was 'an able pupil' though his progress was 'erratic' and he was 'not making all the effort of which he is capable'. The head teacher of the school for the partially sighted remarked, "frankly, his behaviour led to his coming here".

The reports suggest strongly that the ordinary school staff put David's difficult school reaction down to his visual impairment. The previous head had written to the parents: 'We know he has a quick brain and the problems arise because he is necessarily a slow reader and writer'; the geography teacher's report made the same point: 'As soon as the work gets beyond him, he loses concentration and he then becomes a behavioural problem in the class'. Two teachers thought that 'he uses his difficulties as an excuse for bad behaviour', while other remarks suggested this connection was generally made by teachers in the school: 'He needs to be better organized to cope ... needs to get his books ready and his magnifying glass'; '(it is) sad to relate he has not made as much progress as he could — he forgets his lens'; and — from the teacher of religious education who had found David's 'behaviour is no worse than average', this comment: 'However, the nature of the work has not called for much written work or prolonged reading and I appreciate that these are two areas where he may have particular problems which affect his attitude adversely'.

As with Sarah, the head teacher of the special school was at pains to point out how much the ordinary school took it for granted that the partially sighted pupil would be behind the rest of the class academically: (from the history teacher) — 'David's written work is obviously bad ...', (from the English teacher) — 'Spelling and punctuation understandably are very poor'; and (in another report)

'Spelling and punctuation are naturally difficult' — spelling was a problem because 'of a difficulty in visualizing the words'.

The ordinary school had not been indifferent to David's case: they had made attempts to get large print books, 'but it doesn't seem to give him much help'; David had been referred to an educational psychologist who had suggested 'specially printed exercise books from the RNIB, a large print dictionary, a special ruler, felt tip pens, soft lead pencils (for increased legibility)'; the school had intended to put him into an even larger class in order to 'push him harder academically . . . (he would) have to work harder to keep up'. Yet one of the main difficulties was the fact that he *was* in a large class: 'his inabilities seem to have frustrated him however and he likes constant attention which it is hard to maintain under present conditions' (history teacher); 'his progress would have been considerable if we had been able to give him the attention he needs, but this is impossible as we have the rest of the class to consider' (geography teacher).

Finally, in this cursory review of the notes about David from the previous school, a statement from the science teacher that provides a good example, in a few sentences, of the complex of problems that confronts an ordinary school with a severely partially sighted pupil:

'David is an able pupil who, in my opinion, is not gaining as much as he should from the science course. The reasons for this are as follows: (i) his sight defect makes it impossible for him to handle safely most scientific equipment. (ii) He is unable to record his results in a way which is necessary for "good science". (iii) He is unable to read instructions for practical work written on the blackboard. (iv) His science records and notes are so poor that he has to rely too much on memory. (v) His class peers are less able than he and he gets bored very quickly and this results in behavioural problems.'[15]

David, like Sarah, had settled down well in his new school. He could no longer "use his defect as an excuse"; he could be given the special attention he needed; and he was encouraged to use his low vision aids. Sarah and David, and others like them, have received less attention in this study than — viewed in hindsight — they probably deserved. However, we decided that rather than concentrating on retrospective studies, with only school records and memories to go on, we should be studying partially sighted children who currently attended ordinary schools; and this part of the work we discuss in Part IV of the book.

Special schools' reactions to integration

Finally, in this chapter, we discuss briefly the attitude of those in special schools towards the movement to integration. The special schools, in criticizing this trend, have certain espoused and expressed reasons for doing so: the supposed lack of support, a fear about children having a raw deal, and so forth. It is legitimate to ask what other factors are involved in their opposition — what hidden reasons, if any, may be lying beneath the public reservations.

It would be easy to point out that special schools have an interest in keeping themselves in being — all institutions tend to put this as one of their highest priorities among their unspoken objectives. But there are a number of other factors too that can be discerned (we are now being speculative).

It is clear, first, that many teachers enjoy teaching in special schools for the visually impaired: they appreciate the personal nature of the teaching, the somewhat less frenetic and fraught schedule, the smaller classes, and the opportunity to combine pedagogic and 'helping' elements in the same job. In short, it is seen as more satisfying than a post, say, in a larger ordinary school would be, or running a unit peripheral to the main part of the school. There are other factors: there is, within this area of special education, a sense of professional affiliation to a sub-specialty of the teaching profession; the possibility of widescale integration is seen, perhaps, as an unwelcome disruption of this collegiality. Then there is the fact that, following implementation of a major programme of integration, there would be a new function imposed on the special schools: the academically able and perhaps more personable children would be the first candidates for integration; the multiply handicapped, the more disturbed, and less able children would probably remain in the special schools. As happened in Perkins School for the Blind in Watertown, Massachusetts, the nature of the school's population would change: the academic tradition becomes steadily less applicable, and the teacher's role becomes more of a counsellor and social worker and less that of the traditional teacher.

These fears are perfectly understandable. Any major social or organizational change is disruptive of established patterns. This is not meant to pillory those who strongly oppose integration: one could equally ask about the private purposes of those who advocate with vehemence a programme of integration for all when, almost certainly, a sizeable number of visually impaired children could be integrated satis-factorily only with massive levels of support. The pressure for integration stems in part from a general shift in society's attitudes towards the treatment of the handicapped and other minorities: it is not advocated for educational considerations alone. Equally, perhaps, opposition to integration may have deeper roots than simply reservations about the adequacy of support to be found in integrated schemes.

Notes

(1) See Chapter Six.

(2) VERNON, M.D. (1974/5). 'Integrated education of the visually-handicapped', *The Teacher of the Blind*, 63, 2.

(3) KIRK, S. (1975). In a paper entitled 'Where are we in labelling, categorising and mainstreaming?' delivered at the conference 'Special Education 75: The New Frontiers', University of Kent, July 1975.

(4) Tobin (1972) in a study of 189 blind and partially sighted children using a Piagetian-type conservation of substance experiment inferred that 'while the best of them are performing on a par with the best of their sighted peers, the age range in which conservation is attained is more extended for the visually handicapped'. His article draws together data from previous investigations on the effects of visual impairment on development and cognitive skills. TOBIN, J.J. (1972b). 'Conservation of substance in the blind and partially sighted', *The British Journal of Educational Psychology*, 42, 2.

(5) DEPARTMENT OF EDUCATION AND SCIENCE (1972). *The Education of the Visually Handicapped*, (Vernon Report). London: HMSO.

(6) For a radical discussion of the dissemination of technological information see CLARK, L.L. (1974). 'Research Resource Needs for the Future'. Paper presented at the Fifth World Assembly of the World Council for the Welfare of the Blind, August 1974.

(7) At John Aird School for the Partially Sighted in London, the resource room is staffed by a full-time specially trained Media Resource Officer whose responsibility it is to provide materials for teachers, operate equipment, and instruct teachers in its use. Equipment includes television, cassette and tape-recorders, radios, a projector, slide viewers, cameras, a record player, an enlarging machine, and copiers.

(8) The Secretary of State for Education is now committed to making such training compulsory. Details of the pattern and timing of training are still under discussion.

(9) Fine (1968) in a study of 644 blind children discovered that 83 of them used glasses, low vision aids or hand lenses. FINE, S.R. (1968). 'Blind and partially sighted children', *Education Survey*, 4. London: HMSO.

(10) The Vernon Committee attributed inadequate use of LVAs by children to 'low intelligence, lack of self-confidence or persistence, and even vanity, shyness or a psychological inhibition'. DEPARTMENT OF EDUCATION AND SCIENCE (1972). *op. cit.*

(11) These include: 'rocking' (swaying back and forth), 'poking' (constantly touching the eyes), 'praying to heaven' (walking with head held high and eyes directed upwards), 'hand flapping' (constantly shaking hands), and 'spinning' (pirouetting on the spot).

(12) There is no further education provision exclusively for the partially sighted. One head teacher of a special school pointed out that there was "appalling

provision for the (partially sighted) school leaver . . . it's abysmal . . . non-existent". One of his ex-pupils, a partially sighted girl, had recently gone to one of the colleges for the visually impaired. On arrival, "they gave her a white cane and a test for braille".

(13) These comments came from pupils attending special schools for the blind.

(14) At this particular school, a coeducational, all-age special school for the partially sighted, with a catchment area of 17 local education authorities, the proportion of pupils transferring from ordinary schools at the age of 11+ had increased dramatically over recent years. The following table demonstrates this trend.

Academic Year	Transfers at age 5 — 10	Transfers at 11 and over	Total intake
1965 — 66	13	1	14
1966 — 67	14	2	16
1967 — 68	13	2	15
1968 — 69	8	8	16
1969 — 70	10	5	15
1970 — 71	10	2	12
1971 — 72	14	2	16
1972 — 73	19	9	28
1973 — 74	11	8	19
1974 — 75	13	11	24

(15) This last remark from the science teacher is in agreement with the view of the head teacher of the school for the partially sighted who remarked: "he is intelligent but I'm sure he finds life frustrating".

Chapter Twelve

The Visually Impaired Child and the School Milieu

Many of the arguments about integration are difficult to size up and decide about. Advantages are claimed either for ordinary schooling or for special schooling that sound valid on a first hearing, but which prove tendentious or only superficially true when listened to with greater care.

A lot of points raised are to do with the supposed effects of different kinds of school setting. The visually impaired child, it is said, will suffer teasing in the ordinary school and be considered 'odd'; he or she will be socially isolated in the special school and develop a 'handicapped mentality'. Questions about stigma, normality, and the psychological impact of total school experiences form significant parts of the controversy.

In general, detailed evidence is hard to come by. This chapter raises several questions, not so much to recite what evidence there is, for and against, but rather to promote some fresh ways of thinking. These seem a necessary precursor to gathering more sophisticated evidence in the future.

It is increasingly part of educational thought to acknowledge the role of the school context — the social and organizational environment of the pupils — and to consider what it does to them. The child's total surroundings at school include the physical premises; his or her peers and teachers; the activities and formal demands of the curriculum and class work; the school's rituals, local customs, traditions, and ways of doing things; the extracurricular school world; and much else besides.

Each individual naturally relates in a unique fashion to his or her surroundings, but actions and reactions overlap; every child is different, but not completely so. Often there are common patterns of experience and participation, in the same way that different school milieux have many similarities and parallels despite their singularity.

A central assumption is that children in a school milieu are profoundly affected by it. It is a reasonable assumption: they are assailed by a whole variety of signals, cues, and messages about what it is appropriate or not to do, who is rewarded for what, how the school works, what image the school wants to present to the outside community, whether parents are welcome and, if so, at what times and under what circumstances, what academic goals are highly valued, what alternative futures the school foresees for its pupils, and so forth. Some of the messages are transmitted as explicit statements — reiterated at assemblies or in class — others are never spelled out but instead are communicated implicitly, e.g. by noting what activity is stopped or begun, or by drawing inferences from casual remarks.

Those within a milieu may be affected by it through adopting its conventions or rules and internalizing them; by taking certain attitudes towards themselves increasingly for granted as time goes on; or by accepting local definitions and prejudices because they know no others. They may isolate features of their surroundings to criticize or to distance themselves from — not realizing they are still profoundly affected by them, as well as by other elements of which they may not even be conscious.

Development and socialization of the child — the growing up process — proceeds within several different milieux: family and home, schools, settings for community activities, and others different for each child. While schools certainly do not provide the child with all his or her self-definitions, budding interests, habits of mind, aspirations for life, feelings of confidence or inadequacy, they do provide some part of them. Many result from internalizing and taking for granted messages at and from school.

In this chapter we examine three forms of message that visually impaired children receive in their school milieux: some that stem from the wider attitudes, beliefs, prejudices, and reactions present in society generally; some that are mediated by the school as an institution or derive from its corporate self-definition; and, third, some that are not messages to the group so much as messages from those in the school to the individual child — to do with his or her progress, status, capability, and self-definition.

Stereotypes in society

Schools do not exist in isolation, unaffected by society at large. Children in schools live within a local school milieu; at the same time there are numerous influences traceable to further afield — to the wider context of general society. Many of the signals to the individual visually impaired pupil derive from stereotypes about blindness and partial sight that are prevalent in everyday life outside the school. Some of the half-truths and fallacies that are circulated concerning visual impairment have already been referred to. Some of them are entrenched and institutionalized in society's thinking, demonstrating collective ignorance. Others are encountered in more face to face, immediate fashion: almost all visually impaired individuals encountered in this study had at some time met with ill-informed, insensitive, or outright prejudiced reactions.

A detailed discussion of how society-wide beliefs, reactions, labels, and prejudices are formed and maintained is beyond the scope of this account. Goffman's book, *Stigma*,[1] points out how every individual, at some time or other, has experienced being labelled as this or that 'type' — the appellation then serving as an often grossly inaccurate shorthand; how stigmatized individuals suffer, react, defend themselves, retaliate, or internalize the notions that others ascribe to them; how stigmatizing reactions stem from fear of the unknown; and how prejudiced reactions towards minority groups can be worn away by people in the majority discovering that what they share with the minority is greater than what is not shared.

We confine ourselves here to certain ideas and reactions in society that relate to blindness and partial sight and which children with visual impairment encounter, have to learn to live with, and often come to resent. Perhaps the most potent images projected about blindness are ones of dependence and incapacity. There is gross underestimation of what can be done by blind individuals — that they can dress and cook for themselves, use public transport, eat in restaurants, marry and raise children, obtain professional employment, are all sometimes thought surprising. Paradoxically, this general image may be reinforced by specific demonstrations that it is not true: a television news item on blind skiers, while demonstrating that the blind are not generally incapacitated and can lead full and varied lives, also has a strand of what one blind professional person described as "the patronizing logic" of sighted society: "Look at this guy struggling on ... isn't this magnificent".

If, for individuals labelled blind, there is consistent underestimation of what they can do, with the partially sighted it is sometimes the opposite. A head teacher thought that society misunderstood the partially sighted: "They see glasses on; (and) society expects they can see ... They are in a twilight world — worse off than the blind, a world of total ambiguity. All partial problems are those nobody knows about — if they are profound, they are understood ... "

That partial sight is a lesser known handicap than blindness is worth particular note for the following reason. There are far fewer established stereotypes about it, fewer cultural and institutional beliefs surrounding it as a category of disability. It is less of a social state; there is little talk of the 'world of the partially sighted' though the phrase 'the world of the blind' is in very common use.

It is worth examining this latter expression. The world of the blind is a prominent catch-phrase. As such, it can influence the way blind persons think of themselves and how others think of them. People, we found, defined it differently — everybody assuming others knew what it meant. For instance, a special school head teacher defined it as, "that accumulation of experience . . . to which workers for the blind and blind individuals belong". In this sense, the 'world' is surprisingly small-scale. In America, Scott[2] identified the phenomenon of blindness agencies as big business, complete with an attendant profession of work for the blind. He argued that such organizations actively fostered dependency within the blind population, becoming a crucial mainstay in their lives.

A second meaning points to the sense of separation and distance purported to exist between itself and 'the world of the sighted'.[3] The implication is that each is exclusive of the other. The blind world, thought several blind people, was perceived by sighted people as a "cut-off world" characterized by "funny behaviours", inhabited by "a strange sort of species" with its own habits and culture. It lacked a visual element. Similar comments were frequently made: one blind girl remarked, "In the blind world you don't do the visual things" — while a teacher in a further education establishment for the blind defined it as "a closed world which the blind live in". An adviser pointed out: "the whole pattern of learning and individual reactions are different. So many actions, which the sighted do automatically, need to be operationalized. It *is* a different world". This echoes the remark made by a head teacher: "In one sense they *do* belong to it . . . the blind really are handicapped"; certain pursuits (e.g. car driving) are obviously denied them, while other activities and social interactions with sighted people are inevitably more demanding.

We have concentrated on the powerful — and divisive — metaphor of the world of the blind because it is a good example of a major background construct or category for the visually impaired school pupil to come to terms with. The idea that there is such a world represents an established way of thinking that is taken for granted and transmitted to the blind child. Allied to it are implicit expectations: for example, that the young blind person will become part of that world; that he or she will come to terms with the degree of segregation it implies; and that certain opportunities are afforded to those in the world of the sighted that are denied to those in the blind world. Individually, the thinking may be rejected, serving as a focus for expression of independence (one ex-open education pupil regarded integration as a way of "getting away from the blind world") but it still remains as a powerful socializing idea for young persons who are blind.

Deeply entrenched categories of this kind also have effects on other related groups — especially on those designated 'visually handicapped' but not blind. Thus, "partially sighted children have a permanent fear of going blind" (head teacher), of their measured visual acuity diminishing to the point where the label has to change and they move into the blind world. Those concerned with the partially sighted aim to establish some distance between the two categories, partly in order to draw increased recognition to their own special needs.[4]

The school and its messages

The general background messages just discussed are present in society. The visually impaired school pupil is made aware of them in whatever kind of school he or she attends, special or ordinary. However, there are certain differences in the ways the two types of school (special and ordinary) filter these common ideas and stereotypes from outside. And there are also messages from the institution itself, beliefs transmitted about what type of school it is, and what the child is there for. These may be powerfully influential too.

First, let us examine the 'typical' ordinary and special school and the extent to which they may filter societal beliefs and stereotypes.

In the ordinary school, the integrated child is likely to face at least some ignorant and insensitive reactions from other children and occasionally from staff as well.[5] What knowledge others have about visual impairment is likely to be derived from their general knowledge. It could be said, with some justification, that the visually impaired child in an ordinary school has to contend with the full force of societal prejudice and ignorance. There is sometimes hurtful teasing from other children. We interviewed several partially sighted pupils who had at various times been called "freaks", "idiots", or "queers": "They treat you as if you're halfway round the twist", remarked one boy. Another older boy added: "Anything the visually handicapped say is hooted at; if you are a bad case . . . then it's constant mockery".

As one might expect there was little or no teasing of this kind in the special schools we studied. However, to conclude that the special schools provide full protection from prejudiced or hurtful reactions would be incorrect. Here, remarks related to the individual's disability tend to come from outside: thus, one child was asked by a sighted visitor to the school, "do you do *real* A-levels here?". There was also teasing: "do you use a sonic fork when eating?". More generally, schools often have to contend with a community reaction or assumption that the school's pupils are mentally handicapped. Finally, there are the various images of blindness projected for fund-raising which, for the special schools, are double-edged. A teacher of blind pupils pointed out that "the blind do have certain needs, but they are not those projected for charitable purposes". An ex-open education pupil commented: "people put their money in the stocking for a vision of blindness which I don't fit". The images projected are, again, those of helplessness and dependence — the very opposite of those that special schools want to foster and encourage. As one blind girl put it: "Sighted people have the chance to make an image — we're hampered by an image".

The second area of discussion about the two types of schooling relates to their claims about achieving a sense of normality. In integrated settings, visually impaired pupils are distinctly in a minority; in special schools they are a majority interest, indeed an exclusive one. Yet both claim to make the child feel normal. It is achieved in different ways.

In the ordinary school setting the visually impaired child begins by being 'newsworthy' but this diminishes over time. The teasing and being treated as 'odd' seem to decline — as one might expect — with greater familiarity: a teacher in a PSU pointed out that, "now children talk with them, whereas before they used to stare". Our evidence suggested that in many cases of individual integration[6] children came to be accepted by their peers as 'just other pupils'. Also, among the ex-open education pupils we interviewed, we heard remarks such as: "When I go round with other kids I forget I'm blind", and "you're more normal . . . not in a community of your own (kind)".

The sense of normality engendered in the ordinary school is, however, not automatic and numerous factors make it somewhat precarious. For example, an adverse physical appearance, a group of unsympathetic peers, the occasional ignorant or insensitive teacher, a lack of general understanding over a particular matter, could all upset the child's equilibrium and feeling of being an accepted minority pupil. However, in another way, a sense of normality could definitely be said to be automatic: integrated pupils seem to have — even at the worst moments of teasing — a consciousness of 'being normal' in that they are attending an ordinary school.

While day-to-day acceptance in integrated settings may not be entirely taken for granted, in the special school such acceptance is institutionalized. Here, visual impairment is not newsworthy — "here the last thing you talk about is blindness", said one special school teacher. Using a noisy Perkins brailler in class, or tape-recording a lesson elicits no surprise; the school can absorb these without a murmur. A child with cumbersome or ugly-looking low vision aids is not made fun of — a matter that can be of the greatest importance to sensitive adolescents. The local norm is impaired vision; the child is not continually made conscious of it.

In the previous chapter, when discussing pupils who transferred to a school for the partially sighted, we alluded to the implicit expectation that they — the minority interest in the ordinary school — would perform less well, that there would be things they could not be expected to do. In a special school setting, however, there are different natural expectations.

We found a vivid example of the contrast in what was 'normally' expected in the two settings. In a school for the blind the handicraft teacher had introduced power tools in woodwork. While acknowledging an "element of danger", he argued that blind children were "unfamiliar with machines, so they (needed to) get used to them". He articulated this principle: "You have to put them at some risk to teach them anything". We contrast this philosophy — typical of the down-to-earth approach of the school generally — with what happened in one of the integration schemes we investigated. Here, visually impaired pupils, for a variety of practical reasons, were not allowed this kind of experience. One partially sighted boy commented, "they've got some great woodwork and metalwork sheds . . . but we can't use them. They're frightened you might chop your hand off".

The working norms of the special school, its supportiveness, its consciousness of the needs of the visually impaired, are all embedded in the institution — it is what it is all about: "If you have special schools they've really got to be special" (head teacher of a special school). At the same time, although the cues and signals from the school to its pupils are those of acceptance and understanding, there is one other particular message that the school can do nothing about. Visually impaired pupils in ordinary schools seem to derive a sense of confidence from knowing they are attending a 'normal' school. Similarly, special school pupils are conscious of the kind of school they are attending, realize they are in an institution that lies outside the main system of schooling: "I say absolutely nothing about this school to my mates — they don't know where it is or what it is" (pupil at a school for the partially sighted).

To summarize so far, we have dwelt briefly on some of the messages or ideas communicated by the two types of school to visually impaired pupils. In one case — the ordinary school milieu — the pupil is conscious of being a minority interest, special or odd, receiving help and perhaps having allowances made. The visual condition may cut him or her off from some of the school's activities, but the child derives certain gratification from being in the school at all. In the other case — that of the special school — the pupil is not, in general, treated differently from his or her school peers, pressures are perhaps greater, expectations can be higher; and instead of being reminded constantly of his or her condition and the limitations it imposes, the pupil finds it treated in a matter-of-fact way, as a 'given' of school life. At the same time — offsetting this — the pupil is aware that the school itself is not a 'normal' school.

We recognize that to summarize in this way is dangerous — it may suggest (wrongly) that we believe there are neat systematic differences between the two types of schooling. We do not wish to gloss over the great differences that exist between integration schemes, in the quality of special schools, and the variation in school milieux generally. These provisos should be borne in mind as we move to the third realm of difference.

This relates to the amount of background information and specialized knowledge that different kinds of schools have about visual impairment. Special schools, as noted in the last chapter, have a good deal of practical 'know-how', a certain lore, experience, and a bank of memories and precedents to draw upon. Ordinary schools (unless they form part of an integration scheme) are likely to have little of this: they may have had a hearing impaired or physically handicapped child in the past, and teachers may refer back to these, drawing upon recollections of them for help in deciding what to do. But this is far-removed from the often highly complex, differentiated, and refined practical theorizing and reflection that form part of what makes special schools special.

We can say, therefore, with some confidence, that if two visually impaired pupils enrol as new arrivals at school — one in a special school, one in an ordinary school — they will from the start be picking up fundamentally different kinds of signals from the school milieu. The reason for this is quite straightforward: they will be thought about in significantly different ways.

Specifically, for the child arriving in the special school, ophthalmological details will be studied; the likely prognosis and its long-term educational implications will be considered; requirements in terms of aids, lighting, and so forth will be met. The child will soon be slotted into general informal categories or types — particularly in terms of general behaviour, attitude to his or her handicap, and personal adaptation. In special schools, we often heard references to various 'types' — e.g. those who "want to get their own back"; those who "appear balanced but often are not — (it's) manifested in a frame of mind of being against everything"; others who are "bottled up — they play games among themselves that sighted children would have grown out of earlier"; the independent ones who "want to go round on their own (and) not mix with blind boys"; and the 'non-acceptors' — "his problem is that he won't admit to needing this place but he needs our one-to-one teaching".

The induction and early days of the child who goes to an ordinary school will differ quite markedly from this pattern. Detailed attention to records concerning vision is unlikely to occur – the terminology itself may seem strange to the school staff; no particular associations and connections are likely to be conjured up; the way the child is classified informally in teachers' minds will be more tentative, probably less worked out. In some senses, it is as if the ordinary school has to develop a mode of thinking about the new pupil from scratch, by modifying its usual patterns and categories, rather than having a way of thinking and talking about visually impaired children already established and ready to draw upon.

This is, of course, all very speculative. It may not appear to all readers to be relevant or important. But it touches on one of the most basic – if difficult to pin down – contrasts between ordinary and special schooling. If a special school is characterized by pre-existing knowledge of an elaborate kind, numerous distinct advantages are likely to accrue to its pupils in terms of having their educational needs properly catered for. They will have, for instance, specialized and knowledgeable careers advice; a carefully tailored curriculum; opportunities to take part in sports that have been specifically devised for them; and, moreover, their hesitations, worries, ambitions, resentments, and sense of achievement, will be recognized, appreciated, and understood.

By contrast, in the ordinary school – where the informal professional knowledge lacks this specialized component – the pupil has to fare without such a finely tuned set of understandings. He or she will not have access to teachers with the same store of codified or semi-codified experience as his or her counterpart in the special school. Advice given about careers will be less grounded in knowledge of alternative opportunities; decisions about what subjects the child should take are likely to be far more 'hit or miss'; and there may be a tendency for teachers to exclude the child from ordinary school practice if he or she cannot contend with it, unaware of the possible modifications to that practice that could easily be made in order to include the child.

However, as we should now have come to expect in this labyrinth of subtleties, there are no 'quick-fire' conclusions to be drawn from all this. Unquestionably, the special school has a repository of refined practical knowledge and it can deploy its collective wisdom to meet individual demands, visual requirements, special needs, and to deal with classroom management questions. This may be far less possible for ordinary schools with their more limited and more diffuse knowledge. The advantage is seen to rest, in this instance at least, with the special schools. However, there is a small potential snag. Greater knowledge can also constrain. It defines opportunities but also suggests limits.

Nowhere is this possibility clearer than with careers counselling: it may be here that awareness of precedents, of what is normal, discourages the *avant-garde* or unusual, and that where there is less knowledge there is also, paradoxically, more freedom. The same principle may hold more widely: a mass of experience may lead to expectations about how a visually impaired child should behave, react, and develop, if he or she is to be 'normal'. Such expectations — conveyed inadvertently and in the least obtrusive of ways — may subtly serve to socialize the child into responding as expected.[7] The idea that one trains someone to be visually handicapped is preposterous — yet, in the special school setting, there may be elements of this. It is an intriguing point.

The commonalities and disparities of different school milieux
We come, in the final section of this chapter, to discuss the messages from the milieux that are the most local and personal — those that are communicated to individual children about how well they are doing, what the school thinks of them, whether they are popular, and the like.

It is not meant to devalue the potential impact on visually impaired pupils of societal or institutional messages of the kind already discussed, to say that this third category may be the most influential upon them. It is not to play down the differences between ordinary and special schools to point out that this third level of messages may well transcend the special / ordinary distinction.

Special and ordinary establishments have important differences, but they are all schools. They share many common characteristics. Children with visual impairment will encounter — irrespective of the school they attend — both more and less sensitive teachers, both supportive and non-supportive traditions and procedures, both friendly and unfriendly reactions. In particular, there are children thought 'unusual' in both settings; both types of school have their 'problem' children; both inevitably sort out 'successes' from 'failures'.

Children at school receive numerous messages of this kind — about others and about themselves. The individual child may develop a feeling of being encouraged and supported, approved of by some or all teachers; or, alternatively, of being up against a set of more critical and less sympathetic reactions. All schools dispense this kind of informal message and no visually impaired child in either kind of establishment is going to avoid being labelled and signalled to in one way or another.[8]

The messages referred to so far, whether deriving from society or from the institution, have tended to be related to the child as someone with a severe problem. The messages to which we now refer are of a different ilk: they may still be connected in people's minds with the impairment, but they involve categories used in all school settings which are deeply entrenched in the corporate everyday thinking of teaching staff, and other professionals involved with children. The visually impaired child will receive messages about whether he or she is regarded as a success or failure, as a problem or not, as an asset or an embarrassment to the school. It is not unreasonable to assume that epithets such as 'backward', 'doing well', 'likeable', 'difficult', may have at least some effect on the child — reinforcing what in Chapter Nineteen we shall discuss as cycles of a diminishing or of an enhancing kind.

These categories pervade both kinds of school. We heard about a number of specialized types that had been identified; in special schools we also heard pupils being described as 'doing marvellously' or 'proving very difficult'. Special schools may differ greatly from ordinary ones, but not in this respect: there is still a hierarchy of expressed pride, still a pool of pupils that teachers find discouraging; there are still stars and high-fliers, still a number whom the school would rather be without. There are also instances of teachers in ordinary schools expressing pride and enthusiasm over their integrated pupils — they may be considered special, but as 'successfully special'. Similarly, we noted examples of teachers in special schools regarding a pupil not only as not special, but as not successful in the school's terms, as 'needing a lot of attention or help'. The messages in the former case may foster increased self-confidence; in the latter they may further erode it. Signals picked up most readily may be those that slot the child into a perceived level of capability, a calibration which is then internalized.

If there is any validity in these ideas at all, the implications are clear. Moreover they accord with certain inescapable conclusions from this investigation. In the last chapter, we documented instances of children who were being considered as having behaviour problems or as being at an academical standstill in their ordinary schools. Moved to a special school they began to do better. Was this to do with their new school being special? Perhaps not; in later chapters we document the opposite transition: of children being moved from special schools, where they were doing poorly, to ordinary schools where they flourished.

In a particular school setting or milieu, the definitions and labels may all add up to a shared view — that the child is, say, troublesome in class: counter-examples of responses and behaviour on the part of the child are overlooked as the exception rather than the rule. If the child moves elsewhere, he or she has a new chance to shine, an opportunity to shed old labels. In short, we are saying this: there is a lot of talk about the differential effects of special and ordinary schooling, and certainly there *are* differences of the kinds already discussed in this chapter. But there are similarities too. Each provides a series of 'micro-milieux' for its pupils — classes, groups, or personal tuition. Although the school as a larger milieu may inculcate certain ideas — and these may differ from special to ordinary — the most powerful set of inputs to the child's sense of identity may come from the most immediate surround, the micro-milieu. The differences at this level are very great indeed: the individual patterns of interaction between teacher and pupils, relations with other children, and small group definitions applied to individual members, are open to wide variation. The range of difference is so great that it is pointless to pretend that the set of micro-milieux in one kind of school can be compared with that found in another kind of school.

The policy implications of these ideas may be far-reaching. What we are saying is that it is impossible to state conclusively that a child will automatically be better off in an ordinary or a special school. To do so would be a crude generalization: a visually impaired child in one class, in one school, with one group of teachers, may be well-off; shifted elsewhere — whether to a similar or different kind of school — he or she could end up either better or worse off. It would depend far more on the particular micro-milieu the child was absorbed in, rather than on the kind of school it was.

This may seem an entirely unsatisfactory conclusion to have reached. It may seem — for those who seek simplicity in these affairs — to dodge the major policy questions entirely and to provide a 'non-answer'. But this is not so: instead, we are suggesting that the wrong policy questions are usually asked, questions for which there are simply no sensible answers. Instead of asking which kind of provision for visually impaired children is 'better', the questions ought perhaps to be more on the following lines: how can the wider system provide the micro-systems of schools with greater support, information, advice, and active encouragement? How can early warning systems of potential difficulties be rendered more efficient? What can be done to ease transfers from unsuitable school settings to ones that might be more suitable for the individual concerned? How can ordinary and special schools work together — to provide different children with a variety of school opportunities? They have, after all, a variety of individual needs.

Notes

(1) Goffman (1968) writes: 'Society establishes the means of categorizing persons and the complement of attributes felt to be ordinary and natural for members of each of these categories'. He argues that we have certain anticipations about a person's 'social identity' and we transform these anticipations into 'normative expectations' or 'righteously presented demands'. So, if society labels a blind man as such, we, in turn, attach this 'stigma' to that person, expecting him to behave in a particular way and conform to certain expectations, e.g. to be totally immobile, a source of pity, etc. Thus a handicap becomes a stigma which creates a discrepancy

between that handicapped person's 'virtual social identity' i.e. the demands we make of him as a handicapped person, and his 'actual social identity' — the attributes he could be proved to possess. Goffman continues:

> 'By definition . . . we believe the person with the stigma is not quite human. On this assumption we exercise varieties of discrimination, through which we effectively, if often unthinkingly, reduce his life chances. We construct a stigma theory, an ideology to explain his inferiority and account for the danger he represents . . . The central feature of the stigmatised individual situation . . . is "acceptance". Those who have dealings with him fail to accord him the respect and regard which the uncontaminated aspects of his social identity have led them to anticipate extending, and have led him to anticipate receiving; he echoes this denial by finding that some of his own attributes warrant it'.

Thus a person may conform to the expectations of blindness by adhering to blind mannerisms and to the 'world of the blind'. All this results, says Goffman, when there is little continual mixing between 'normal' and 'stigmatized'.

> 'Persons who have a particular stigma tend to have similar learning experiences regarding their plight, and similar changes in conception of self — a similar 'moral career' that is both cause and effect of commitment to a similar sequence of personal adjustment.'

GOFFMAN, E. (1968). *Stigma: Notes on the Management of Spoiled Identity*. Harmondsworth: Penguin.

(2) SCOTT, R.A. (1969). *The Making of Blind Men: A Study of Adult Socialization*. New York: Russell Sage Foundation. The situation in Britain is very different, partly because there are far fewer agencies. The RNIB commands a dominant position with regard to the social welfare and education of the blind.

(3) Whether this meaning of the term originated within the blind population itself, or was attributed to them because of the geographical isolation of schools for the blind, is difficult to ascertain.

(4) The growth of such bodies as the Partially Sighted Society, together with the acknowledgement that teachers of the partially sighted need specialist training, are two examples of the increasing consciousness that the partially sighted are a separate group with their own special needs.

(5) See Chapter Seventeen.

(6) See Part IV.

(7) Lukoff and Whiteman (1970) write:

> 'The decision to send a blind child, particularly one blinded at an early age, to a segregated school has many ramifications for the way in which the blind person ultimately responds to his handicap. (The) choice of education directions . . . can influence the kind of identification the

child develops as a blind person, his patterns of social relations, even his achievement of different kinds of adjustment patterns'.

Their study concluded that blind children in special schools displayed a lower degree of independence than those in schools for the sighted, but that where family expectations were not oriented towards independence, the congenitally blind benefited from attendance at residential schools:

'Schools established for blind persons, in addition to attenuating the achievement of social-role independence, also lay the ground-work for life-long patterns of social affiliation which are significant for many classes of behaviour. It is not so much the attitudes of others that result in the segregation of some of the blind but the institutions established for the blind that provide the essential ingredient for a group response'.

LUKOFF, I.F. and WHITEMAN, M. (1970). 'Socialization and segregated education', *American Foundation for the Blind, Research Bulletin*, 20.

(8) This is not the place to discuss the controversy over the effects of labelling and expectations on school performance, explored in detail by Rosenthal and Jacobson. ROSENTHAL, R. and JACOBSON, L. (1968). *Pygmalion in the Classroom: Teacher Expectations and Pupils' Intellectual Development*. New York: Holt, Rinehart and Winston Inc. For a further discussion see NASH, R. (1973). *Classrooms Observed: Teacher's Perception and the Pupil's Performance*. London: Routledge. Several experimental studies in this area have produced ambiguous results.

Part Four

The Experience of Individual Integration

The issues surrounding integration are complicated; and so much depends on particular cases and local circumstances. We have sought in this research to unravel complexity. But readers should also encounter complexity first hand, how the various questions interlock. We can think of no better way of doing this than by presenting detailed information about four individual partially sighted children and their ordinary schooling.

Part IV therefore differs drastically from the rest of the book. It concentrates on the individual experiences of four visually impaired children who attend ordinary schools. It is our intention to bring to life issues discussed in other chapters — drawing on the words, opinions, and subjective experiences of children, parents, and teachers. The tone and style is deliberately more personal and freer than elsewhere in the book.

We decided to present four studies at length because there was a danger of losing all the advantages of individual data if we did not — it is important to see how numerous factors converge on a child to affect his or her educational experience. There is obviously enormous variation between children in their problems, personal backgrounds, school circumstances, perceived needs, extent of family encouragement, and individual personality characteristics. The case study captures some of the texture of all this idiosyncracy.

The origins of this part of our work go back to Phase I of the project. During the period of consultation and deciding on areas of concentration, we heard of one particular area where little was known — the academic, social, and personal experiences of partially sighted children integrated individually in ordinary schools, with or without peripatetic support. There was no shortage of conjecture and glib generalization. But there was little said that was based on systematic study of children integrated in their local schools, or of their teachers, or their home backgrounds.

We decided to locate visually impaired children who were integrated on a 'one off' basis in ordinary schools and study what happened to them. The number of such pupils was thought to be sizeable but nobody knew for sure — there was a paucity of statistical records.

We began by sending letters to local education authorities asking for 'numbers of visually impaired children attending ordinary schools in their authority'. The returns varied dramatically, ranging from over 50 in one case to only one in another. Some authorities seemed to list registered children only; others included all children with known visual difficulties. Where children were listed who were blind — as opposed to being partially sighted — they were either of pre-school age or in further education: both groups fell outside the bounds of our research brief — to study visually impaired children at primary and secondary levels. We decided, therefore, that this part of the study should be restricted to the partially sighted.

Initial inquiries seemed discouraging: we shelved the problem and only later realized how we could proceed. We identified two different groups of partially sighted children to whom we could obtain access: the first, some patients at a well-known eye hospital; the second, a group concentrated in one local education authority, the responsibility of a peripatetic advisory teacher whom we had already studied at work (see Chapter Eight).

To contact the two samples was a delicate operation. We had no knowledge of who these children were, the nature of their problems, or whether schools and families would agree to assist us in our research. We proceeded as follows. With the 'hospital' group we asked the principal ophthalmic optician in charge of the low vision clinic to work through her records, selecting patients who were known to be at ordinary schools. This she did, choosing a group of 14 in all. After obtaining permission from the medical authorities and each patient's consultant ophthalmologist, she sent to the parents a letter from us with a covering note from her. The letters described our research and asked volunteer families to contact us directly. Until they did so, we had no means of identifying them. This procedure was obviously not ideal: the case load of integrated children was small (many young patients at the hospital attended special schools); we had no access to medical records beforehand on grounds of confidentiality; and the principal ophthalmic optician decided to exclude in advance those with parents known to be uncooperative and those with consultants unlikely to give their consent.

We pursued a parallel but slightly different strategy with the 'local education authority' group. Again we negotiated the sample, in this instance with their advisory teacher. In this case, she sent the team a list of integrated pupils within the authority; we selected a group of 10 candidates broadly balanced in terms of sex, age, and type of school (i.e. primary and secondary); she then made a final choice, suggesting alternatives to those parents who would be unlikely to agree to take part. Again, we sent a letter to parents via the advisory teacher, who added her own letter of introduction.

With both samples, the response was overwhelming. Of 24 invitations to participate, there were only two refusals. As soon as we obtained parental consent, we began arranging visits to the pupils' homes and schools.

The 'hospital' sample had in common only their attendance at the same low vision clinic. They came from a wide geographical area and from several different local education authorities. None, at the time of our initial visits, had the benefit of an advisory teacher or peripatetic service. The 'LEA' group, though also placed individually, were given support to varying degrees; the peripatetic advisory teacher visited some of them occasionally, others regularly, to give extra tuition, remedial help and mobility training. Nearly all the children in both groups were attending schools in their locality,[1] though not always their most local school, since not all schools are willing to accept a handicapped child and in some cases are not deemed suitable (even if willing).

It was not the intention to match or compare the two groups, nor even to draw collective conclusions necessarily. For most purposes, we were going to treat the 22 studied as separate histories, acknowledging their diversity and the individuality of their circumstances. Our purpose was to concentrate on the practical problems encountered, any doubts or misgivings about integration, what the school's expectations were, and what restrictions on normal school activities were necessary or imposed. We had heard reservations about both the quality and quantity of support these children received in ordinary schools; and there were many questions. How well did children cope? Were teachers worried by having a partially sighted child in the class? These and many other questions were in our minds as we set about constructing each case history. We collected information from conversations and interviews with the pupils themselves; from talks with their parents and teachers; and from our own observations at home and at school.[2]

We have had difficulty in deciding how to present our case history material. In the end we fixed on a pattern: we would include four case histories in detail in this part of the book and draw heavily on the remaining 18 for the discussion that follows in Part V.

Presenting only four histories in full raises several questions. How did we make the choice of which four? And to what extent can one generalize from the four to the 22 as a whole? And from the 22 to the whole of this population?

There are several points to make in answer. First, obviously no individual history or case study can be said to be truly 'typical'. The four pupils cannot be considered representative in the technical sense of that term. The term has little meaning here. Those chosen certainly embody a typicality of issues: they are included because, in some ways at least, their experiences, reactions, and school situations are sharply reminiscent of those of other children. Despite the uniqueness of each child's history and milieu there were many common issues, recurrent patterns, and parallel phenomena that were identified as we proceeded. We therefore selected children for inclusion who best demonstrated some of the sub-themes encountered in the group as a whole, and which are discussed as such in Part V. We wanted to avoid presenting cases that — in terms of our group of 22 as a whole — were obviously 'extreme': we include, therefore, no child whose progress at school was either totally smooth or full of severe problems. In this respect, it is important to underline the fact that in the event of 'total failure' in an integrated setting, the child would be transferred to a special school and, naturally therefore, would not appear in this sample. Officially speaking, all 22 studied were broadly regarded as 'successes'.

A second point to make is this. Embodied in questions about representativeness and generalization are certain ideas about human phenomena and affairs and the way to study them. These ideas are those most conventionally held; but there are other approaches, differing sets of assumptions about what can be learned from considering the particular. Robert Stake, the distinguished American researcher, has recently written ' . . . our methods of studying human affairs need to capitalize upon the natural powers of people to experience and to understand'.[3] He advocates increased use of case studies. These may not provide the form of generalization based on 'underlying attributes, objective observables, and universal forces' but can provide a basis for what he calls 'naturalistic generalization'. This kind of generalization is arrived at 'by recognizing the similarities of objects and issues in and out of context and by sensing the natural covariations of happenings . . . Naturalistic generalizations develop within a person as a result of experience'. Stake argues that case histories are 'epistemologically in harmony with the reader's experience and thus to that person a natural basis for generalization'; they have been 'found to be a direct and satisfying way of adding to experience and improving understanding'.

This fits closely with our intention and methods of work. It is a case of illuminating the general by detailed consideration of the particular. In other sections of the book we discuss general questions, including some that might appear dramatic or sensational if presented in isolation. Here they are put in individual contexts.

There are examples of general issues such as: concern about 'normality'; uninformed expectations about the partially sighted; theories about coping after school; availability of resources; and the varying degrees of classroom integration. The case studies also raise a great variety of new general questions, some of which receive attention later. Some concern parents: for example, their role in decisions about their child and the quality of advice they were given.

In conclusion, this section is *not* designed as an evaluation of the educational benefits of integrated provision but, rather, is designed to convey in a vivid fashion a little of the life of the ordinary classroom and school, when a partially sighted child is present within them.

The case studies themselves need little introduction: each tells a complete story. All names have been changed to protect the identity of those concerned, with medical and educational details included only after permission had been given. The reader may not wish to read them all or all at once. Simply to read one is to be reminded that we are dealing with real children and not just issues.

Notes

(1) Three of the 'hospital' group were at boarding school.

(2) An average of one complete working school day and an evening were allocated to each of the 22 case studies for observation, a school visit, and talks with parents. Wherever necessary we made follow-up visits to the families. Any queries still outstanding were checked by letter and telephone. The families of the four pupils were asked to comment on the manuscript, suggesting any changes they wished.

(3) STAKE, R.E. (1975). The Case Study Method in Social Inquiry. Unpublished paper. CIRCE, University of Illinois at Champaign-Urbana.

Chapter Thirteen

Clare

Clare was the daughter of a professional family, the younger of two children. There was no obvious indication that she was visually impaired; although she wore fairly heavy glasses, they did not immediately suggest serious vision loss. She was a mature 14-year-old: lively, uninhibited and seemed confident. She spoke with ease about her school experiences, describing them in a reasoned and intelligent manner. At school, she appeared a popular member of the class, had many friends, and was definitely no outsider. That she was an attractive girl with "a beautiful smile" (a teacher), may have had much to do with reinforcing her confidence.

Clare was an albino, but did not have white hair. Her measured visual acuity for distance was 6/36, for both eyes, and for near vision it was N4.5. With the use of low vision aids, her near vision could be greatly improved.

Outside of school Clare enjoyed cooking, watching television, collecting foreign dolls, attending Red Cross classes, swimming and going out with her friends. On Saturday mornings she worked in a sweetshop. The only thing she was not allowed to do was to ride her bicycle on the road, her parents having explained to her the reasons why not. She went to discotheques, had a "healthy attitude towards boys", was dress conscious and helped in the home.

Clare's parents first noticed that she was not focusing normally when she was about three months old. They immediately consulted a specialist at the local hospital. He confirmed she had a visual defect but could not say what it was.[1] At the age of four, Clare underwent minor surgery to correct a squint.

Turning to Clare's educational history, we discovered she had attended both ordinary and special schools. She started in a sighted nursery school where, according to her father "they didn't do a lot" and where her visual defect "made little difference". Her difficulties began when she was five years old with the "learning aspects" of her infant school: "It was obvious from the outset that she had a problem" (father). She could not see sufficiently well nor was she mixing very much with other children. She could not join in many activities requiring sight: "Feeling an outsider . . . she developed a complex . . . lurking in the corner of the playground". She was prescribed glasses, but these seemed to have little effect. In time, she confided to her parents how unhappy she was at seeing others doing things she could not do.

At the age of seven, a consultant ophthalmologist recommended that Clare go to a special school for the partially sighted since she was having problems with her reading. This was most apparent during project work at school when Clare experienced great difficulty in consulting reference books. Her parents abided by this decision, although they were reluctant for their daughter to leave home. They felt obliged to comply with the advice given by "experts". It was not until much later, when "things got very difficult", that they felt the need "to assert themselves".

Clare spent about 15 months at a special school for the partially sighted. She was required to board, even though the school was only a few miles from her home. Her parents described this period as "tremendously retrograde" and Clare "went downhill rapidly". The school was "very regimented . . . like an army institution". It lacked any "feeling of family", there was "no love or affection". After some months, the head teacher informed Clare's parents that their daughter was "beyond being educated" and that her future employment lay, if anywhere, in a simple manual job.

At the age of nine, while still at the special school, Clare was caught shop-lifting. The head teacher summed her up as a "bad influence, naughty and wicked". Her parents "were at a loss to decide what to do for the best". Shortly after this incident Clare left the school.

Her parents considered that Clare had been very unhappy at the special school. She was upset by other pupils whose range of sight defects varied enormously. Many of them were additionally handicapped, and Clare began asking, "Am I like these girls?". In addition, some of the other children were resentful of the number of weekends Clare spent at home and of the frequent visits her family made to the school. Because she was virtually separated from contact with sighted children and her home, her parents "began to dread her mixing with normal children".

Clare's parents also felt the special school gave insufficient time or concern to the '3Rs' — which had surprised them. They assumed the main priority "at a school like that" would be to teach pupils to read. They also doubted whether "the school encouraged the use of its pupils' sight . . . They appeared to be working downwards on a vision scale": it was intended that Clare should learn braille, but she did not. Not surprisingly, her father summed up the family's reaction to this phase of Clare's schooling as "bitter".

However, before taking Clare away from the special school, her parents sought further specialist medical advice. A consultant ophthalmologist now suggested that although Clare "had sight difficulties, she would be better off in a sighted school if a place could be found". The local education authority resisted the proposed move despite the specialist's recommendation, but her parents persisted. It was at this stage that they began "asserting themselves", as they felt the situation had become extremely serious.

At nine years, then, Clare moved to a local primary school where, in her parents' words, "she was in a normal school with normal people". Her parents described her stay there in the following way:

> 'Clare was placed in a remedial group for reading . . . under a teacher who, we were told, had been specially selected for his kindliness and understanding. Under this teacher Clare made more progress in the first month than during the whole period spent at the special school . . . Although no very large print books were available, we are in no doubt that the four months spent in this primary school and particularly the progress made in reading made possible the dramatic progress that was to follow in Australia.'[2]

A few months later, Clare's father was posted to Australia and the family accompanied him. They found that Australia had "a very refreshing approach towards this problem" (i.e. the education of the partially sighted). Special schools were regarded as a "last resort", so Clare automatically went to an ordinary school. Initially, she lagged behind her peers academically, but within a year had shown a very marked improvement; she "even went ahead of her age group". She was also "very happy . . . everything you could wish for had happened".

Her parents were then, and still are, convinced that this "dramatic change around was entirely due to normal education". Clare herself described the Australian experience as "disconcerting" for the first few weeks, because the school was "much stricter" and had a "very high standard . . . I was afraid to get things wrong". However, within a month she had settled down and made several friends.

Fifteen months later, the family returned to England. Clare went back to her former primary school where she spent six months before moving on to a comprehensive. This latter move was "not at all traumatic" as by now, Clare was used to attending schools for sighted children. In addition, she had made a close friend in the primary school before going to Australia, and this girl now accompanied her to the comprehensive.[3]

When Clare's parents first approached the comprehensive school, the only information required of them was an estimate "as to how well she could see". They were advised by the head of the lower school not to become impatient if she had problems in managing. However, he did not anticipate any difficulties: the primary school had assured him that Clare had adapted well.

At the time of our visit, Clare had been at the comprehensive for three years. The school was a large, urban, coeducational, eight-form entry school where pupils were banded in the first three years and later settled for particular subjects. Her teachers described her as an "intelligent girl for her class". Her position was usually among the top three. Because she was "a lot brighter than the rest of her class", her teachers felt that her visual defect was not so obvious: "she performs so well that her visual handicap does not hamper her . . . it has never really been noticed". If she had been a problem or been unable "to cope", most teachers felt that it would have been difficult to contain her in the school. She was described as "interested in everything". Teachers agreed, however, that she could achieve a higher standard academically than had been demanded of her. Retaining Clare in her present class was deliberate – precisely because she was on top and thus gained respect from her peers as one of the brightest among them. Also, both her parents and teachers were concerned to keep her and her friend together.

Clare described herself as "happy at school", the people were "nice" and the teachers "understanding". She felt it helped considerably that she was successful in her work, but stressed the importance of having "a friend to help her when the need arises". In fact, Clare's close friend clearly did help her "an enormous amount". She read things off the blackboard and tidied up after Clare in domestic science and art lessons. The two girls were friends both in and out of school.

Having Clare in their class was seen by her teachers as making no difference to teaching methods. All were satisfied that she received the attention she required. Some concern was expressed about the slowness of her reading but teachers agreed that she worked hard at it and that "her own efforts get her through". She was about to embark on a two-year GCE / CSE course taking geography, French, maths, English, history, human biology and possibly German. Her favourite subject at school was maths, which seemed to present her with few difficulties. Reading maps in geography – even with the use of a magnifier – was, however, often difficult. Of the subjects she disliked, she cited physics, chemistry and needlework, all of which she found "too difficult to see".

Some subjects which are frequently quoted as difficult for a visually impaired child to handle seemed to present Clare with minimal problems: for instance, her art teacher stated that she managed very well, although "she tended to draw with the paper close to her face". Her work was of good quality. Her music teacher reiterated this. The PE teacher felt that Clare was able "to cope with everything except tennis and other ball games" although she was perhaps "a bit slow". She had never asked to be let off PE and was "enthusiastic about everything", though sometimes afraid of "holding people up".

Perhaps the most important factor contributing to Clare's success at the comprehensive was that she was "intelligent . . . not backward . . . and diligent at her work, not considering it a chore". A few teachers were concerned about public exams and how far Clare's visual defect would hinder her. The school was however aware of the concessions available to visually impaired pupils[4] and would investigate them in detail nearer the time.

In her daily school work, Clare had made use of both low vision aids and large print material. At the time of meeting her, Clare had had binoculars for six months. Before this, for close work, she had used only magnifiers (obtained commercially by her parents). She now wore glasses, although she did not like them. (She had been prescribed her binoculars by the low vision clinic through which we had located her. She had reached this clinic in the following way: her usual ophthalmologist had been away at the time of her regular visit and the locum in charge referred her to the specialist hospital because he happened to have a colleague there studying her particular optical condition. Such are the chance events that so often seem to determine what kind of aid and provision an individual child receives.) Although Clare still had to hold books very close to her face, and preferred to take dictation rather than look at the board, the only major effect of this was that she was slower than her classmates. Her teachers however agreed that "her brightness makes up for it". She sat at the front or back of the class as necessary, using binoculars to see the blackboard. Large print books had been obtained when appropriate.

Although the school had been informed of Clare's visual impairment, it often only became apparent to her teachers when she used her low vision aids in class. Some teachers had queried the use of binoculars, and astonishingly some still did. Clare's parents expressed surprise that teachers had not thoroughly realized the extent of her vision loss. Once the seriousness of her impairment became more widely known, teachers had made more adjustments; for example, allowing Clare to receive assistance from other pupils whenever necessary. Her teachers all felt that she was "very open" about her visual defect, and perhaps because she was so interested in learning, made efforts to ensure she could participate in everything going on.

Her teachers acknowledged the importance of Clare's being willing "to laugh at herself". In the early days of attending an ordinary school, Clare had been acutely aware that she was "different" from her sighted classmates; she had worried that they would tease her about her glasses. They did not. When, at the comprehensive, she obtained her new low vision aids, the initial reaction of her class was one of curiosity. In order to prevent people from asking too many questions, Clare let each of her classmates try out the aids and explained what they were for. (This was done on the advice of the low vision clinic.) As a result, Clare's condition and her low vision aids were both accepted as commonplace, though she still tended to hide them when there were pupils around who were not in her class. Some surprise was expressed by three of Clare's teachers at the fact that other children made no fun of her. It was thought "remarkable", given that there were some "tough" children in the class. The fact that she was "well accepted" at school, and had "gained the respect" of her classmates was seen to explain this.

However, Clare was still occasionally the victim of some potentially hurtful remarks from teachers, with thoughtless references on occasion to the fact that she could not see well. A recent instance was when plans were being made for an outing to Boulogne. When asked who was going, Clare raised her hand: her teacher remarked, "You won't be able to see anything".

Unquestionably, the foremost landmark in Clare's school career was her transfer from the special to the ordinary primary school, a move that beforehand she had been afraid of. But people had "not been mean" and there had been less teasing than anticipated. Clare herself remarked that she had not really noticed any difference academically between the special and the ordinary school, other than that the latter offered a wider subject range. Unlike her parents, she did not feel that she had been held back academically by attending a special school.

Teachers at the comprehensive felt that parental attitudes towards Clare's schooling were "positive" and that she "received a lot of support". Evidently, the school encouraged communication with parents; but the head of the lower school had had no more contact with Clare's parents than with those of other pupils. Nor had he had contact with any kind of agency for the visually impaired, or received any medical details. This did not seem to him to have hampered the school's appreciation of Clare's problem and their ability to offer her the attention she needed. Staff felt confident that they could handle Clare until such time as her sight severely deteriorated, if it ever did.[5]

The head of the lower school pointed out that dealing with Clare was the responsibility of each individual teacher. He or she had to "organize the class in such a way that *all* children are able to keep up with what is being taught". It was up to the teacher to adjust the amount of attention given to particular children. But teachers "need to be reminded of pupils' problems" because a teacher might see at least 240 pupils per week, each with his or her own peculiarities. There was no peripatetic advisory teacher to assist the school, nor — in the school's view — was there a need for one. No formal special provision for any handicapped children existed at the school, although there was a remedial unit to which children could be withdrawn if necessary. Clare had had no need of it.

Both Clare's parents and Clare herself were optimistic about the future. At one time, they had dreaded the prospect of Clare remaining in a special school until the age of 16. Now she hoped to stay on at the comprehensive until the sixth form and take A-levels if she could. In the course of organizing Clare's school career, her parents had had no contact with any kind of specialist educational agency, and only in the case of medical diagnoses had they ever sought a second opinion.

Her parents clearly played a central role by getting Clare into ordinary education; by maintaining a close interest in her progress; and by no longer accepting everything they were told by "the authorities". They were not initially aware that they had any "choice as to where Clare could go to school". They "just knew" that Clare was not right in a special school and that in order to try something else they had to "risk it . . . we couldn't have done any *more* harm". Integrated education had provided her with "an environment which made her feel as normal as possible". She was "not kept in cotton wool", nor "treated as special". Her father added: "All her friends now are normal". He felt that it was important that parents should be better informed, as most parents did not have sufficient knowledge "to question authority". In addition, local education authorities, parents, and teachers in ordinary schools could all be far "better educated about visual handicaps".

The above account, the first of the four individual histories, documents what seems to have been widely regarded as a successful experience of individual integration. Clare's personality, manner, enthusiasm, and academic ability clearly were advantages, as were her parents' middle class status, support and rugged persistence. Her current school was hospitable and seemed to treat her assimiliation in a straightforward, almost routine manner. It is of interest that no peripatetic or advisory support was considered necessary. Of course, if Clare had been doing less well, this might have changed. Clare also derived a good deal of advice and support from the low vision clinic she was attending and this was greater than many partially sighted children probably receive. In the classroom, minor adaptations were called for;

and her progress and acceptance by peers was probably significantly enhanced by her academic ability. We find, in this account, evidence of the essential role that low vision aids can play: Clare was enabled to take part in almost all activities through the use of her aids.

Finally, we found out that the special school, so roundly condemned by Clare's parents, had undergone a massive overhaul and change of head teacher since the time that Clare attended it.

Notes

(1) Although albinism was diagnosed, the exact cause of her rare condition of it was not firmly established until she was 13-years-old.

(2) Letter to the research team.

(3) At first, the two girls had been allocated to different secondary schools but Clare's parents had persuaded the local education authority to allow Clare to change schools. The authorities were somewhat reluctant, finally agreeing because there was a busy and dangerous main road that Clare would otherwise have had to cross.

(4) Concessions on public exams vary with examination boards and with the subjects being examined. Concessions for partially sighted pupils can include: extra time allowances, large print question papers, permission to type answers, rest periods, and if necessary, an amanuensis to whom answers can be dictated.

(5) The prognosis of her condition does not suggest any further deterioration of vision.

Chapter Fourteen

Alan

At the time of this study, Alan was nine and a half years old, the youngest of three children in an Air Force family, the only one whose vision was impaired. His family gave the impression of being close-knit, all concerned doing everything they could to help Alan.

First impressions of Alan belied the severity of his vision loss. There was no outward indication of any visual impairment. He was a physically good looking child, smart in appearance, although smaller and more delicate than many boys of his age group. At first, Alan seemed shy, rather reserved, possibly suspicious of the researcher. However, as he relaxed, he became more outgoing, and at home he was at times almost cheeky. Conversation however remained somewhat limited, mainly because of his age. Overall, he was polite and quiet, speaking only in response to specific questions. It transpired he was a fairly introverted child in public settings, but was lively and well-accepted by his peers. For a child with marked vision loss and slight spasticity as well, his energy and alacrity were quite remarkable.

Alan had optic atrophy as a result of cerebral palsy, itself the outcome of injury at premature birth. He also had an alternating squint. On a test of visual acuity, he registered readings of less that 6/60 with his right eye and 3/60 with his left eye with the aid of correcting glasses. He was registered partially sighted at the age of eight and a half years, but was now on the borderline between partial sight and blindness.

At his birth, Alan's mother had been assured he would be a "perfectly normal" child despite the prematurity. But six months later she was told he was brain damaged and would "always be retarded". At 12 months he was "dismissed as a cabbage" by a paediatrician, who advised placement in an institution. His mother had refused to accept this, although Alan "behaved like a cabbage for the next 18 months".

At this stage, the only eye defect that had become apparent was a squint. The conviction that Alan was brain damaged at birth ruled out any search for other handicaps. In his mother's words, "the eyes have never been classed as important". By the age of two years, some degree of physical handicap had also become evident: Alan lacked full control of his left leg and hand. This was identified as cerebral palsy, and seen to justify the earlier diagnosis of mental handicap.

It was not until Alan was three years old, and the family had moved to an air base in the Far East, that he first visited an ophthalmologist. He was prescribed glasses, and an operation was carried out to correct his squint.[1]

The "breakthrough" the family had longed for, came just before Alan was five. He had to take "an assessment test to see if he could cope with a normal school — Alan came out with an IQ of about 120 so it was obvious that it couldn't be mental handicap". He was placed in an ordinary local infants school, but further setbacks soon arose. For example, although not naturally left-handed, it was noticed that he used his left hand a great deal. His right hand was found to be the more spastic. His mother was then told by a physiotherapist that "he would never be able to write, although he could be taught to type". However, in other areas Alan made rapid progress: for instance, "he quickly picked up reading".

This steady progress was interrupted by the family returning to England. Alan by then was six and a half years old. There was a delay in re-entering him at an ordinary school. His parents were convinced that "with an IQ of 120, nothing other than an ordinary school made sense". At this point they were unaware of how serious his vision problem was: "We did not realize that he might require specialist schooling . . . had not been advised that he might . . . had not considered anything other than ordinary schooling".

It was not until Alan entered his current school (at the age of seven and a half years) that "real medical progress came about". His parents informed the school medical officer that Alan's vision was the main problem. The medical officer, in turn, notified a peripatetic advisory teacher for the visually impaired, who assumed responsibility for Alan — in particular, pressing for further medical attention. Alan began attending an eye clinic, where tests disclosed his vision was deteriorating.

Alan has always been 'individually integrated'. Interestingly, his mother felt that going to an ordinary school had highlighted opposing viewpoints: thus, medical opinion had queried "how could he possibly cope?"; the lay point of view tended to assume "he was perfectly normal" and treated him as such. She believed he had suffered as a result of the latter: there were certain inescapable consequences of visual impairment.

Alan's parents had no difficulty in getting him taken on at his present school — his neighbourhood school. This was a small school (of about 220 pupils) of very modern design, situated in a predominantly middle class suburb. They discussed the situation beforehand with the head teacher who met Alan before accepting him. Alan's mother felt the head "saw it as a challenge". However she acknowledged that the support of the advisory teacher had been crucial in getting Alan accepted, particularly since the ophthalmologist involved had not favoured integration.[2]

The head of Alan's school expressed sympathy and concern: "Most children, irrespective of handicap, have some compensating features . . . Any child deserves the opportunity to show what he is capable of when given appropriate assistance". He had imposed only one condition of entry — that the LEA provide some specialist assistance. Since Alan was the school's first pupil with a severe vision loss, he thought staff would need some expert help and guidance. In retrospect, he considered they had been most hampered by a lack of medical knowledge about Alan's condition. He described contact with medical authorities as "pretty poor"; the school was "not allowed to keep a copy of a child's medical record".[3] In Alan's case, they had had to rely on his mother and the advisory teacher to "ferret out" medical details. This was considered insufficient.

Although Alan came to his present school as a first year junior, "in effect, he was a first year infant" (head teacher). This was seen as resulting from his being "allowed to drift" at infants school. His mother remarked that no one there "had really known what to do with him" nor been particularly concerned to find out: "It was a case of as long as he's in a corner and pretty happy then leave him".

Alan's junior school took decisive steps to improve basic skills, fixing upon reading for the first year. By the close, his reading age had risen to seven years (his chronological age was eight years).[4] In his second year, they turned attention to his maths.

In his first year at the school, Alan's mother felt he "did not get on particularly well" with his class teacher. She sensed that this person had not approved of Alan being at the school. Alan had become very emotionally distressed, and the advisory teacher, at one stage, had considered transferring him to a unit for the partially sighted. His mother had not favoured this — "it would mean his adapting to another new environment". Alan had eventually settled down though and the matter was taken no further.

While Alan's mother believed education was "more than the 3Rs", she was very pleased that he had "come on a bundle" academically. Socially, he had friends both in and out of school: "He plays with children from the neighbourhood, he's invited to parties, and does many of the things they do . . . he stresses very much that he is normal . . . he is not overawed by anything or anyone". She admitted that Alan suffered periodic teasing — for example, his friends occasionally hid his possessions — but did not consider this a major problem. A counter example was that he joined in PE activities with enthusiasm and confidence and experienced no ridicule when he did something wrong.

At the time of our study, Alan was nearing the end of his second year. He was a full member of an ordinary class but was withdrawn daily for an hour of individualized tuition,[5] in "the normal sort of school work (reading, writing, number work), modified to his needs". This prompted his class teacher's comment: "Invaluable though it might be, it disrupts his participation in class-based activities". Another teacher considered it "too narrowly remedial", an attempt simply to "catch up", rather than to put him on an equal footing with his peers.[6] In class, Alan's teacher claimed, "My whole working approach needs to be different since he can neither work from the blackboard, nor independently from books . . . there is nothing he can do with the rest of the class". She thought more time spent on oral work would have helped him, but felt this was impossible in practical terms.

Another form of special help was instruction in braille. This was introduced by the advisory teacher, and later continued by a peripatetic supply teacher. Reasons given for introducing braille conflicted: one teacher saw it as "a preparation for the possibility of future blindness"; another as a means of extending the range of potential reading material. In fact, the advisory teacher introduced it partly because of Alan's deteriorating sight, partly because he was having problems with writing on account of his spasticity. Despite considerable enthusiasm at first, Alan had subsequently lost interest, and braille teaching had been abandoned. The supply teacher felt this was because it had not been "sufficiently meaningful as a means of communication" for him. However, the advisory teacher stated, "It was stopped purposely as he had had the fillip needed to work harder at his sighted work".

Alan's ability to contend with ordinary classroom activities depended partly on the use of low vision aids. He had two pairs of spectacles, provided by the eye clinic — one with strong lenses for distance vision, the second (with one lens blacked out and a telescopic attachment on the other) which he used for reading. His personal tutor remarked on his reluctance to wear these reading glasses in public. While they enabled him to read small print, a potential disadvantage was that they needed constant refocussing whenever attention was transferred from one object to another. Alan also used aids provided by the advisory teacher — including an abacus, a flat-field magnifier, and a large scale magnifier.[7]

Altogether, Alan's mother was appreciative of the education he was getting. However, she had certain fears: "I don't think the class teacher really understands . . . (the personal tutor) does understand the problem, but doesn't know how to go about it". More serious was the fact that Alan was now "beginning to fall behind the general level of his class", and was aware of this — "He's bright enough to realize that the standard of work he's producing is not good enough, even though we tend to say it's fine" (mother). She put his slow progress down to insufficient time rather than any lack of ability.

She was also worried by forthcoming staff turnover: the personal tutor, the peripatetic supply teacher, and the head were all leaving shortly. Alan's class teacher would be assuming responsibility for his personal tuition.

Of Alan's various teachers, only the peripatetic supply teacher had undertaken any training in visual impairment. Other teachers felt they needed specialized help and that they did not receive enough. They criticized the advisory teacher for not visiting them more often and considered it "a complete waste of human resources" for her to arrive unexpectedly when they might be unavailable. This teacher pays periodic visits to the school to monitor Alan's progress and to advise on any problems.[8] Staff were also critical of the inadequate resources within the school and LEA. There was no centralized resource centre, and it was very much a case of individual staff "having to make do".

Some teachers wondered if they had done enough for Alan: "His schooling, such as it is, is constant. He has been very happy here, his parents are happy he can stay . . . perhaps we have filled the gap but . . . we have felt that perhaps we have been doing the wrong thing sometimes . . . " (personal tutor). The supply teacher believed, "Schools have got to see the day as a whole rather than just in terms of a little bit (of provision) here and there". She thought that integrating Alan was a good example of "a well meant innovation insufficiently thought out".

Turning now to more general reactions, Alan's mother felt that handicapped people were given too little opportunity to demonstrate what they could achieve: "There must be a way to tap this (potential) but a lot of people are only too willing to treat them as idiots".

She was, not surprisingly, strongly in favour of integration: "There was no way that anybody was going to persuade me integration was not a good thing". However, she emphasized this was not an inflexible allegiance: she would always ask of herself, "Is it fair to the child? . . . Is he working to the best of his ability?". She believed that "the parent who wants his child integrated is asking for butter on both sides". Both social and academic development were frequently expected, but she doubted whether both could always be realized. It was a matter of determining which was more important. Although she "would not refuse a special school place just because of the social stigma", she regretted that special schools were too often residential: "There is no special school in this area which is in daily commuting distance . . . The choice for Alan was mainstream schooling or separation from his family . . . Alan has been a very dependent child, hating change and any separation . . . To have sent him to a residential school at the tender age of five or even nine years would . . . have been such a traumatic experience that he might never have recovered". However, she accepted that at the secondary level, special schooling might well become necessary.

The head teacher confirmed that there was some doubt about Alan's future in an ordinary school: "I feel that having given the basic skills, more expertise is needed . . . the fact that he is a boy who cannot really help himself on tasks which demand self-initiative will act against him". He regarded the middle junior stage as particularly appropriate for transferring a child from ordinary to special schooling, should it become really necessary.

Nevertheless, whatever happens in the future, school staff widely agreed that accepting Alan had been justified both educationally and socially. He had made good academic progress, and his classmates had "grown accustomed to him". Being "a bright child with a high IQ" was considered a distinct advantage. According to the head, Alan had always been left "to fight his own battles". He felt this was invaluable experience. He disagreed that children were inevitably cruel toward their handicapped peers: "Kids are just as astute as grown ups. Ninety-nine per cent are aware of the problem (without being told), and will help . . . most of them realize that the best help they can give is to treat him as a normal child".

Teachers thought Alan's "understanding and supportive home" had significantly helped. His mother's enthusiasm was particularly commended: at one point she had even begun to learn braille. The family read extensively to him, assisted him with homework, verbalized television programmes, copied school material into larger print, and took him on educational outings. Alan's mother thought that parents generally "ought to, and could do, more", but they needed assistance: "If only parents could be given a day's tuition to help them aid their children . . . ".

Of the future, she hoped that "in 10 years' time Alan ought to be contributing something to society . . . He's got to be independent and he's got to make it in his own way. I don't want charity in any form". She believed independence was best fostered by his remaining in ordinary schools. However, she was concerned that "he might be striving for the impossible" in denying, wherever possible, the reality of his handicap — "It's nonsense pretending that being visually handicapped makes no difference". She also wondered whether they, as parents, were too demanding and whether they fully acknowledged the extent of his condition.

We find in this history some of the problems of individual integration. Although no one interviewed described Alan's experiences in the ordinary school in terms of failure, nevertheless there were several causes for concern: e.g. the attitude and commitment of the ordinary class teacher; that wearing low vision aids in this milieu was embarrassing; the advisory teacher's visits were seen as being too infrequent and unpredictable to be as helpful as they could have been; and staff turnover was going to remove a number of those who had been most closely concerned with Alan heretofore.

While many were enthusiastic about the overall success of the scheme, there was a feeling that it was becoming increasingly difficult to keep Alan in ordinary schooling. It is very clear that the parents favoured integration. They did, however, acknowledge that transfer to a residential special school might prove necessary in the end, although the boarding aspect particularly disturbed them. Alan's mother thought that attending a special school carried at least some social stigma — underlining the fact that many parents may favour integration because it is proof that their child is 'normal': an entirely comprehensible reaction though not, perhaps, always to the child's advantage. However, all this said, it is by no means clear that Alan would be better off at this stage in a residential school: he would miss out, for a start, on the daily support and active encouragement of his parents.

At Alan's school, in contrast to Clare's school (discussed in the last chapter), the need for effective outside support was given emphasis. This reflected, perhaps, significant differences between the two children, as much as between the schools: Alan was younger than Clare, his vision loss was more severe, and he was slightly multiply-handicapped. But it may also simply be due to there being an advisory teacher available in Alan's local authority.

Finally, this history demonstrates, as do the others in this series, the medical uncertainties that parents so often have to live with, and the large areas of responsibility that, despite medical and educational advice, still rest on parents' shoulders.

Notes
(1) An operation to correct a squint makes no difference to visual function. The individual continues to use one eye at a time.

(2) Until about two years ago, educational placement decisions within this local authority rested almost exclusively upon ophthalmologists' recommendations. The appointment of a peripatetic advisory teacher altered this procedure.

(3) Medical records, which are highly confidential, are not made available to schools or other bodies without the permission of the child's parents. Certain medical details — e.g. information about visual functioning — are more likely to be disclosed if requested by schools.

(4) A reading age can be attributed to a person on the basis of a score on a test of reading. A child may have a reading age of eight, although his chronological or actual age is 10, because he scores at the level of the average eight-year-old.

(5) This is provided by a member of the school staff whose job is to give personal or small group tuition. She is not a specialist in the education of the visually impaired.

(6) It should be remembered that Alan came to the school virtually unable to read or write. The tuition was to teach him basic skills of reading, writing and numeracy, and was not perceived as remedial teaching. That he was behind with his schooling was only partly a consequence of his partial sight.

(7) This can magnify a full page of a book if necessary. However, magnification of this order cannot be very great, probably less than twofold.

(8) Her working policy is to spread the workload among school staff as much as possible, so that the scheme is not totally dependent upon her personally.

Chapter Fifteen

Judith

Judith, aged 16 at the time of our study, was the younger daughter of non-professional parents, the only one in her family with serious vision loss. Her visual impairment was not obvious but she tended to stare a great deal. She seemed a quiet, rather nervous girl, difficult to engage in conversation, and was slightly embarrassed at discussing her vision. Nevertheless, she spoke about her educational experience in a thoughtful and mature fashion.

Judith had aniridia and nystagmus; both visual acuity and field of vision were seriously affected. She had Snellen test readings of 5/60 in each eye, with correcting glasses worn. Her visual acuity had varied considerably over the preceding six years.[1]

Judith's mother "felt there was something wrong (with Judith) at birth". Their family doctor had been uncertain about Judith's condition, so her mother requested referral to a well-known eye hospital.[2] Judith was admitted at the age of seven months for detailed assessment. Even at this early time, it was suggested that she would need special schooling.

However, Judith remained at home until she was five, when she went for a short time to a local infants school. Her parents soon became unhappy with this: "Kind and tolerant as teachers were, it led to increasing frustration on both sides". The sole alternative appeared to be residential special schooling, although Judith's parents did not want her to leave home: "The home environment for Judith was *the* most important thing, but she had an abundance for learning. This was why we (agreed to) the early separation". They gradually came to realize that the benefits of living at home "could not make up for the educational disadvantage" of attending a school that did not know how best to help Judith. With reluctance, they sent Judith to the nearest residential school for the partially sighted when she was six: "We were determined not to institutionalize her. Going there meant she could come home at weekends".

Initially, Judith settled in well at this special school: "Going away was a game". However, in the words of her parents, "The school was run on formal, old-fashioned, boarding school lines", and going home at weekends "led to resentment among the school authorities". This caused Judith considerable conflict, and culminated — according to her parents — in "a nervous breakdown" in her tenth year. They had been aware of her increasing unhappiness, but had convinced themselves it was "nothing more than home sickness . . . We like to think we saw it coming, but the sad fact is we didn't".

Just before this crisis, the special school closed. Judith's mother felt this had "just saved the day". While Judith recovered at home, the local education authority worked on finding some alternative educational placement.[3] With the help of an adviser for special education, Judith's parents tried to enter her in another school for the partially sighted — one they felt was altogether different from the first one. Judith sat the entrance exam, was offered a place, but could not start immediately because the school was full. In the interim, the adviser suggested they try a nearby comprehensive school.

Judith's parents were impressed by their initial interview with the head teacher. They were informed that they would be able to visit the school monthly for up-to-date reports on her progress. They decided that she should attend the comprehensive school for one year. Judith began when she was 11½ years old. It was at a time when her parents had become very conscious of her frustration with her poor vision: she could not play with other children, and was jealous of her elder sister (then 14 years old) who had perfect sight.

Once at the comprehensive, Judith found a very different educational climate from the one she had been used to. At the special school, "she had been made to work extremely hard", and had benefited academically; now, by comparison, limited demands were made on her. As a result, she "became very lazy", despite her parents urging her to work hard. However, as the year progressed, she regained "a working frame of mind" (mother), encouraged particularly by new friendships. At the end of the year, school and parents assessed the options: "We as parents tried to think of her working years. If she was prepared to have a go, then the way things were going it looked promising. We thought surely it could only go forward". The school was willing to persevere; Judith herself was happy. Staying on was indicated, though — perhaps significantly — Judith's mother felt their attitude toward their daughter changed at that time: "We began to feel that perhaps education wasn't so important as her happiness".

What kind of school was to provide Judith with the rest of her education? It was a small (about 750 pupils), modern, coeducational comprehensive, situated in a new town. It claimed a tradition of accepting children whom many schools rejected — the emotionally or culturally deprived and some physically handicapped. The head teacher's philosophy was one of "equality and equal treatment for all". There was mixed ability grouping — this is discussed later. The head teacher considered the school's atmosphere was conducive to the gradual integration of handicapped children: "We are the kind of school that deals with *all* children . . . We're tackling problems now that we wouldn't have done 10 years ago. I would hope that with more experience we can tackle those with a greater degree of handicap". In Judith's case, though her vision had deteriorated since arriving there, "her personality and general attitude toward the school more than compensate for this". He believed it was rarely the disability *per se* that caused most difficulty, but the psychological problems that often went with it: "Handicap usually affects personality . . . you get a sort of spiky personality".

The head teacher remarked that Judith was very much an ordinary member of the school: "These kids come as full members of the school and we feed them into the normal class and a normal programme". However, she received a certain amount of daily individual tuition within the school's unit for the partially hearing.[4] Staff and parents agreed that this personal tuition had benefited Judith greatly.

The teacher in charge of the unit had experience and training with the partially hearing and deaf, but none with the partially sighted. Nevertheless, she willingly accepted Judith: "Both handicaps have a lot in common". She explained: "A deaf child can see objects although he might not know their names; a partially sighted child will hear objects talked about, but might not be able to see them in order to associate name and object . . . both children share a language problem". Also, "both handicaps involve the basic issue of how humans use their senses together . . . Often with these children you are coping with lots of problems. You can't have the attitude of 'I'll cope with your deafness but ignore your other difficulties . . . '".

The unit teacher described as her "primary aim . . . keeping the handicapped child ahead of his or her class". Her task at first (she arrived in Judith's second year) had been to discover how Judith had managed in her first year, and to identify any problems she was having. She learnt that Judith had entered the school as "an extremely introverted child" who had "blossomed socially". In terms of school work, she considered Judith "was at a standstill". She put this down, in part, to Judith's previous "very structured" education at the special school. In addition, she thought many of the school staff seemed to hold the attitude, "Oh, you're partially sighted, you needn't do it". She held strong views on this: "If you're in a normal school, then you should be a normal child and get favours only where it's needed".

Overall, she felt it had been good for Judith to have had "a year's social development before concentrating on educational matters".

Her strategy now was two-fold: first, "to develop a positive relationship with Judith"; second, to get other teachers "to regard her as a normal child". Her academic policy was "to concentrate on English and maths for any pupil", although not at the expense of their other needs. Judith dropped some periods of physical education, needlework, and her weakest subject, French. She was also withdrawn from certain English lessons for practice in reading and handwriting.

At the time of this study, Judith's main problems in the classroom were difficulty in seeing the blackboard, and insufficient time to complete set work. The unit teacher had encouraged her to use a carbon copy of another child's notes. However, this was not successful: Judith had been reluctant to ask her classmates for such help. Next, she had been encouraged to record her lessons but, again, had not been enthusiastic. Judith had a close friend in the class who helped her a great deal, and this mitigated some of these problems.

When questioned, Judith's subject teachers generally did not seem uneasy about her presence in their classes; nor did they feel she was an imposition. For most, it had simply meant making sure that Judith could see the blackboard, and that her progress was carefully watched. A few modifications to teaching methods or materials had been made: for instance, providing Judith with individual workcards, a specially adapted protractor, and plastic graph paper embossed with a raised grid; they had enlarged and thickened map outlines for her and allowed her to use a tape recorder. Certain subjects posed more specific problems, notably geography — mapwork was extremely difficult — and science practical work. However, the consensus among teachers was that "the little extra didn't interfere with the rest of the children". In her CSE examinations she was allowed extra time, and exam papers were enlarged.

As noted earlier, most subjects at this comprehensive were taught in mixed ability groups and this was thought to be to Judith's advantage. Had she been in a streamed class, "she would inevitably have fallen into a lower stream because of (her) slower rate of progress" (head teacher). But in a mixed ability class, "Judith's innate intelligence means she isn't the weakest pupil, despite the limitations of her visual condition". Staff also pointed out that mixed ability grouping allowed for individualized teaching: "You try to prepare your work scrupulously (using graded worksheets, linking themes from one lesson to the next, etc.) so that most are catered for". It also meant "she's integrated with a true cross-section of children". This was considered "socially important; a child's social progress is a barometer of other things as well". Most teachers felt Judith had "coped quite adequately" educationally speaking, in the last two or three years, and also that she had made friends at school. Her peers had "never complained that she was a drawback".

Her "favourable personality" and "determination to succeed" were frequently mentioned. One teacher spoke of these as "both pathetic and a strength" — but admitted it had encouraged him to do everything he could to help her. However, some questioned Judith's "sense of normality": one commented, "I feel there's a certain element present of Judith being unwilling to acknowledge the reality of her condition". She did not think Judith enjoyed going to the unit because "everyone knows that only special pupils go there". In addition, Judith had a long cane, "but she firmly refuses to use it because it shows her as blind".

Judith has made extensive use of low vision aids in school. She has attended a low vision clinic since the age of 14 and currently has four types of aids[5] for use in the classroom. Several teachers referred to Judith's reluctance to use her aids: "they make her conspicuous"; her Keeler aid in particular "makes her look ghastly". Her mother thought low vision aids were "fine indoors, but what happens when you go outside?".

Almost without exception, teachers at the school totally lacked previous experience of teaching visually impaired pupils. Some were concerned that this meant they "couldn't do the best for her". Although they were encouraged to go on courses, only one was known to have done so — a day-long course of lectures and discussion covering both visual and hearing impairment. This person considered it had been strikingly helpful — "I don't think any of us really realized the problem". She thought it would be useful "to get experts to address the staff as a whole": this had yet to happen.

Staff at the school, particularly the unit teacher, also expressed concern that they had received so few details about Judith's visual condition. Information had come largely from Judith herself or her parents.[6] Medical authorities were perceived as "very reluctant to pass on information".

However, the school was not left without any external support. Judith's overall progress was monitored by an advisory teacher who had considerable experience with visually impaired children and was in close contact with medical experts. She made monthly visits to the school and had issued a standing invitation to teachers to contact her whenever they felt the need. In the past, she had also provided Judith with various optical and non-optical[7] aids. At one point she had also begun to teach Judith braille — at a time when her sight had got worse. This was subsequently abandoned and typing substituted. Reasons for this included "the pressures of CSEs", and Judith's own lack of enthusiasm:

"I wanted to write and read from books. I wanted to use my eyes, but I had to understand that it would help me to do it (learn braille)". The advisory teacher had also tried to arrange mobility training for Judith who was "very nervous" at having to use public highways. This request, however, could not be met, as mobility training by specialists was only provided for those registered as blind.[8] The advisory teacher finally provided some training herself, convinced that it was essential for Judith's independence and confidence.

At the time of our study, Judith was preparing to leave school in a few months time. Her occupational prospects concerned both her parents and teachers. Preparation for possible careers generally begins earlier for handicapped pupils.[9] Although there was a careers mistress at the school, she had not sought out Judith in advance of a specialist careers officer becoming involved. She explained why: "Judith was a prototype, the first of the severely handicapped. I suppose I shied away from it". Judith's parents were aware that Judith displayed "a great tenderness for handicapped children", but unfortunately, training courses in this area had all been full. Her parents' suggestion was that she should train as a secretary. Judith was not enthusiastic. She noted that "even the blind are doing typing in my dad's factory". Her parents claimed that settling on a job was ultimately for Judith to decide. Judith was present when they said this and promptly added, "Well, the choice *is* very limited". This led the parents to admit that "perhaps we have talked her into it, but although she might not be that keen on it, surely it wouldn't hurt to begin with". To them it was important that she should be "self-sufficient and enjoy life", and they accepted her own evaluation that she had gone as far as she could academically. Taking her CSEs had been "a very real struggle" (mother). Her results in fact proved to be very good.

Throughout her school career — and indeed life — Judith's parents thought they had tried to help her as much as possible. They had emphasized social activities, seeing these as a good way of building her confidence, but had also helped with school work, especially reading and domestic science. They cautioned, however, that "giving our attention mustn't be confused with spoiling. We try to help but we also seek to make her help herself". She had been encouraged to try everything, but where "unfair demands were being made on her" (like being sent on cross-country runs or doing needlework) they had intervened: "Intervention isn't for ourselves. We've only ever done what we felt was right". With regard to her visual condition, they had insisted on being fully informed from the moment it was first diagnosed. Judith's father remarked, "How can you help a child if you don't know the facts?"

They recounted one particular incident which they felt amply justified their readiness to intervene. When Judith was 14½ years old, she had complained that her sight was getting worse. They had at once arranged a hospital appointment: the diagnosis was cataracts. Dissatisfied with this, Judith's parents had sought a second opinion. The second examination revealed patches of scarring on the cornea, suggesting possible corneal ulceration. Eye drops were prescribed and these appeared to cure the condition, although it further reduced Judith's visual acuity. The hospital had been reluctant to offer any firm prognosis as Judith suffered a rare complication of aniridia.[10] Nevertheless, the confusion over the diagnosis convinced Judith's parents of the need for their active involvement with doctors: "If we'd sat back, they would have said it was a slow cataract leading to blindness within 10 years".

Judith herself claimed she had been very happy at the comprehensive. However, in retrospect, she was glad she had attended a special school when younger, despite having "disliked being away from home". Not only had she benefited from "the high standard of work" demanded at the school for the partially sighted, but she was convinced that as a junior she would have found it much harder to mix with sighted peers: "If I'd seen kids doing things I wasn't able to do, then I think I'd have felt left out". As an adolescent, however, there were "so many things to do which did not demand perfect sight".

Judith singled out for special praise a close friend at the comprehensive school who helped her a lot. To begin with, she had met with "a good deal of teasing". This had been distressing, reminding her that she "was different from the majority". With time, the teasing ended. She also expressed her debt to the unit teacher for all the assistance she had provided, and to her various subject teachers for the concern they had shown toward her. They were the first to agree that "most of the hard work had been done by the time she came here".

In conclusion and summary, both parents and teachers considered Judith had derived benefit from attending an ordinary school for her secondary education. Her mother's opinion was: "Where it's at all possible you must integrate to help them (handicapped persons) live a normal life — but it's not always practical". The unit teacher confirmed this view: "These children behave so much more normally when they are with ordinary children . . . in terms of their stance and social poise. As soon as you isolate anyone then they start behaving differently".

Two factors were clearly important in bringing about a successful end to Judith's schooling. First, despite the emotional distress which accompanied her earlier special schooling, undoubtedly she benefited academically, and continued to trade off this throughout her secondary education. Second, the presence in the school of a specialist teacher, who provided Judith with extensive individual tuition, as well as easing the load that making suitable provision for Judith might otherwise have been for other members of staff. This teacher is a good example of the peripatetic advisory teacher's working policy to delegate responsibility, wherever possible, to someone within the handicapped child's school. This frees the advisory teacher to carry out an overseer's role — although she had been prompt in providing practical help wherever necessary, for example, introducing braille tuition and low vision aids.

Having built a sound academic footing in the special school, it may well be that the social and personal development which accompanied Judith's switch to integrated schooling, came at just the right time. Certainly, her balanced personality and determination to overcome her handicap were critical factors in encouraging teachers' commitment toward her.

Finally, although Judith was not seen as a burden or a nuisance by teachers, clearly they knew relatively little about her visual condition, or of the techniques of teaching that might be usefully employed. It is interesting to speculate about whether — if staff had known more — they would have treated Judith less naturally.

Notes

(1) The visual acuity of her left eye had been as low as 1/60. There had been some improvement of late, and she now has an acuity of 2/60 in each eye.

(2) Regular contact with this hospital has been maintained ever since.

(3) As one of the last educational authorities to be informed of the closure, they found that all available special school places for that school year had been filled.

(4) This unit was founded in Judith's second year at the school. Its working practice is still evolving. Pupils attend singly or in pairs for individualized attention as, and when, necessary. It is the policy of the local authority to offer partially sighted children assistance from different kinds of unit if this "allows for greater integration".

(5) She uses a Keeler aid or a hand-held monocular for reading the blackboard, street names etc., and a flat-field magnifier for near-vision tasks — reading print, doing map exercises etc. She also has a pair of face-mounted distance binoculars.

(6) Some medical details were provided by the advisory teacher.

(7) Optical aids include various kinds of magnificatory instruments. Non-optical aids include such equipment as large print typewriters.

(8) Appreciation of the needs of the partially sighted to have mobility training is growing.

(9) Careers advice in schools usually begins in the penultimate year of compulsory schooling and is arranged by the school careers officer. In the case of handicapped pupils, vocational guidance is normally initiated one year earlier, the child being seen by the school's careers officer and then ordinarily referred to the specialist employment services of the local authority.

(10) A very small percentage of people with aniridia develop reduced sensitivity of the cornea. In Judith's case, this meant she was not particularly aware of the pain caused by the corneal ulceration.

Chapter Sixteen

Mary

Mary was ten, and came from a professional, middle class home. She had one younger brother. No one else in the family was visually impaired. Mary impressed the researcher as a lively, confident, intelligent and independent girl. She was neither shy nor withdrawn, but warm and friendly. She was thought to be a mature child for her age with an excellent grasp of general knowledge and a wide vocabulary; she was, indeed, remarkably articulate. She appeared to have 'adjusted' to her visual impairment, taking its consequences in her stride. Mary was an attractive girl whose visual impairment was not noticeable.

She suffered from macular degeneration. Her measured visual acuity was 6/60 for distance and N6 for near vision. Low vision aids improved her sight to 6/12 and N4.5 respectively, but her field of vision remained limited.

Mary's condition did not become evident until she was ten. Before this she wore spectacles but was not considered to have any serious problem with her sight. She began to complain that she could no longer see the blackboard clearly. At first, her parents thought that she simply needed new glasses. They decided to consult the local ophthalmologist; he noticed a macular change. The following day, her parents made an appointment with a Harley Street specialist. He confirmed the diagnosis and offered a pessimistic prognosis – that Mary might no longer be able to see to read at all within the space of three months. An appointment for a further medical check could not be made for four to six weeks. With a prognosis of what Mary's parents believed to be one of such rapid deterioration, they decided to seek help elsewhere. They departed for a prestigious eye clinic abroad. This clinic confirmed the diagnosis, but disputed the cause of the disease – suggesting it could be a viral infection. However, attempts to isolate a virus proved fruitless and Mary was referred back to a renowned London paediatric hospital for further consultation. On returning to England, thorough neurological tests were made, again confirming Mary's condition. A consultant ophthalmologist was called in. He confirmed the earlier diagnosis made at Harley Street and referred the child to a low vision clinic. Now it was thought she would not lose her vision before middle adolescence.

Mary's parents expressed strong criticism of what they saw as the lack of understanding of their anxiety shown by medical advisers in England.[1] Their appeal to a medical clinic overseas had been frowned upon, and their choice of this hospital criticized. But going there had been psychologically very important to them: they wanted "to pursue the problem more urgently" and have "a real opportunity to understand her condition . . . and be more alert to the opportunities which might arise . . . We knew too little about Mary's condition to feel that we were sufficiently involved". The great value of the foreign clinic was that it "showed some concern". Seven consultants had discussed the diagnosis, and they felt they were "being treated as people by being given medical information about her condition". In contrast, the diagnosis in England had resulted from a 10 minute session with only one specialist,[2] and they felt that they were "just a statistic in the statistics of macular degeneration". In England, they felt they had been asked more questions about how they "came to be referred to particular hospitals than about ourselves, our problems, fears and concerns and how these could be helped". Mary's parents felt that probably they had been labelled as "panicky parents" by medical authorities. However, to them, any panic they may have shown was understandable, they felt, "in view of the pessimistic prognosis originally offered".

The sudden discovery of Mary's visual impairment was a traumatic experience for the whole family. It brought an element of tension into their lives which they had not experienced before. "Every day you wake up wondering is it worse?". The stress led to differing parental reactions: her father welcomed every opportunity to "get it off his chest"; her mother, on the other hand, found it too difficult to talk about. Mary's father also noticed a change in himself: previously he had "taken his children for granted"; now he was probably "over-indulgent and over-concerned". His daughter's difficulty was "ultimately her own", but it was one for them as well: "When Mary is older, she will have to deal with her own problems. While she is a child, everything will be related to her problems and ours". He was acutely aware of his own "fear of the unknown": he needed now to establish greater rapport with his daughter; she needed "an overt expression of security".

The feelings that Mary's parents experienced included "helplessness, bitterness, resentment and desperation". They had felt "inadequate, deficient, and hopeless". They had learnt to stop asking Mary "what she can and cannot see", and were prepared to infer this from observing her. One of the worst aspects had been watching Mary cope with her handicap: "her bravery hurts". She had never been known "to express any bitterness", but her parents felt that it might almost help them if she had.

When Mary's condition was first diagnosed, her parents saw it as their responsibility to seek both educational and medical advice. Over education, they had no idea where to begin: "We were totally at a loss as to where to look for advice. One isn't geared to coping with something out of the ordinary".[3] The parents agreed that it was not up to doctors "to offer educational advice", but they now thought they might have been directed to agencies who could.[4]

Seeking the relevant advice became the prerogative of Mary's mother. She described herself as "the kind of person who will get on the phone and find out things". Most information she acquired through being referred from one person to another. The family were told (by the LEA) that an "alternative form of schooling" was available, i.e. special schools for the partially sighted. When they realized there was no cure, they began to "think seriously about a special school". They contacted one which suggested they should apply immediately.

Meanwhile, her mother had contacted the Partially Sighted Society. A representative visited the family and suggested Mary might in fact stay at the school she was already attending. Continuously, since the age of four, Mary had gone to a small, denominational, fee-paying local school. After careful weighing of the pros and cons, Mary's parents decided that, if possible, she should stay where she was: she was, after all, "managing to cope". But they did not want to "pressurize her teachers" into keeping Mary on. However, attending a local school would enable deficiencies to be made up at home, and she would be "treated normally" — they "would be aware of Mary's potential".

The school, in fact, raised no objection; since Mary was expected to have reasonable sight until 15 or 16, the school felt "able to contain her". It helped (the parents said) that it was a small private school with small classes; staff felt they could offer Mary "the security of an environment to which she (was) accustomed".

Mary's parents — at the time we met them — had been satisfied so far with the education offered at this school. However, they felt that a special school could still not be ruled out "should the situation require it". But they would need to be convinced about the quality of the education offered; and they would prefer not to "inflict" on Mary the experience of living away from home; they believed in "the educational value of the home environment".

No fundamental changes had been made in the way that teaching was carried out at Mary's school because of her condition. Of course, there were minor ones: she was occasionally helped to copy out work, and given a rough copy of blackboard notes. Teachers had been instructed to "keep an unobtrusive careful watch" so that she did not fall behind. The main problems were in seeing the blackboard and taking part in physical education. She was considered intelligent and "able to cope well academically", although her writing was still "untidy" and "does not always stay on the line". The local authority had arranged typing lessons — at the mother's request; the school had also agreed to provide braille teaching, if necessary.

Mary's parents had throughout been concerned that the school might lower their academic expectations: "Our main worries are that Mary will not realize her academic potential, especially now that she is visually handicapped". They acknowledged that Mary's teachers possessed a "very real understanding", but there remained a "nagging feeling" that "insufficient might be expected" of Mary. On the other hand, her teachers felt that the parents were, if anything, "pressuring the child" and were being careful not to do so themselves.

Despite the keenness of parents and teachers to ensure continuation of a full school experience, Mary's visual impairment had caused some tricky problems — most notably in maths. This was partly because of time lost when she went abroad to consult doctors, but there were other difficulties. For instance, because of her restricted field of vision, she could not always see a long sequence of figures — "I don't find fractions difficult to do, I find them difficult to see" — or read the print clearly; italics were visually difficult; low vision aids could sometimes cause confusion because of different print sizes or the juxtaposition of diagrams and print; drawing geometric figures required accurate use of a ruler, which was sometimes difficult. Mapwork in geography also caused trouble: boundary lines were indistinct and colours that were similar seemed to her to merge.[5]

Mary used various low vision aids which helped her to function at school. She had telescopic devices for reading, and binoculars for looking at the blackboard. She occasionally found it "frustrating" if she focused her low vision aids, only to be presented later with a copy of the notes she had been trying laboriously to copy off the blackboard.

Always an avid reader, her parents had feared that, with her vision loss, she might read less, to the general detriment of her educational progress. But with her low vision aids she continued to read a great deal — although lengthy periods of reading tended to make her eyes painful. Her telescope often made her feel "cross-eyed", and her eyes hurt when she looked up suddenly.

Mary had a variety of other kinds of help: extra typing lessons (provided free by the LEA), private French tuition, and the use of her own radio and tape-recorder. Her mother had also obtained talking books which Mary "enjoys tremendously".

Despite difficulties with some school subjects, Mary had not dropped any. But she was excluded from certain activities such as ball games and physical education; these, she claimed, she was "not particularly interested in anyway". She enjoyed swimming and also hoped to learn to ride.

Mary was careful to avoid things generally which highlighted her disability. She had been known, when playing games with friends, to change, very subtly, the nature of the game if she could no longer participate as an equal; she was "anxious to do things she can do and avoid things which she cannot do" (mother). If she could not see something, she would sometimes quietly return later to take a closer look. Mary described herself as a person who "pretends that she knows more than she does". Her parents thought that as an "extrovert . . . able to talk her way out of anything — she can display a kind of total conviction. She was not embarrassed to use her aids; she remarked: "aids are for using not for looks".

Mary's teachers described her classmates as "marvellous in their reaction to her . . . they do everything they can to help her". They did not think she had been the victim of any teasing. Told of her visual condition, her classmates had been "somewhat overprotective" towards her at first. This reaction did disturb Mary: she felt it was "important to overcome it". She wanted to be accepted in the school as "ordinary" and not to "gain sympathy". Her teachers were also on guard to stop her classmates "helping her too much . . . Mary should learn to cope with things alone".

Both parents and teachers agreed that Mary did not appear basically changed by her sudden loss of vision. She had "taken the whole episode marvellously" — it was thought "almost to have made her into a nicer girl"; she had "never been known to complain" and it had not hindered her social life. She was described as an "unusual girl", "well-adjusted", "anxious that people should in no way think that she *had* been changed by her condition", and as having a "positive attitude towards life and people". At first, Mary may have thought her condition was temporary, that eventually it might be cured, but she had later come to accept that it would not.

Any overview of Mary's life in school has to take into account that she still attended the same school: it was considered altogether different from her moving to a new school where she would have been "a new girl in a new situation" (instead of "an old girl in a new situation") and more likely "to be labelled as visually handicapped". It was important, perhaps, that Mary's outward physical appearance was not affected: this was considered "a great advantage" by both parents and teachers.

The school had not had contact with any agency involved with the partially sighted. They had received no reports directly from medical personnel, but felt that it would have made little difference if they had. Their information had come via the parents, and this had proved sufficient.

Mary's parents now anticipated other, perhaps greater, problems for her in the future. They felt there was "insufficient guidance about the educational value of integrated education"; that there was no one available to monitor her progress, like a peripatetic advisory teacher who could "recognize inequalities or problems which might not be immediately apparent to the parent".[6] There were problems of puberty and adolescence looming up that might create complications; her emotional problems might well increase. Her parents had now revised their ambitions for Mary's secondary education, to "approach the problem from a totally new viewpoint". Mary's mother felt there was a need to look ahead: the situation was "an evolving one". She believed that if you wanted to get your children into a particular school, you had to "start making decisions and taking action fairly early on".

Her parents still felt somewhat hampered by their lack of understanding of Mary's visual condition: "There should be an information service made available to parents on medical research into the (eye) condition, for example, centres specializing in the condition throughout the world". Whatever happened at the secondary stage Mary's parents were concerned that she should be "able to enjoy a congenial environment within which she can find fulfillment". On balance, Mary's parents realized that although their situation had been "traumatic", they, as parents, had also been "fairly bold and outgoing . . . and knew where to start looking for information". This had proved a tremendous advantage.

Important in Mary's success was the attitude of her school, the fact that she was well-established there, familiar with school routine, staff and other pupils, and they with her. Her pleasant, well-balanced personality, and remarkable maturity for a 10-year-old were also crucial contributory factors. Accepting the restrictions which visual impairment imposed, developing strategies which capitalized on individual strengths, and taking care to avoid those areas which emphasized her disability, were Mary's own significant contribution. They built confidence and a positive self-identity — and they won her the respect and acceptance of her peers.

Low vision aids had certainly helped Mary to stay in the ordinary school. She differed markedly from both Alan and Judith (for whom aids were an embarrassment) in the rational attitude she had developed toward having to use them. At the same time, her experience shows that aids are not always an unqualified success: in enabling a child to cope, they may present new problems. For instance, where print and diagrams were juxtaposed, aids had continually to be readjusted; and aids intensified the concentration demanded, which she was unable to sustain for very long.

Finally, Mary has much to thank her parents for. Not only had they offered consistent help and encouragement, but they took the initiative from the outset. Their assistance surpassed day-to-day practical help, like reading aloud. Mary's mother, for instance, obtained talking books; she arranged for typing lessons; she contacted agencies for the visually impaired; she sought out medical advice. It helped further that parents and school worked broadly in harmony, knowing each other well.

Notes

(1) To define a diagnosis or prognosis accurately is a long process and may require up to one-and-a-half days' intensive testing, some of it painful. For this reason, such testing may be delayed if the child is managing and is expected to do so for the next two or three years.

(2) In England, there is only one ophthalmologist per 150,000 of the population. This is in sharp contrast to the usual European ratio of 1:20,000. This discrepancy is partly due to the fact that opticians are responsible for refraction work in England.

(3) Mary was not registered as partially sighted at the time.

(4) Ophthalmologists may not be able to provide advice about particular schools but they should be able to suggest whether a child's visual functioning is sufficiently good for him or her to attend an ordinary school.

(5) Colour discrimination is frequently very much reduced in partially sighted people, including those suffering from macular degeneration.

(6) Since this case history was completed, a peripatetic advisory teacher has taken on responsibility for supervising Mary's progress.

Part Five

Supporting and Coping

Chapter Seventeen

School Support for the Integrated Child

We return frequently, in this chapter and the next, to Clare, Alan, Judith and Mary. But we also draw extensively on material from the other 18 case histories we completed. Although each history is unique — and we have concentrated on their particularities — we can also discern a number of common elements. This and the following chapter concentrate on the inputs from school and home that, separately or in combination, may help determine whether a child with a severe loss of vision can be assimilated into an ordinary school and thrive there. We shall examine the commonplace problems that children encounter, and how (if at all) they contend with them.

In this chapter we discuss schools: 'successful integration' — however defined — does not depend simply on the child; there are also demands on the school that need to be explored.

Just as children, sight defects, and family attitudes vary enormously, so do different schools. The 22 children investigated came from a great variety — primary and secondary, single sex and coeducational, fee paying and state, selective and comprehensive. As we noted earlier, each school has its own specific attitude and response toward the integrated child. Here we are seeking patterns amidst all the variation. We believe there are many.

Accepting the visually impaired child in the ordinary school

Not unnaturally, schools are not all equally keen or able to take on children with handicaps. Placement of visually impaired children in ordinary schools comes about in various ways. In the case of the 'Hospital' group of children we studied, it was largely the outcome of parental initiative; with the 'LEA' group, on the other hand, the advisory teacher played a large part in negotiating suitable placement. However, irrespective of who proposes that a child go there, a response and decision from the school concerned is always required.

Whether a school is amenable to the idea of accepting a handicapped child often depends on the attitude of the head teacher. Some see it as a challenge. This was certainly true for Alan's head teacher who thought that handicapped children had "compensating features" which it was his responsibility to ensure were capitalized upon. Another head teacher was equally accepting: "Let's encourage a positive attitude. A person might lack arms and legs, but I say ignore that and emphasize what that person can do". Some linked accepting a child with the climate of their schools: "It is a professional problem which we hope, as professionals, to be able to overcome . . . If I can create the right atmosphere among my teachers, I feel . . . (they) can enjoy the new problems it throws up". Sometimes it was a case of a general philosophy of equal opportunity: "I would hope we are the kind of school that deals with all children", stated Judith's head teacher.

In deciding whether or not to accept a child, head teachers often have to rely on the advice tendered them, not all of which is necessarily of the highest quality. In the case of one 14-year-old boy, an educational psychologist had assured the head that the boy was suitable, despite a highly pessimistic prognosis — the child was almost certain to go blind sometime in the future. The head teacher "took him on the understanding that we should give him a normal intermediate year's education and make allowances where necessary"; but whether or not the full circumstances were known to him is distinctly questionable.

There were instances where active parental pressure for a place at a particular school or for a particular type of education had clearly been influential — as in the case of Anthony (one of the 18 children in the group not discussed at length). His parents claimed they were being pressured by the head teacher of the school he was attending — whom they described as "a panicker" — to remove Anthony to a school for the partially sighted. They were determined to resist this pressure for special schooling. Their assertiveness paid off in the end, when the head teacher of a second (ordinary) school accepted Anthony and he subsequently made good progress there.

If a child's admission to a school has a lot to do with the head teacher, the subsequent full acceptance of the child and his difficulty has much more to do with individual teachers. Instances of overt hostility were rare, and where apparent, seemed more related to the child's personality than to the visual impairment itself — although the two were often related. Thus, one child was described as "a misfit . . . an introverted character who often does something horrid to provoke retaliation". In one disturbing instance, a boy of 13 was called a "blind bat" by one member of staff.

A larger proportion of teachers, although not unwelcoming to individual children, expressed reservations about integration: "It may be fine for some kids, (but) for others all you're offering them is the chance to fail". Rather than adopting integration wholesale, these teachers cautioned that there was a need to judge each child on his or her merits and to ask, "What can (he or she) get out of the school?"

Some consequences of the visually impaired child in the ordinary class

Uncertainty was far more prevalent than antipathy among teachers: for instance, uncertainty about the nature of the child's visual impairment, about what could be expected of the child, or about what extra attention should be laid on. The vast majority of teachers of the 22 children studied had no previous experience of teaching a child designated 'visually handicapped'; many had been told nothing about special teaching techniques or modifications required, and their professional training had often included only the odd lecture on the handicapped pupil.

Naturally, there were questions about whether specialized training ought to be provided for teachers in ordinary schools with a visually impaired pupil. There was some disagreement over this. Many regarded it as desirable. Even a one-day in-service course, organized by an advisory teacher, was thought to have been "highly instructive" by the teacher who had attended. At times we encountered naivety and plain ignorance displayed by teachers unaccustomed to having a visually impaired child in their class: one teacher remarked about a partially sighted boy of eight and a half years, "I find him quite enlightening. You imagine someone who can't see much wouldn't have much inside". On the other hand, some teachers disputed the need for training of any kind: for them, experience — "you only learn practical shortcuts by doing" — and "the teacher's attitudes" were all-important.

If giving information to teachers is to become more widespread, practical guidance and medical details would appear to be the two aspects that would be most appreciated. With regard to the former, teachers complained about the lack of advice concerning, for instance, the use of low vision aids; the importance of lighting conditions; the fact that residual vision could not be 'used up'; the longer time needed by the partially sighted child for experiencing visually pictures in books or biological organisms under the microscope; and the more intense concentration demanded which reduced the time for which it could be sustained.

With regard to specific medical details, one teacher voiced what many felt: "Unless you are obnoxious you don't discover anything about the child". However, even where medical details were passed on, it was apparent that teachers had not always fully understood and internalized their implications. There were several instances of teachers not appearing to know of a child's defective vision at all (obviously

among those children whose visual condition was not readily apparent).
Sometimes these children were subject to hurtful remarks — for
example, teachers querying whether they were blind when they could
not read the blackboard, or questioning the use of low vision aids. Or
again, the child was asked to perform the impossible — for instance, a
child with a severely reduced field of vision was expected to use a plane
in woodwork.

Teachers' uncertainty about exactly what to do with visually
impaired children was revealed in several ways. Their usual working
assumptions tended to be rendered invalid by a partially sighted pupil.
They were less at ease and confident about what they were doing. One
of Alan's teachers had wondered whether they were not "doing the
wrong thing sometimes". Other comments reinforced the same notion
— of teachers 'working in the dark' — "all the time we are feeling our
way". Of course, channels do exist for teachers eager to become better
informed, but few appeared to take positive steps to do so.

The sense of slight vagueness and not being sure may not be
particularly harmful, but one suspects it is hardly an ideal basis for
good teaching. It led, almost certainly, in a number of the cases studied,
to failure to give sufficient attention. An attitude prevailed: "If he
seemed to be working happily, I left him to it". Some teachers had no
qualms about this: "As long as he keeps up with the class then there's
nothing to worry about". This ignores the fact that simply keeping up
may mean a child is under-achieving relative to his or her educational
potential. It is perhaps this reduced ambition for the child, on the part
of teachers, that most alarms the critics of integration.

Not knowing quite what to do also affected how much
independence a child was given. Many teachers acted in the belief that
handicapped pupils were integrated in order to be treated as 'normal'
children. This meant that in certain situations, a child was expected to
assert himself or herself against physically, and perhaps emotionally,
stronger peers. Susan was a case in point. She was a particularly reticent
11-year-old, yet her class teacher commented, "It does her good to
fight her own battles". And, in Mary's case, staff were concerned about
her peers giving her too much assistance. They thought she should cope
by herself. Of course, one major objective for integration is to
encourage independence. But in practice, expecting integrated pupils to
fend for themselves, irrespective of the circumstances, may be
unacceptably non-interventionist. The teacher has to decide what is
best — and it is not easy: "What is important is knowing where a
situation arises that the child cannot cope with, and developing
alternatives".

The teacher also has to determine what demands can legitimately be made on the child with impaired vision. If the teacher is unsure, there is perhaps a natural tendency to 'play safe' and lower expectations. This may take several forms: not expecting work of such high quality; excusing the child from certain academic tasks or from homework; excluding him or her from project work; and taking it for granted that certain subjects (e.g. sewing) are impossible. Some teachers sounded unduly dismissive. Take, for instance, the earlier quoted remark of Alan's class teacher: "He can neither work from the blackboard, nor independently from books . . . there is nothing he can do with the rest of the class".

We encountered a great deal of parental concern that teachers should not lower expectations or standards. These were not altogether without foundation: we found instances of a willingness to 'bend the rules', and in some cases, a remarkable lack of concern on the part of teachers. One head teacher remarked, "There may be a slight under-functioning but I would accept that as tolerable". Sometimes these lowered expectations had become institutionalized, a child being deliberately retained in a band or stream that was below his or her educational potential. In Clare's case, this was justified on the grounds that, at that particular level, she was one of the "brightest" pupils and thereby commanded peer respect. Certainly her own awareness of her academic success helped sustain her confidence, and — arguably — served to reduce the impact of her visual impairment.

However, lack of knowledge about a child's condition is not always a complete disadvantage: it has a positive dimension too. For example, in those cases where teachers are not informed, or fail to realize a child is visually impaired, their expectations are unlikely to be founded on visual grounds. Stuart, a boy of 16 years with an extremely outgoing personality, exemplified this. Unaware of his visual condition, his art teacher had, on one notable occasion, asked him to "sharpen" his drawing which was "woolly" and "indistinct". This led to some exceptional work which, once the teacher found out about the boy's condition, had greatly alarmed him. He was concerned that unwittingly he might have imposed visual strain on Stuart. Stuart himself was adamant that this had not been the case, and was delighted that his work had been so well received. What is interesting is that the teacher said he was uncertain whether he would have made the same demand had he known about the boy's condition in advance.

Much of the teachers' uncertainty about what are appropriate reactions reflects worries that concern handicapped people in general. These have been discussed in earlier chapters. Central is the familiar tension between wanting to 'normalize' the child's presence — by not extensively modifying the environment or separating the child off in any way and, pulling in the opposite direction, also wanting to ensure that the requisite attention is given and proper allowances are made. In fact, this is a tension that underlines all educational practice: but teaching children with manifestly special needs often seems to increase the conflict.

One of the central 'management' questions for the ordinary school to resolve relates directly to these competing goals: if a child is maintained in integration only by a great deal of special support, does this make educational or economic sense? Without the support the child could be at a distinct disadvantage; yet, whisking the child off repeatedly for special instruction serves to disrupt his or her chances of enjoying a 'normal school life in an ordinary school'. It may even prove isolating. Alan is a good illustration of how a lot of extra attention can fragment a child's involvement as a full class member. The issue to be resolved is characterized as one of 'where to draw the line' or 'how to strike a balance'. Advocates of special schools often criticize integration on the grounds that all the necessary specialized elements cannot possibly be introduced to an ordinary school setting. Arguably, however, were such 'special' support to be introduced on a massive scale, it would create an imbalance. In any case, the case histories by and large demonstrate that this degree of support was not necessary for most children to function at a level considered satisfactory. This is not to deny that pupils might, in theory, have achieved more academically if levels of support (characteristic of special schooling) had been forthcoming in the ordinary school. One thing is certain, that if children with more severe visual deficiencies or with additional handicaps are integrated in the future, more support than that typically found at present would become obligatory.

'Special' provision in the ordinary school

A good number of the 22 children investigated received little extra support. The group seemed to fall into three categories: a group of 12 children — those who received no organized support whatsoever; a second group of six who received occasional special support involving someone other than the child's class or subject teacher(s); and a small group of four children who received some daily support involving remedial or specialist teachers. Children in this last group were, in all cases, the responsibility of the LEA advisory teacher.

There were various kinds of extra provision. For example, both Alan and Judith had been introduced to braille, partly in case their vision deteriorated further. Another boy, Robert, a 15-year-old who had recently begun at a senior high school, received typing lessons, as did Judith. In Robert's case, this was provided at a school for the partially sighted. Three pupils from the 'LEA group', other than Judith, received additional tuition in the basic subjects from teachers in charge of units for the partially hearing. In other instances, integrated pupils were introduced to new subjects earlier than their peers in an attempt to give them a head start; Mary began French lessons for this reason.

Otherwise, most integrated pupils played a full part in the curriculum. Few teachers felt that catering for them was an excessive burden, or that it demanded extensive modification to their teaching method. As noted before, the obvious and most prevalent difficulty was being unable to see the blackboard clearly. The availability and use of low vision aids made a great difference, and these − perhaps more than any other single factor − helped keep modifications to teaching practice to a minimum.

A number of minor alterations in teaching were reported by teachers. These included: (i) reduced use of the blackboard − this partly mirrors a change in contemporary educational practice; (ii) a correspondingly greater reliance on individual worksheets; (iii) more teacher verbalization; (iv) wider use of group discussion; (v) particular emphasis on questioning integrated pupils to ensure they were following and understanding lesson material; (vi) providing pupils with their own copies of notes; (vii) enlarging maps and diagrams; (viii) allowing them to receive the assistance of peers on certain tasks − e.g. copying up notes or undertaking practical experiments; (ix) providing large print materials − log tables, maths books etc.; (x) cooperating in the tape-recording of lesson material; and (xi) keeping an unobtrusive but close watch on their progress. At least some of these minor modifications could be held to be general improvements that might benefit all class members − a point that is generally overlooked.

Undesirable side-effects of special support

We have already alluded to the fact that massive extra provision can disrupt the education of a child who is individually integrated: support may hinder as well as help. Another difficulty is that it can lead to serious imbalance: concentration in one area may lead to neglect in another. Thus, Susan (who, like Alan, had been similarly "neglected" at infants school) received a great deal of compensatory attention when she reached junior school, mainly with reading and writing. Unfortunately, this meant she had to miss out almost completely on maths and English sessions with her class. This hardly facilitated her sense of identity as a full class member.

Another unanticipated disadvantage arose where integrated pupils had been assigned to the smallest teaching groups in order to have maximum contact with the teacher. But quite often these groups contained pupils with little academic motivation, or pupils who were more desperately in need of the teacher's attention than the child who simply had difficulty in seeing.

There are other unintended consequences in providing additional support. It is possible that class teachers may seize on the availability of a support teacher as an excuse for minimizing their own efforts. Susan's head teacher commented, "I think the class teacher feels justified at giving her less attention in class because of the home tutor". This kind of evasion or misunderstanding may be reinforced when — as sometimes occurs — poor communication exists between class and support teachers. The most effective coordination of support was apparent when some form of unit was involved. Responsibilities were then more often divided in systematic fashion. But such a support facility is no guarantee that a child's needs are adequately met. For instance, several unit staff complained about the constraints they worked under: one remarked, "I spend more time copying out materials for my children to use than I spend teaching them". In summary, another comment deserves note: "Schools have got to see the day as a whole rather than just in terms of a little bit (of provision) here and there".

The various adaptations and extra effort a school has to make, on accepting a handicapped child, can be viewed all the way from the trivial and straightforward to the 'excessive'. What is often not overtly expressed is that the school is less likely to resent this extra effort provided some clear 'pay off' is apparent — usually concerning the response of the pupil. Often an implicit contract exists between school and child. Thus, in the case of Michael, a 14-year-old with an extremely restricted field of vision, some teachers felt he had 'used' his visual impairment as an excuse for dropping technical drawing and craftwork: "There's a world of difference between a kid who's not got it (aptitude) but who keeps having a go, and one who doesn't bother . . . he was perhaps too ready to relinquish the challenge". Sometimes this contract is expressed in explicit, even forthright terms. Thus Peter's present head teacher commented, "We'll steam on as best we can . . . within the normal scope of the system, but he must keep up with the convoy" — implying that the child, as well as the school, needed to be seen to be making a positive response. A number of the children studied fully met their side of the contract: for instance, a housemaster remarked of a 13-year-old with severely limited vision, "He . . . is prepared to cause himself more inconvenience in order to be like ordinary people . . . (he) could go through school life without anyone working hard".

In this chapter we have concentrated on the ordinary school's role in integration, pointing out how teachers' attitudes and their knowledge or ignorance about visual impairment may affect the integrated pupil's 'success' in school. Staff in ordinary schools are often unaware of how best to help a child with a severe vision loss, and the need for more information and advice seems imperative if integrated education is to become a viable, alternative form of schooling for the visually impaired.

Chapter Eighteen

Support from Home

It is generally agreed that a child's school experience cannot be viewed in isolation from what goes on at home. We accept that to divide discussion of school and home influences, between this chapter and the last one, is a somewhat artificial exercise. Nevertheless, certain points can be made about home and family support for integration and we raise a number of them here. In speaking of the components of support we acknowledge, of course, that most are not confined to families with a handicapped child. However, the importance of support is heightened in the presence of a handicap, particularly if the child is attending an ordinary school. A special school environment, as noted earlier, may be all-encompassing, regulated, and systematically modified. An ordinary school is not. In this chapter we discuss the role of parents in getting the child into the ordinary school system, and what role they play in assisting the child once there.

The special role of parents

Numerous signals alerted us to the importance of the supportive home. It was notable, in the group of 22 children studied, that in the instances of integration held to be most successful, teachers remarked favourably on the amount of home support. This is not surprising: parents often opt for integration and presumably many are concerned actively to assist their child thereafter. If they were less interested on a day-to-day basis they might have sought to get their child into a residential special school. (This is not to suggest that parents who opt for special provision — presuming there is a real choice — are less interested in helping their child. Reference was earlier made to a mother who fought hard and long for her child, who was doing poorly in an ordinary school setting, to be admitted to a residential special school.)

Another kind of signal was the number of references made by members of the educational and medical professions to the need for greater recognition of the value of the 'good' home environment: parents should be helped to play a fuller role, they should perhaps be provided with more guidance and advisory services. The acknowledgement of the importance of parents seems long overdue. They manifestly have a unique role: they are often the only guaranteed constants in their child's life; in contrast, teachers, ophthalmic and other medical personnel, educational psychologists, advisers and advisory teachers, may all change over time.

There is one notable difference — among all the obvious ones — between the response of the school and that of the home towards the individually integrated child. At school, he or she is inevitably a minority interest — one of the many school pupils and an unusual pupil at that. By contrast, for a great many parents, the child is the centre of their world. Parents of handicapped children are not unique in this respect, but unlike many other parents there is less that they can take for granted. Having a strong emotional tie in a context of uncertainty and insecurity was widely considered to make it "worse emotionally to have a blind daughter than to be a blind daughter" (special school teacher).

It is also possible that each party — home and school — places greater emphasis upon different ends. The school, lacking the emotional attachment that parents have, may emphasize academic ends; their working assumption is that a handicapped child needs to be seen to be better than non-handicapped peers if he or she is to obtain reasonable employment. Parents, by contrast, may see little beyond the immediate future, desiring only that their child be content with the present. Thus the parents of Jeremy, a 12-year-old who had experienced both ordinary and special schooling, claimed they were "unconcerned" about academic qualifications: as long as he was experiencing a "normal and decent" education they were satisfied — in contrast to Jeremy's school which placed high value on the academic side. It is clearly more complicated than this suggests, with immense variation from case to case. Other parents, for example, were intensely concerned over future careers, and some — as noted before — put great academic pressure on their children.

In the case of a home background being unsupportive rather than supportive, there are obvious difficulties. A residential special school can more easily 'bail out' a child from a difficult home situation. The ordinary school, like the day special school, is more 'vulnerable' to the input from home — whether help or hindrance. Special schools — both day and residential — claim to have close contact with parents, not least because they are smaller and more intimate places. The head teacher of a special school for the partially sighted claimed he had met and talked with parents of all his 80-odd pupils and that it constituted another area of his specialized expertise: he knew how to deal with the common parental anxieties; he was able to talk about the medical side as well as the school side; and he could alert parents to issues of the longer term.

What can families do?

Typically, parents of children who are integrated provide both general and specific forms of support, in both medical and educational spheres. We look first at the general support. One area that emerged was that parents acted as collectors of medical and educational details, liaising between 'professionals' and making contact with professional agencies. General back-up of other kinds included boosting confidence, encouraging maximum use of residual vision, and fostering independence. As an example of the latter, one teenage boy's parents admitted they encouraged him to use busy roads, even though "it screws our guts up". They argued that ultimately it was "better for him to be independent and let something happen", than that he be "molly-coddled".

We discovered that parents' interactions with schools and hospitals differed greatly, parents ranging from the demanding and 'pushy' to the extremely deferential. The more assertive sometimes seemed to be acting as "pressure groups" on behalf of their child. For example, Brian's parents were informed when he was 11 months old that he had cataracts, but that surgery was "out of the question" until he was older. Fortunately, they sought a second opinion which was that immediate surgery was needed if blindness was to be avoided. The parallel here with Judith's case (Chapter Fifteen) is striking. Other parents intervened because they felt too little was expected of their child at school — "if it's left to drift in the beginning, we're afraid of it drifting for ever more" — or they objected to the way their child seemed to have been dismissed by officials of one kind or another. For instance, Anthony had been withdrawn by his parents from a state school when he was seven years old, once it was intimated that he would be better off in a special school. They believed that if they had failed to act, "he would have been parcelled off to a (special) school, like a geriatric ward".

We encountered many forms of more specific educational support. Families helped in enlarging print, reading aloud, assisting with homework, and verbalizing many aspects of everyday life which a fully sighted child would pick up incidentally. Sometimes, parents bought tape recorders and other such apparatus; some even obtained and paid for low vision aids.[1]

Two cautions about parental support need to be made. First, as noted above, not all parents find it easy to assert themselves. Clare's parents, for instance, admitted their compunction to follow professional advice given for several years before breaking with the experts and removing her from the special school. Second, even if they are willing and able, parents are not always encouraged to pursue their inquiries and interventions. Our evidence points to this being a more typical response of hospitals than of schools. Thus, one set of parents, who persisted in seeking information about their son's medical condition, claimed that they were given "highly technical sermons" that were deliberately "barely comprehensible"; the father felt he had been treated "like a leper", as if he had "done something wrong, but all I wanted to do was to keep my child alive". Several others voiced similar frustrations – indeed some spoke bitterly – of the way they were "patronized", "ridiculed", or simply ignored by hospital authorities.

By contrast, most schools – even if cautiously – appeared to encourage an active parental role. A number of head teachers firmly expressed their belief that it helped the child's commitment, although some teachers pointed to the potential dangers from the "emotional factor" that came into play when parents got involved. There was also a feeling that too much contact between parents and school could be a disadvantage. It was a case of the familiar dilemma – i.e. that increased attention undermines the goal of winning normality. Here it was extended to include parents: in the words of one head teacher: "We try not to make them feel different to anyone else".

It is hard to find instances where parental persistence – both in wanting to be informed and actively involved – has not paid dividends in the end. Brian and Judith, cited above, are both cases where a more hopeful prognosis was achieved, simply through parents insisting on their right to know more about their child's condition. Another set of parents were constantly thwarted in their attempts to obtain referral to a specialist hospital; they commented, "Some of the experts concerned have great trouble in handling a particular situation they don't understand. Each . . . guards his own expertise, and there's a lack of communication between them. We had to . . . draw the various experts together". In passing, we find here evidence of the potentially fragmentary way that children can become perceived by professionals. As one mother remarked of her son, "I want someone to look at him as a whole person and then tell me". It underlines the parents' special position. In the words of one father, "Parents know the child both at home and through its life, and know it better than any experts . . . The parent must be used as a sounding board".

However, with regard to education, it is not clear that parental support is always an undiluted asset. When parents constantly exhort a child of moderate ability toward an academic goal that is beyond him, the disadvantage may be both lasting and cumulative. One complication is where parents seem to have failed to accept the reality of their child's visual impairment. Terry, an 11-year-old with vision in only one eye, is a case in point. He was not considered by the staff of his primary school to have made a particular success of integration so far — either socially or academically. His father asserted, "As far as we're concerned, he's not got a serious handicap. Don't you go saying he's got something wrong with him". This conviction appeared to be responsible for their maintaining unrealistically high expectations for him: "He is intelligent but his eyes have let him down . . . if he sets his mind to it, his writing improves. I have to threaten him to get it good".

Such an extreme reaction was a minority response among the parents we interviewed. Nevertheless, along with other parents who seemed basically ineffective through simple ignorance about how to assist their child, they represent a group for whom a formally organized system of counselling and practical help might be of great benefit. A handicapped child is invariably a source of strain for the family, not least because of the limitations imposed on its group activities. With increased integration, such help might become essential. Our evidence strongly suggests that more visually impaired children could make a success of integrated education if they received optimum support from home.

Attitudes towards integration

Many parents of the children we investigated had either deliberately sought integration or had been convinced by experts — both educational and medical — that it would benefit their child. Overall, therefore, they were enthusiastic. Many remarks were passed about the relative merits of integrated and special school provision. A sample is given below:

"Stephen feels less handicapped now that he attends a normal school, and so do we."

"He's got to be independent and he's got to make it in his own way. I don't want charity in any form."

"She has gained much more (from not) . . . being isolated into disabilities."

"No kids like another that's different. The mere fact of going to a special school would put up barriers."

"Feeling normal spurs her along. It's an incentive to cope and to keep up with the others."

"Any child should be given the opportunity at competitiveness that they wouldn't get in a special school."

"They'll not bring 35 kids down to his level, they'll raise him to theirs."

What is striking in these and other comments is the degree of disfavour accorded to special schools — at least by implication. Some reactions were founded on little more than hearsay; others in the sample had in fact experienced both integrated and special schooling. In these cases, parental opinion was likely to be more informed.

One view was particularly prominent. Typically, the pupil at the special school was considered by many parents to be "handicapped from the start". Consequently they talked about how their child would be "pulled down to their level" were he or she to go to such a school. This level was regarded as inevitably lower because special schools catered for the full ability range, and because staff would be obliged to attend "to those worse off" — visually, mentally, and perhaps physically. Parents were also greatly concerned about the child's sense of himself or herself as being handicapped. This factor had led to considerable anguish for some of the children, who had been at special schools in the past.

Another common fear was the likelihood of lowered teacher expectations and a slower work rate in special schools. Again, parents advanced evidence to support their beliefs. Jeremy was a 12-year-old whose parents withdrew him from a school for the partially sighted after three years. The staff had evidently been "marvellous" and "patient" but it "didn't help Jeremy". Those with more serious conditions had upset him. He would ask "'Why does Tommy do that? They act silly . . .'". He had been "very keen to learn" and had found the work below his intellectual capacity — "He used to ask: 'Why are you giving me baby sums?'".

To sum up, this group of parents tended to regard special schools as artificial, sheltered environments, as 'institutional', and as lacking in stimulation: "Even if you don't get a complex, you tend to build a shell about you and therefore don't take the knocks of everyday life", remarked one parent. These reactions are not surprising given that many of the parents had chosen or willingly agreed to integration, and some had fought hard to keep their child out of special schooling. At the same time, too, they were aware of a number of advantages that special schools had. They agreed that they allowed for individualized, specialized attention from teachers who understood the child's difficulties and problems; and that special schools were often in a better position to do something about them. Special schools were considered as appropriate for children whose vision was fast deteriorating, or whose academic progress seemed in severe jeopardy. The special schools could also establish a personalized work rate for the physically delicate and emotionally immature, and promote independence by means of specific training in such areas as mobility and social skills. However, all in all, parents seemed genuinely convinced that their children were getting the right kind of education and that the advantages of integration outweighed its disadvantages. Part of its attraction was, perhaps, that it permitted parents who wanted to, to play a more active part in promoting their child's development.

Notes
(1) Any low vision aid which is deemed 'clinically necessary' by an ophthalmologist can be obtained 'on loan' from a low vision clinic without charge.

Chapter Nineteen

How Children Cope

The preceding two chapters have concentrated on the contributions — both real and desired — that the school and home can make to successful integration. But the personal attitudes and attributes which the visually impaired pupil brings to the ordinary school are also important and it is to these that we now turn our attention.

What is 'coping'?

Persistently, throughout our study, the question was raised about whether or not visually impaired pupils could 'cope' in ordinary school settings, especially when they received little or no support. We discovered, too, that a major component in decisions about retaining children in integrated settings was an evaluation of how well the child was 'coping'. The term 'coping' seems to have become an important if not crucial one in the lexicon of discussions about integration. Virtually a 'catch-phrase', it is used to describe, question and shed doubt or light upon a visually impaired pupil's ability to relate to the many different facets of his or her life at school.

As researchers new to this field of study, we were surprised by how often the term was used and by the variety of meanings it seemed to have acquired. People used the term 'coping' in arguments, they talked about it, were concerned about it — as if it meant something precise and specific, clearly understood by all involved. In reality, however, the term means different things to different people; it is a convenient 'umbrella word' embracing a whole host of personal and educational adaptations. Coping may mean no more than 'keeping your head above water', a response very different from 'full achievement of academic and social potential'. It may denote 'distinct progress' or merely 'survival'. Our research has shown that 'successful integration' was frequently defined by both teachers and parents as a situation in which a pupil 'coped'. For them, coping and success had become synonymous.

In order to gain a better understanding of the concept, it is necessary to bear in mind several points. *First*, every visually impaired child's condition, circumstances, personality, strength, and adaptation are different. We have been constantly reminded of the importance of considering "the individual needs of the child". Coping, ultimately, relates to individual response. *Second*, in assessing the demands made upon a visually impaired child, the sighted cannot fully transpose themselves into the shoes of the blind or partially sighted and may not understand how difficult or easy particular concepts or demands are for them. Factors that facilitate or undermine adequate coping may be difficult to fathom. *Third*, as soon as a visually impaired child enters an ordinary school, he or she faces the demands of a dominant 'culture' where dependence upon sight is the norm — that child is immediately at a disadvantage, called upon to 'prove' him or herself before being granted a licence to continue. Coping, in this milieu, is defined quite differently from the way it would be in, say, a school for the blind. Definitions of coping vary with different social expectations. *Fourth*, there are two realms of activity in which integrated pupils are expected to cope if they are to be judged successful; 'achieving academic potential' and 'deriving social benefit' are the coveted goals. In practice, a pupil may be held to be coping in one sphere and not in the other without being labelled a 'failure'. Coping is divisible.

In unravelling the widescale use of 'coping', let us consider in more detail what the integrated pupil is required to deal with at school. First, some teacher-governed and formal tasks or demands: that the child follow lessons on the blackboard (a possible visual problem); that the child read, write and possibly draw to a certain standard, with limited allowance perhaps made for speed, legibility and clarity; that the child join in the majority of curriculum activities and participate in most class projects (be 'of' the class, not just 'in' it). Second, there are other, implicit rather than explicit adaptations called for: being expected to form reciprocal relationships with peers; making friends, being accepted, participating with peers in classroom and extracurricular activities; not becoming too dependent upon peers; gaining their respect; and putting up with the teasing inevitably encountered. Integrated pupils also need to be able to handle the 'singling out' which they may experience as a result of sitting at the front of the class in order to see; to accept 'missing out' on activities which fall beyond their scope of vision; and finally they may periodically have to put up with the natural expectation that they can see when they cannot and, when they cannot, to make some explicit and public acknowledgement of this.

To meet the formal requirements, a number of physical resources are available, including low vision aids, and technical aids such as tape recorders, large print books, typewriters and magnifiers. There are also certain widely understood and accepted procedural modifications to teaching practices. These include greater verbalization on the part of the teacher, less reliance on blackboard work, permitting the child to have lesson notes, and making concessions for his or her slowness. There are other related allowances that can be made: for instance, the child may be given extra attention, either by being withdrawn from the class, or within the class itself by a supply teacher or the class teacher if he or she has time. There are additional 'resources' available to help the child handle the less explicit adaptations required: peers may be (indeed often are) sympathetic; the child's condition may be carefully explained so that its severity is properly understood; peers may make allowances both in the playground and the classroom; and singling the child out for particular activities or constantly placing him at the front of the class can be deliberately played down.

We can identify, therefore, a number of 'adaptations demanded' and 'supports proffered', some of which are spelled out and others that are known about by the parties concerned but are not always widely acknowledged. Some children will need more of the supports than others to make the adaptations; some will use the supports with more fluency or public visibility than others. Certain teachers or particular circumstances may call for a greater degree of adjustment by the child, and the child's degree of adaptation will be affected by the rigour of the demands made, the accessibility of useful supports, and by the child's own capacity to deploy supports to meet demands.

Judgments about a child's ability to cope in the ordinary school draw in other factors — particularly the child's 'personality', 'the influence of home' and 'the allowances made by the school'. The last two dimensions have already been discussed in Chapters Seventeen and Eighteen. The remainder of this chapter will, therefore, concentrate on the child's personality — particularly those aspects that may be influential in determining how well a child with a vision loss contends with an integrated school life.

The critical role of 'confidence'

The four case histories included in Part IV highlighted some of the most influential 'personal characteristics' thought to be significant in contributing to 'successful integration': intelligence, confidence, independence, sociability, an ability to come to terms with impaired vision, were some of them. Some of these characteristics are more basic than others and have a more general effect upon a child's total adaptation. In particular, we can single out 'confidence'.

Confidence — however difficult for psychologists to define, operation-alize, or adequately measure — seems to affect every facet of a child's life. Pupils in our study, who were consistently identified as lacking confidence, were those held to be coping less well than others. Often their future in integrated education was in doubt.

It is clearly artificial to isolate personal characteristics from home attitudes, school concessions, the severity of vision loss, and the external constraints and demands. Nevertheless, for purposes of the present discussion, let us examine the central factor of confidence by looking at one or two further case histories.

Susan was an 11-year-old suffering from congenital cataracts on both eyes. She attended her local junior school. She was registered as partially sighted, had a visual acuity of 6/24 with correcting glasses and a severely contracted field of vision. Although Susan continued in integrated education, her future there was questionable. She was thought to have 'little confidence'. Here are some extracts from case notes written up at the time of our visit.

'On transferring to infants school at the age of five, the nursery teacher told Susan's infant teacher that she was "nearly blind". Susan was not a "particularly active child", and these two problems combined resulted in her being left by herself, largely ignored, since she was little trouble to the staff. Her mother clearly felt that she had been "held back" by not being allowed to play under the same conditions as non-handicapped children. She claimed that the infants head had made fun of Susan because of her visual difficulties and her "reticent personality".'[1]

Susan appeared to have been ignored, teased, and defined as "a clinging child" during her first school experience. At junior school, 'much of the first year seems to have been spent in undoing the harm that the negative approach of the infants school had resulted in'.[2] She joined an ordinary class but also received individual attention from a home tutor. But educational progress was slow. Since a psychologist had once assured Susan's mother that she was a "very bright child", she blamed the schools for Susan's lack of confidence. Her teachers described Susan as "sluggish . . . totally lacking any initiative": her mother, on the other hand, saw her as "very active, never still". Her mother was confident that "it is just a question of gaining her interest", yet her class teacher described Susan as "in her class, but not *of* it. It may seem that I'm ignoring her, but there's not much she can do with the rest". She claimed that Susan had an "inflated view of herself" and attributed this to "too much help" in the past. Her reticence and "sluggishness", it was agreed, were the result of a total "lack of independence" rather than of vision loss *per se*.

Peer relations were also affected by Susan's personality: she was described as "withdrawn" and "immature", she had "done nothing" to gain respect or admiration from her classmates. Not surprisingly, she was excluded from many informal activities. That she was an "outsider", an "isolate", was not perhaps helped by her physical appearance, (she was overweight and wore thick glasses). Of her classmates, her class teacher commented, "some have got used to her, but some still regard her as a freak". She had no "real friends" and "the ones (children) on her table (are those who) tolerate her the most". She was the victim of considerable teasing.

In short, Susan's case demonstrates how easily children with an added educational handicap may come to have a "dented morale". Susan was not particularly gifted academically and she certainly lacked confidence – manifested in her questionable independence, her reticence to capitalize upon special help, and her social immaturity.

Our second example is Karen, a 10-year-old girl, with dislocated lenses.[3] She was described as "a happy youngster". Until recently she attended an ordinary school and was thought perfectly able 'to cope' by both her parents and teachers. The latter felt that academically she had "kept her head above water quite well". No one felt that she was being unduly teased nor that she was unhappy. She was, however, variously described as a "very quiet girl . . . timid . . . wary . . . afraid . . . reserved . . . does not mix well". Her friends often tended to be other "isolates" in the school and friendship was thought often to be based on "friendly consideration". While both her parents and teachers acknowledged Karen's visual impairment, they made every attempt to treat her "normally".

It was, in fact, Karen who recently decided that she did not want to remain in the ordinary school. She did not feel she was achieving as well as she might academically and would prefer to be in a school where those around her would "know" of her situation and where there would be no need to "explain it". Her mother finally agreed that a special school "would encourage Karen to go out more and gain greater confidence". There would be "activities designed to boost confidence, for example, doing the shopping for old people". At present, she only went out with her brother, too afraid to be "caught out" by giving the wrong money or by mis-identifying the article she wanted to buy.

At the time of transfer it was found that there was in fact considerable teasing by her peer group and that she was over-dependent upon friends to shield and protect her from it: "She cannot always stand up for herself completely on her own . . . Karen still lacks confidence . . . We (her parents) did not realize how dependent she was upon Dick (her brother) until he went to school . . . She is only confident with friends".

A number of the individual case histories reflect the same emphasis on the fundamental need for confidence. Confidence so often forms the

basis of further adaptations, in particular, a realistic acceptance of
visual impairment and adjusting to its limitations. Consider Robert's
success. He was 15, partially sighted[4] and attended a local comprehensive.
His teachers enumerated a number of factors that had helped him: in all
of them one sees evidence of (and further reinforcement for) a sense of
personal confidence.

> "He is conscientious, determined, hard-working . . . he tries all the
> time . . . his disability has forced him to think in original ways . . . he
> is as bright, if not brighter than those in his class . . . he likes to
> please . . . he is determined to do well . . . he is prepared to accept
> his handicap and to soldier on . . . he is in a good class, with
> sympathetic classmates — half the battle is being in a class with a
> good atmosphere . . . if he were unaware of his limitations, more
> withdrawn or less intelligent, he would not integrate — he would be
> a partially sighted delinquent . . . he gets a tremendous drive from
> home."

Robert himself felt that integration was not the panacea for everyone.
In order to succeed he felt it was necessary to be intelligent and, also,
confident — "have a nerve, be determined, not frightened, not shy, and
not imagine that I couldn't do all the things that others do".

Understanding coping

We have focused on coping for several reasons. There was our swift
discovery of its frequent use, already mentioned. Second, in advocating
more integrated provision, one argument is that children with vision
loss should 'learn to cope' with an environment that is as normal — i.e.
sighted — as possible; yet here again, 'learning to cope' is rarely
examined with any precision. Third, many of those holding a
middle-ground position advocate a modest increase of integrated
provision for 'suitable children who can cope', with special schools held
in reserve for children who cannot. Lastly, the topic seems a general
one, certainly applicable throughout special education and to a lesser
extent in perhaps all spheres of schooling. Moreover, coping — as
tolerably successful self-management — is not even confined to the
domain of education but recurs, as an idea, throughout the helping
professions.[5] Arguably, if coping is so predominant an idea in currency,
it should be better understood than it is.

What we have done so far is to point out a number of different
concomitants or contributory resources that favour successful coping
for children with a vision loss in local schools. Some of these resources
are personal: the child's intellectual capability and self-confidence being
pre-eminent, along with the degree of functional vision. Some of the

resources derive from the family, from a child's pre-school experience, early assessment, diagnosis and guidance. Parents and siblings may give practical assistance, encouragement, and can inject positive attitudes. (Some parents may, however, be over-protective, neglectful, un-informed. Failure to encourage independence, activity and self-reliance may have far-reaching effects on a child's personal resources.) Other resources are institutional: the school or itinerant advisory teacher can provide assistance – e.g. aids, concessions, timetable modifications, special tutoring, as well as encouragement and a high level of acceptance.

Although we appear to have picked upon a single factor, confidence, and to have elevated it into first place, all the evidence points towards a complicated interaction of many different factors. On the one side are all the resources, the pluses; on the other, all the demands to be met and difficulties to be overcome, the minuses.

A boy with reasonable functional vision, who has academic interests, is able and confident; who comes from a supportive, relaxed, and interested home, who is personable and physically good looking; who has a teacher who is interested in him but does not draw attention to his poor sight, is sensitive to his special requirements and explains why, on a particular occasion, these requirements cannot be met; who is in a class that is supportive but that does not fuss or pamper him, is – almost by definition – successfully coping with the classroom reality of integration: the pluses clearly outweigh the minuses.

Another boy, however, more retiring and without marked ability; with less functional vision and perhaps a slight physical handicap as well; coming from a home, say, where the parents have separated and there are several siblings; and attending a school where the teacher does not appreciate how little he can see but draws attention to his unusual status or lets him drift along behind the rest of the class, is – in terms of integration – a child 'at risk': the pluses are fewer and the minuses may easily come to outweigh them.

This kind of simple 'cost accounting' exercise can be useful, (and is applicable to decisions both about special and ordinary education). When it is said 'that attention is given to the total needs of the child' (in placement or school transfer decisions), the professional is more than likely to be running through some similar kind of mental checklist and drawing up a balance sheet of pluses and minuses. If a child comes from 'a supportive home', has 'the right kind of personality', 'has a good school history', and 'does not read too slowly', then the prognosis for a successful integrated experience seems good: the child will cope. However, if the child has had a previously poor school experience, is lacking in confidence, reads slowly, and has, say, a slight impairment of hearing as well, the prognosis is less favourable and special schooling may be indicated.

The 'cost accounting' and 'checklist' approaches to predicting a child's coping capacity (or to explaining present coping or non-coping) have much to commend them. They embody a straightforward and easily understood principle; they recognize the multiplicity of potentially relevant influences, and the dangers of generalizing from one case to another. There is also the recognition of 'trade-off': a child with a severe vision loss but with supportive parents and school, a determined personality, and so forth, may do better than another child with a comparatively minor defect of vision but with other 'minus' factors strongly evident. However, there are also limitations to the cost accounting model and these need to be understood.

The first caution is that it is difficult to draw up the accounts. Even with a one or two day study of the school and family circumstances, such as we were able to conduct, it was not always easy to delineate all the possible pluses and minuses. There is a pronounced danger that busy professionals, called upon to make a recommendation about placement, will have at their fingertips only a small part of the relevant information. Systemizing procedures of evaluation might offset this somewhat, and the present day trend is towards more far-ranging and detailed review of the child's total circumstances.[6]

A second point to consider is that though two independent cost accounting kinds of evaluation might reveal similar patterns of plus and minus factors, two independent evaluators might well differ in their decision criteria: one may require evidence of many plus factors before recommending that a child attend a local school for the sighted; the other may be willing to take more of a risk and 'give the child the benefit of the doubt'. It appears that there is a general, slow shift in the decision criteria being applied in such evaluations. Now, fewer partially sighted children are thought to require placement in a special residential school. Different countries and regions have different prevailing norms: almost every partially sighted child in Massachusetts and in Denmark, for instance, attends an ordinary school.

A third reservation about the cost accounting model is that it is simplistic. Although it acknowledges that there are many different influences, it treats them as separate and distinct from one another, and this is false. Manifestly, they do not act in isolation but together. They interlock and interweave: academic performance cannot be divorced from confidence, confidence from personality, expression of personality from the quality of peer relations, the kind of relations with classmates from the prevailing attitudes of the school. Not only do all the various resources complement and reinforce each other, but the demands and difficulties can also combine together, so that the child has little chance. As well as tending to ignore how much the various factors interact, the cost accounting model is also basically a static one, an interpretation fixed in time: it describes the various influential forces acting upon the individual (in this instance, in an integrated school setting) at one point in time. This, again, violates common sense. The various resources do not remain constant: teachers move, confidence wanes, a crucial friend moves abroad. The cost accounting kind of thinking is no longer so applicable: a new audit is necessary.

We wish to suggest here a variant of the above way of thinking about coping — one that accepts the inter-relatedness of the various influences and is dynamic rather than static.

What characterized Robert, our last example, was that he had many plus factors: we heard that he was conscientious, determined, bright, accepted handicap and soldiered on, had sympathetic classmates, got tremendous drive from home, and so on. These clearly interacted and enhanced each other: they formed a constellation of relevant influences. In a preceding example, Susan, one found a different constellation, a diminishing rather than enhancing one: thus, we were told, she was withdrawn, immature, had no real friends, was a victim of teasing, reticent, lacked independence, and so on. In both cases it is easy to see how the existence of a constellation can become a fixed fact of everyday existence — Robert has a great deal going for him, Susan has very little; Robert's upsets, if any, may be dismissed as uncharacteristic whereas Susan's may be seen as further evidence of her inadequacy; Robert's lot, if anything, may improve as increased confidence leads to even greater independence which in turn may prompt even better academic work, whereas Susan's chances could easily deteriorate, each setback reducing her confidence and making the next setback more likely.

Cycles such as these are often referred to as vicious circles or 'positive feedback loops'. They rarely exist in such pronounced form. Doubtless Robert, if he became over-confident, would over-reach himself or be 'taken down a peg or two'; Susan, if she seemed to be noticeably unhappy or academically unsuccessful, would hopefully be given extra support and help. The systems, in cybernetic jargon, are 'error-correcting'. Most of the time, for the children we studied, there were both 'enhancing' connections (e.g. the presence of a friend made for greater academic effort and more success) and 'diminishing' connections (e.g. necessary exclusion from certain activities leading to a sense of feeling 'odd') that were affecting individuals simultaneously. Robert and Susan were unusual in our sample in that their cases were extreme.

The main practical implication of the foregoing is that instead of straightforwardly tabulating pluses and minuses, the assessment of present or future degrees of coping might include a simple analysis to see how the various influences may be interacting. It might be possible to look more systematically at 'enhancing' and 'diminishing' connections. More specifically, we found in the histories of individual children, examples of both 'the setback' and 'the leap forward'. These were instances of where a sudden and noticeable change had occurred in how well the child was coping at school. Customarily, such changes followed a shift of class or school, the arrival of a new teacher, a sudden change in the extent of vision, a long school absence, the making of a close friend or the departure of an old one. In our terms, each of these represents a major shift in the constellation of influences acting upon the child.[7] It means that what might have once been an enhancing connection (e.g. a teacher offering encouragement that fostered independence) may have become a diminishing one (e.g. a teacher being indifferent and thereby discouraging initiatives) — or vice versa. A shift of school (a massive change in the constellation) can be the beginning of a successful new phase (as it was for Clare in Chapter Thirteen) or may be a severe setback.

Attention to enhancing and diminishing connections, to setbacks and leaps forward, suggests somewhat different priorities when assessing the degree of coping. It may be useful to bear in mind that sometimes all that pupils may need is some shift in the constellation of influences surrounding them to release an enhancing cycle in place of one that diminishes. These ideas are speculative and deserve more extended elaboration. But at least they demonstrate that behind even a commonly voiced and little thought about term, coping, there lie several highly significant issues.

Notes

(1)   Fieldnotes, 18/6/75.

(2)   Fieldnotes, *ibid*.

(3)   Karen had a visual acuity of 60/60 for distance, but could see well at a distance of 8".

(4)   Robert suffered from congenital cataracts and aphakia. He had a visual acuity of 6/36 for distance and N6 for near vision. His vision was improved with the help of low vision aids.

(5)   A social worker, met during the writing of this report, was heard remarking that "being able to cope" was critical. Asked to define what she meant, she replied — saying how difficult it was to be precise — that to cope was "to recognize your limitations and not go under".

(6)   Such a development has its own dangers — i.e. of making the procedure rigid

and bureaucratic, so that a child who might bring some strong personal qualities to offset his or her handicaps might in fact be denied opportunities because the 'situation profile' revealed a high minus score.

(7) The impact of changing school and class milieux was discussed in Chapter Twelve.

Part Six

Towards Integration

Chapter Twenty

Overview

This book has examined educational provision in England and Wales for children with impaired vision. We have concentrated on integration, the contemporary movement toward educating blind and partially sighted children in ordinary schools. Using the approach of illuminative research (discussed more fully in Appendix 1), we have sought to examine integration as a debate, a movement, a set of schemes, an educational goal, and as a group of interrelated policy questions. We hope we have produced a relatively detached and straightforward discussion and analysis of what has often seemed to generate both confusion and controversy.

The book has been divided into six parts. *Part I* (Chapters One – Three) introduced basic background information about blindness and partial sight, registration, discovery, the use of remaining vision, and the potential revolutions in educational practice through increased use of low vision aids and the advent of perceptual training.

Chapter One sketched in the background to the study: how it was commissioned; how it was carried out; and the audience we hoped to reach with this report. Chapter Two focused on certain erroneous assumptions and misunderstandings about the visually impaired, held by wider society. Chapter Three discussed the inadequacies of traditional screening procedures. We introduced the term 'visual impairment' to replace 'visual handicap'.

Part II of the book (Chapters Four – Nine) was full of basic descriptions of schemes of integration, in this country and abroad; their organization and working philosophies. Chapter Four traced the practice of integration as it was developed towards the end of the nineteenth century and which subsequently disappeared altogether from the educational scene. Chapter Five discussed the imprecise and elusive nature of the term 'integration', itself so suggestive of a single, tangible entity but full of diverse meanings when closely examined. We also identified a number of fundamental axes or dimensions along which forms of integration varied: and in Chapters Six to Nine we provided basic documentation of these various schemes. We fixed on the more significant aspects of their history, organization, special claims and working difficulties, and summarized these. These chapters, though containing some interpretative and critical comment, were not intended to be evaluative in the traditional sense.

Part III of the book (Chapters Ten — Twelve) discussed integration against the backdrop of special education generally. Chapter Ten concentrated on the main arguments for and against special and integrated education; Chapter Eleven examined the various 'special' elements claimed for special schooling; Chapter Twelve discussed fundamental issues to do with how schools of various kinds had different impacts on visually impaired pupils.

Part IV (Chapters Thirteen — Sixteen) differed from everything that had gone before. It consisted of four extended case histories of partially sighted children who were individually integrated in ordinary schools. The case histories were designed to impart some of the 'real-life' flavour of the issues surrounding integration, and thereby, perhaps to bring the discussion more down to earth.

If the case histories represent the particular, they also contain generalizable elements. In *Part V* (Chapters Seventeen — Nineteen) we drew on the data from the 22 case histories that we carried out in all, selecting material designed to illuminate some of the issues where misgivings about independent integration were greatest. Chapter Seventeen concentrated on issues that concerned the school; Chapter Eighteen, on issues to do with the home; Chapter Nineteen analysed the conditions and factors that contributed to a child successfully coping with ordinary school life.

Finally, in *Part VI* (Chapters Twenty and Twenty-One), we attempt, first, to draw together various separate strands that have turned up at several points in the book and, second, to present conclusions. Chapter Twenty summarizes certain central ideas and spells out a major conclusion we have reached. In Chapter Twenty-One we introduce a set of concerns more directly to do with educational policy in this area. The points and themes chosen for the concluding chapter strike us as the most significant of all the numerous themes explored in the course of study.

The move to integrate

At the beginning of this study we had not bargained on the full complexity of the issues we were to encounter in its course. The integration debate represents a tangled configuration of related arguments that draw together questions about virtually every aspect of how visually impaired children should be educated. Discussion and analysis is necessary at many separate levels; we have had to range from town hall resource management issues at one end, to intimate interactions in classroom settings at the other. Given the variety of issues involved, any presumption of there being obvious solutions, proofs, or easily validated conclusions, is unwarranted.

Underpinning the debate are ideological disagreements that are highly charged. We can say with confidence that there are valid and powerful arguments on both sides. Many observations in summary can be made. It is clear that, overall, the move to integrate is seen as a threat to the existing *status quo* — a questioning of traditional systems and structures; the objectives of special schools are closely examined: the schools feel threatened, their survival seems at stake. From a different standpoint, the capability of the ordinary school to assume responsibility for special provision is seriously questioned — can ordinary schools even begin to replicate the extensive technical and personal support systems that special schools are able to offer their pupils? At once, we find ourselves slipping into subsidiary groups of questions — like, for instance, the dilemma about whether or not specialized support in the ordinary school undercuts the intentions of the integration exercise.

Any decision to extend integration, or not to extend it, has to be based on practical considerations as well as on philosophy and principle. It pays to remember — in discussions of policy — that integration is not a single system but rather a movement characterized by alternative routes to a common goal — the goal itself being imprecisely and variously defined. Each approach to, or scheme of, integration embodies merits, uncertainties and disadvantages at the level of detailed practicalities.

Our intention has never been to evaluate integration, in the sense of passing judgment on it. We set out instead to marshall and coordinate the various views and opinions of those directly or indirectly involved in the policy arena; distilling arguments, raising questions and assembling data in such a way as to help identify issues central to the discussion. There was a great deal of consensus on certain points. We summarize two here.

First, while it is difficult to define precisely what factors affect or determine 'successful integration', the following seem generally, if loosely, agreed upon: the child should be confident and able to cope, not be socially isolated, or left behind sighted peers in academic terms; nor should the child with visual impairment be given so much help or extra support that school life amounts to being in a special school in miniature; the host school should be willing to accept the child, prepared to seek advice and offer help if necessary, have access to specialist equipment or materials if the need arises, and its teachers should be kept informed of the child's condition, progress, and special needs. Integration also benefits from a supportive home. Finally, integration should not be prohibitive in terms of cost or volunteer time.

The second area of consensus was that most people agreed that certain disadvantages could — but not necessarily would — befall a child who was integrated. These included inadequate monitoring of progress; insufficient support of a specialist or non-specialist variety; a lowering of academic expectations; social isolation and teasing; and insufficient regard being paid to visual problems.

The integration movement also highlights wider questions about the ways in which educational policies evolve. Changes in policy and practice come about in many overlapping ways. New ideas can be traced to the activities of pressure groups or committed innovators; to publicity that is given to showcase schools and schemes; to campaigns in the educational press, to books, to research, and — most notably perhaps — to reports of government committees and Royal Commissions.

It would take us too far afield to examine the curious means by which educational ideas originate, circulate, get taken up, become absorbed in mainstream thinking, and so become the generally accepted beliefs of the day; or — alternatively — why others never catch on, get off the ground, or acquire the status of the legitimate, the reasonable, or the established point of view. That notions come and go in cyclical fashions is well appreciated — though knowledge of the cycles does not seem to prevent their returning, as if for the first time. Similarly, that educational controversies rage for the duration of a few years and then die down is also understood — though, again, understanding rarely seems to disperse the heat that is temporarily generated.

Such observations allude to complex sociological phenomena that deserve more attention than they usually receive. They need to be sketched as basic contours on the integration map because here, *par excellence*, is an educational controversy with all the usual features. For example, the argument is about an organizational format, integration, which is not wholly new and unprecedented — it had a lengthy and honourable earlier innings, albeit with different antecedents and justifications. Second, it is a public debate that will probably not stay at fever pitch for very long — middle ground, compromise positions are already in evidence. Third, while the debate continues, we can see the customary tendency to simplify issues into either/or forms and for the disputants to take a more extreme stance publicly (to "make an impact") than as individuals they will accord with privately.

Finally, in this chapter, we spell out a major conclusion of our study. We believe that the movement to integrate visually impaired children in ordinary schools is here to stay — that it is unlikely, in the medium-term future, to be arrested, and almost certainly will not be reversed. This needs explaining.

When asked whether our title *Towards Integration* should not have a question mark following it — on the grounds that we had said that we were not taking sides over the issue — we replied that it should not. There *is* a shift towards integration whether it is approved of or not. Our detached research stance does not prevent us from having and expressing the view that present day currents of public attitude in educational thinking favour integration, and that it has become — or is becoming — a fact of educational life in the visual impairment community. *The real questions are not so much 'whether and why integration?' as 'how, when, where, and for whom integration?'*

There are a number of different factors involved. *First*, there is the general trend in society towards de-isolating the handicapped, and the wish to absorb them into the community whenever possible. This is accompanied by a new emphasis on acknowledging an individual's disability with greater openness than did previous generations. Paradoxically perhaps, the greater frankness about the disability itself reinforces the person's otherwise normal characteristics. *Second*, there is the widespread application of the general comprehensive principle. One LEA saw its commitment to integration as a logical and necessary extension of its abolishing selectivity throughout the schools in the authority. *Third*, there is increasing acknowledgement that children's special educational needs do not follow closely the neat, official categories of statutory handicaps. To insist that a partially sighted child, well-adjusted and from a good home, should attend a special school simply on account of his or her low vision, no longer makes so much sense — given that many other children may be hampered more, in overall educational terms, because of, say, a disturbed home background or general social deprivation. The latter, unless unduly severe, would not qualify as reasons for removing the child to a special school.

Fourth, as noted in Chapter Three, there are two relevant recent major developments, both affecting treatment and management of young people with visual impairment. One entails the maximization of the vision that remains, linked to improving perceptual efficiency and acknowledging that measures of visual acuity inadequately indicate how much functional vision an individual has or may acquire through training. A second, almost revolutionary development, involves the increased use of more sophisticated optical aids than were prescribed in the past. These twin developments may reduce the number of braille-users and permit a greater proportion of the visually impaired population of school age to function in ordinary classrooms without extensive specialized help.

Fifth, (and of a slightly different nature) there are similar developments elsewhere. It is unlikely that Britain would move strongly against the gathering international groundswell in favour of extending or introducing integration for the partially sighted and blind. To do so would probably require a powerful countermovement in favour of *increased* segregation of the visually impaired. Such a position would ally us probably with the Soviet Union alone. Relatedly, and closer to home, there are similar developments favouring increased integration throughout the field of education for the handicapped in Britain. The fact that our study restricted itself to the visually impaired should not lead us to overlook the fact that many — though not all — the issues discussed here have their counterparts among other handicaps.

To point out that forces exist that favour expansion of integrated provision in the long run, does not mean that this arrangement is shortly to sweep the board and that the system based on special schools will disappear. Unless the Warnock Committee were to propose radical changes — such as centralized direction of education for the handicapped, or a national corps of specialist advisory teachers — the most likely picture for the future is gradual, piecemeal change with cautious innovations and small local initiatives. In this way, integration could become a common practice without a sudden, system-wide change replete with fanfares.

Chapter Twenty-One

Final Points

In this chapter we present a number of concluding observations. They come in a variety of forms: as inferences, morals, warnings, discoveries, points we wish to underline. They are not recommendations for action, but they are selected as having relevance in the adjudication and making of policy in this arena. Most follow directly from points already noted — but sometimes we introduce, even at this stage, new material when it makes sense to do so.

i. A word of caution

We begin by noting the hazards in extrapolating from the experience of presently existing schemes to draw general conclusions about the likely workings of integration, were it to be more generally applied.

These hazards should not be disregarded: the basis for comparison and analysis is, after all, not large. For instance, there are few different examples of any one design of scheme. In particular, in the only two organized English examples of integrating the blind — as opposed to the partially sighted — numbers have been extremely small and the individuals carefully selected; above all, there was a commitment that the open education schemes should not 'fail', a laudable policy because of the 'tinkering with people's lives' argument but difficult for helping to decide how far such schemes might have wider applicability. The schemes observed in Massachusetts and in Denmark suggest that selection criteria may not have to be quite so rigorous, but these schemes operate within different educational systems; so there is danger here, too, in drawing firm conclusions.

A second hazard is that several of the organized schemes examined were still largely 'person-dependent' or were initiated and sustained by 'gentlemen's agreements' — some had yet to pass to the second generation stage of development.

A third point to remember is that some of the features of the early schemes might have been a function of their being unusual departures from the norm. Thus, with increasing acceptance of integration, the tendency of special schools — when linking up with an ordinary school — to make no demands upon it, may appear unnecessarily self-denying.

Finally, each scheme has to be seen in the light of its own local circumstances, founding motivations, historical background, detailed organizational rationale, and official, technical, and financial support. The various features, of both the scheme and its institutional surround, interlock in complicated ways. It is unwise, therefore, to speak of schemes of integration as if they exist in abstract, insubstantial form. Generalizing from one scheme as the basis for designing another can never mean exact replication. Successful transfer of a scheme's design depends on taking the assembly of elements found in one locus, and reconstituting them appropriately for the individual circumstances pertaining in another locus. In short, a scheme can provide ideas for elsewhere, but not a detailed blueprint.

ii. Differentiating forms of integration

There is a natural tendency in discussion to refer to integration as if it were a single pattern. We have tried to show that this can be seriously misleading, by exploring the slides and shifts in meaning that the word itself accommodates and demonstrating the variation in design and practice. What needs underlining here is that in discussions of policy about integration, there should be clear differentiations made: and also that choices of what kind of scheme might be implemented should be carefully weighed.

What is decided upon — whether it is a unit, a peripatetic service, a link-up with a local special school or some other approach — has much to do with the following: (a) the existing provision, if any; (b) the incidence of visual impairment in the area and the level of demand, at present and as projected; (c) the local education committee's general policy regarding possible changes in special education; the priority they give to needs in this field of special education; and, within special education, how they decide between 'competing handicaps'; (d) whether or not there is a strong advisory team in the LEA responsible for special education; and whether there are innovation-minded head teachers, cooperative teachers, and interested schools likely to be hospitable to either the setting up of an organized programme or to the arrival of individually integrated children; (e) the local geography and distribution of population, and whether or not a proposed scheme permits easy access and transport for the children likely to be involved; (f) the availability of possible supplementary sources of support and expertise — e.g. a special school, eye hospital, low vision clinic, parents' group, research unit on visual impairment, or college of education with a strong interest in special education — and whether ways can be found to utilize these resources in a scheme.

This list of considerations is not meant to imply that practicalities and pragmatism must decide all. Complex arguments about the suitability of different schemes can be advanced that are un-ambiguously educational in nature. But whatever particular stance is assumed by those initiating a new scheme of integration with regard to detailed issues, the devising of any new programme or service must inevitably take account of the local opportunities as well as of the possible administrative problems.

iii. Competition or cooperation?

We have been struck by how thinking on integration has overlooked the special schools. The two systems are seen as competitors and rivals when they could be seen as complementary — exchanging information, expertise, and technical resources. In Denmark there is constant reference to "the ordinary and special school and (the) interplay between the two"; there is no reason why this collaborative spirit should not obtain in this country. There are a number of ways in which special schools could complement integrated education if it were adopted on a larger scale. They could (a) become regional resource centres, developing and producing educational materials and holding technical equipment and optical aids readily available for loan; (b) organize short courses and demonstrations for teachers in ordinary schools; (c) run intensive 'booster' courses for integrated pupils with particular goals in mind e.g. mobility or typing, or make provision for pupils to spend longer periods at the special school in order to do concentrated work in certain academic subjects, and provide vocational training programmes; (d) serve as assessment centres, for evaluating pupils' educational needs and special problems, for spotting children whose conditions have not been diagnosed, and for aiding decisions about placement and referral; (e) serve as an organizational base for peripatetic advisory teachers (using special school staff as additional expert advisers in ordinary schools); (f) become centres for research and development (e.g. in methods to improve visual perceptual efficiency along the lines of work described in Chapter Three); (g) provide pre-school training and counselling for parents with young visually impaired children.

To implement these kinds of activity would inevitably require that the two systems — integrated schemes and special schooling — collaborate closely together, perhaps in some overall national framework, as proposed by the Vernon Committee.[2]

iv. A question of cost

One of the newcomer's first questions — more than usually

prominent in the present economic climate — is whether integration is more, or less, expensive per pupil than education in special schools. This is an area we investigated. However, we soon decided we could not do justice to the issue without its becoming an overriding research concern — and this, we decided, was not warranted.

The simple question about comparative costs opens a veritable Pandora's Box of complexities. We heard, categorically, that "of course integration is more expensive" and — equally categorically — that "one of the drives for integration is that it's cheaper". The speakers almost certainly had different things in mind. Those who thought of integration as a specialized unit, complete with resource teachers, abundant equipment, and close personal attention, were speaking of a costly operation. Others, who had in mind individual integration with or without peripatetic support, were pointing to something with a lower price tag.

There are other imponderables. For instance, almost any scheme benefits from adding extra resources — though in doing so there is the now familiar question of whether it renders schooling 'special' in all but name. There are clear disagreements, however, about what constitutes an acceptable level of support. Some of the individually integrated children case-studied in Chapters Thirteen to Sixteen clearly made little call on extra resources; others needed much more. A common view — which we endorse — is that the resource that matters the most is the acceptance and enthusiasm of individual teachers, an item that appears in no audit of costs.

In considering costs, we wrote to several local authorities asking for their comparative costings — between special and integrated provision. None had attempted them. Technically speaking, the difficulties of costing, in isolation, one particular strand of total school activity are both formidable and often artificial. To identify benefits (outcomes) resulting from varying the costs (inputs) is to step into even greater difficulty. All that may confidently be said is, first, that costs naturally increase with extra personnel and technical support but that, second, it is not clear that there is any easily definable optimum level for supporting resources — it depends on the severity of the handicaps represented, on numbers, and on the amount of available external back-up and voluntary assistance. A third point of agreement is that to integrate braille-users entails a different order of supporting service than is required for print-users; a fourth, that there are many start-up and non-recurring costs in establishing a scheme. Fifth, degrees of use of centralized resources are difficult to pin down; and, sixth, integrated provision cannot be wholly isolated — for purposes of cost analysis — from the wider special education system from which it draws personnel, expertise, and pupils.

v. Information required

Teachers in ordinary schools with visually impaired children in their classes, represent a group of key participants in almost any scheme of integration. As noted above, their willingness, curiosity, and concern are resources that any scheme depends on for complete success.

We found a pronounced consensus among this group, spread across many schools, that there were insufficient sources of information and advice. We observed that ignorance leads to apprehension and this can lead to the teacher reacting to the child in a way that can be misinterpreted as negative or as indifferent. Teachers want to know where to turn for advice: without some basic instruction the teacher with a visually impaired child is sustained only by popular public knowledge — which is hardly sophisticated.

Again, there may be something to learn from experience in Denmark. There, teachers from ordinary schools attend brief in-service courses (2—3 days) directed at teachers of integrated visually impaired children. We were told about how the courses "broke down the mystique" surrounding the special needs deriving from low vision; teachers reported they felt "more at ease and less afraid". Sometimes fundamental questions had never been answered before: What is visual impairment? How does braille differ from print? What concepts do the visually impaired find troublesome to grasp? Teachers attending these courses no longer felt alone. Back at their school they became 'minor experts' used by other teachers. Altogether what had seemed "overwhelming" was no longer so.

An equivalent exercise in Britain would undoubtedly be welcomed — particularly by those teachers with individually integrated partially sighted children enjoying no peripatetic support at all — a group of unknown size.

vi. System inequalities

One finds — throughout the education of the visually impaired — evidence of certain inequalities and disparities. The partially sighted, for a start, have fewer benefits, less institutional back-up, and a greater degree of public misunderstanding to contend with, than do the blind. Among the special schools there is unequal distribution of sophisticated technical aids, with more present in the elite, selective schools than in other schools. The availability of low vision aids is grossly uneven, the nearer the child lives to a low vision clinic, the greater the probability of his or her obtaining aids and thus having the chance to maximize fully his or her visual capabilities.

Furthermore, there are other, major disparities in access to aids: visually impaired young persons in special schools have far greater opportunity to use low vision and non-optical aids — e.g. high intensity lamps, large print typewriters — than do other pupils who happen to be integrated. That disparities of this kind are used as part of an economic argument, favouring retention of the special school function, is beside the point: the fact remains that there is non-uniform accessibility to aids according to the type of school that a child goes to. Finally, there is another area of inequality of an altogether different kind: children have different chances of being integrated: it depends on which local authority they find themselves in.

Arguably, such discrepancies should not be taken for granted, though they often seem to be. Perhaps what they indicate for the making of policy is that new schemes and proposals should not inadvertently reinforce the same tendencies. For example, the purchase of one new sophisticated aid — such as an audio-calculator (producing an auditory rather than visual output) — might be weighed against providing adjustable angled desks for all individually integrated partially sighted children throughout a county. This is not a plea for a general levelling down but rather for a general levelling up.

If such a pattern were to be established — and under present economic circumstances it does not seem likely — an expansion of integration, backed by a strong political commitment, might carry within itself the seeds of a new major inequality: integrated pupils might become the 'haves', those still in special schools, the 'have nots'. The possibility of this occurring should reinforce the wisdom of developing a unified system, connecting integrated schemes and special schools, with extensive and easy transfer between the two. There seems little to gain from letting the special schools decay; much to gain from their acquiring new responsibilities.

vii. Divergent professional worlds

The education of the handicapped has dimensions both medical and educational. Clearly diagnoses and prognoses, concerning sight itself, are the province of qualified ophthalmologists. In the past, as was discussed in Chapter Three, the ophthalmologist was also responsible — in a *de facto* sense at least — for most decisions about school placement and transfer of visually impaired children: decisions that routinely followed a designation either as blind or as partially sighted. These, in turn, were based on measures of acuity and field of vision, not on an appraisal of functional vision.

While not denying the continuing need for the best ophthalmological advice — especially concerning likely changes in the visual condition — the marked trend of recent years has been towards a more interdisciplinary approach to placement decisions, with educational considerations being weighed to a far greater extent than was done formerly.[3] Yet, despite this trend, there remains some resentment towards the medical profession among those concerned at the educational end: teachers are rarely given medical details — "unless you are obnoxious you don't discover anything about the child", was one reaction already cited; teachers have attended hospital appointments with children but have then been ignored. Instead of medical / educational contacts being seen as collaboration between professional equals, there are references by teachers to non-medical professionals "being excluded" and "talked down to". On the other hand there is concern from the medical end that clinical details might be subject to misuse.

However, much more could be done — in the view of educators — by way of disseminating general medical and optical information, in order to give schools and families better background understanding of defects of vision and of the latest developments in visual aids.

If medical and educational expertise is to be more fruitfully combined, there is clearly some fence mending required — or fence removing. In this respect, the role of advisory teachers (one of whose work was documented in Chapter Eight) may be critical. This is a new role that can straddle the divide — though this partly depends on previous experience or, in the future perhaps, on the form of training. The same kind of new role has been developed in Denmark — called there 'educational counsellor' — and has also been experimented with in Massachusetts — there referred to as a "liaison person schooled in both domains". The advisory teacher can act as a medical / educational information source — he or she knows individual medical histories and is in touch with the local clinic, school doctor, and nurses; counsels parents, especially of pre-school children; informs teachers about special methods and apparatus; conducts special teaching — e.g. of braille or mobility; disseminates information about special school alternatives; ensures generally that adequate support is provided for individually integrated pupils; and has a central role in recommending what is suitable for each individual child.

It may well be necessary to institute such new professional roles more widely, if the worthy objective of paying attention to the whole needs of the child is to become routine operational practice in integration as it expands.

viii. The forgotten experts

Our research vividly demonstrated the value of communicating with parents. In schools and in hospitals, as in educational research, there is a general reluctance to involve parents: they are seen as 'lay' people, sometimes ignorant, often emotionally biased, by no means always 'reliable witnesses'.

There are elements of truth here but, overall, this view of parents is grossly one-sided. It is also the case that parents are highly knowledgeable about their child's development, previous education, and medical history; when confronted sometimes with many different pieces of professional advice, it is they who have to join the pieces together; legally speaking they are responsible for their child's welfare; and they are highly motivated — as well as worried — and want to do more to help their child. They represent, perhaps, the greatest untapped resource in the whole area of education for the visually impaired.

At the same time they are given very little information.[4] We found evidence of parents having to dig hard to obtain detailed information about services, benefits, and different kinds of schooling. A number of parents lacked even basic facts — some did not know of special schools, others that they were not fee-paying. Some parents were discouraged from inquiring about medical matters and had been rebuffed by certain educational authorities when they expressed a preference for integrated schooling.

In fact, expansion of integration — if it occurs — may inevitably entail pressure for greater parental involvement generally. We found that those pupils thought to be successfully integrated often had parents who supported them academically; took them on educational visits; intervened when necessary in school disputes; encouraged independence and the child's social life; and themselves sometimes acted as liaison persons between schools, hospitals, and local authorities.

Finally, there is a clear need for more parents' groups and for other bodies, such as the Partially Sighted Society, to play an even greater part in supporting parents as well as soliciting their help in corporate ways. Attention to, and a proper appreciation of the parental role has direct effects. There may also be an indirect consequence of involving parents more. Parents of visually impaired children have often felt isolated, powerless, and anxious — hardly an auspicious family milieu for any young child to grow up in.

ix. Assessment

Our last concluding point refers to a convergence of several separate trends: first, the movement towards more informative assessment of visual capability; second, the increased tendency to view the child's needs and progress in a wider compass; third, the shift towards team decision-making about placements and transfers; and, fourth, the increased acceptance of alternative educational patterns. These trends converge on the process of assessment.

Assessment involves, for each child, detailing the nature of the visual impairment, the degree of functional vision as it relates to classroom activities, past educational history, family background and the wishes of parents, and the possible and available educational alternatives at this particular stage of the child's school career.

Recent legislation enacted in Massachusetts which made 'main-streaming' mandatory for most handicapped pupils, incorporated new procedures called 'comprehensive evaluations'. A comprehensive evaluation meeting customarily involves − in the case of a child with defective sight − a representative of the ophthalmologist, the school principal, the child's class teacher, any special education teacher directly involved, a liaison advisory teacher, the school nurse, and − most notably − one or both parent(s), who have the right to request such an evaluation procedure at any time. The meeting considers a number of detailed reports − not unlike the new SE forms in this country − and its main function is to decide what kinds of supporting services, remedial attention, special aids or equipment, or other help a child needs, in order to function satisfactorily as a member of an ordinary class.

Revealingly, a massive commitment to achieving integration in Massachusetts has been paralleled by this commitment to making comprehensive evaluations. In other words, it has been acknowledged not only that integration needs adequate support, but that the kind and extent of support also has to be carefully tuned to the circumstances of each child.

Few in this country at the present time − even among those favouring integration − regard it as a suitable avenue for every child; and no country has given up its special schools altogether. There will always be a sizeable proportion of the very severely or multiply handicapped, for whom integrated education is straightforwardly out of the question. Given this fact, it follows that there are many borderline cases where, again, a full assessment procedure becomes essential.

The moves towards comprehensive evaluation or assessment have other potential benefits: they provide for fuller records being kept and for transfer of these when a child moves to another area; furthermore, periodic re-assessment can both benefit from such records as well as updating them. Concentration on assessment also emphasizes the obligation to consider each child's educational needs, independently, and to think of resources and other kinds of support in a more flexible fashion.

These notes in conclusion are − as we have said earlier − not recommendations but are chiefly an exercise in underlining and drawing together. They do not, by any means, contain and summarize all that has gone before, nor are they the only points that deserve emphasis and invite action.

Notes

(1) Alternatively, the National Health Service in England and Wales could be solely responsible for the distribution of optical aids.

(2)   'A national plan should be drawn up for the distribution, organisation and management of special schools and other educational services for the visually handicapped . . . To this end, committees representing the local education authorities should be set up, in regions designated by the Department of Education and Science, to prepare plans on both a short-term and a long-term basis for their region, after consultation with representatives of voluntary bodies and the health services . . . The Department should co-ordinate the regional plans, determine which schools should have a countrywide intake, and establish a national committee to promote and oversee the execution of the national plan."

DEPARTMENT OF EDUCATION AND SCIENCE (1972). *The Education of the Visually Handicapped*, (Vernon Report). London: HMSO.

(3) Area Health Authorities do have specialists in their Child Health divisions who are responsible for examining children suspected of being handicapped and who are requested to give a medical opinion about the pupil on the newly introduced SE assessment forms.

(4) Mr Iain Davidson and his colleagues in the Pre-school Blind Project in Toronto are, at the time of going to press, in the process of producing a handbook for parents of young blind children in Canada. This might well serve as a model for a similar handbook for parents in Britain. The RNIB in Britain also provides helpful literature for parents of pre-school blind children.

APPENDIX 1

Illuminative Evaluation and Research

This note outlines the research style adopted for this study. It is written for those with methodological interests in educational research. It is not to be regarded as a comprehensive nor a final account of the illuminative approach. Its origins, design characteristics, and theoretical stance, and a variety of methodological assumptions and problems are introduced. That it constitutes only a provisional statement reflects the fact that illuminative evaluation and research have undergone progressive redefinition and elaboration and are still evolving rapidly.

This particular approach to the study of education (e.g. Parlett and Hamilton, 1972, and Hamilton, Jenkins, King, MacDonald, and Parlett, 1976) has several ancestors and close kinship with several parallel traditions and developments in the social sciences and in educational research. There are, for instance, strong family resemblances to case study approaches to curriculum evaluation (MacDonald and Walker, 1975); to Stake's (1976) responsive evaluation; to the participant observation-based fieldwork research into schools developed by Smith (e.g. Smith and Pohland, 1974); and to the 'naturalistic-ethological' and 'qualitative-phenomenological' perspectives combined in what Wilson *et al.* (1974) have referred to as their 'ethnographic methodology' for educational research.

Also related, if not so closely, are the sociological investigations of schools and colleges and their students (e.g. Becker *et al.*, 1968; Lacey, 1970); the work of the 'new' sociologists of education (e.g. Young, 1971); recent work in classroom research (e.g. Hamilton and Delamont, 1974; Chanan and Delamont, 1975); and studies of students from the point of view of educational and social psychiatry (e.g. Snyder, 1971).

Major common elements of these approaches are that studies made tend to be holistic; they are often process- rather than product-orientated; they are carried out under naturalistic or 'field' conditions rather than under more contrived 'laboratory-type' experimental conditions; they utilize observational and interview techniques extensively; they often give less than usual prominence to quantitative measurement procedures; and they are concerned to study educational phenomena and processes in conjunction with wider social and institutional contexts.

The Social Anthropology Paradigm

The illuminative approach lies within what has been called the 'social anthropology' paradigm of educational investigation (Parlett and Hamilton, 1972). The term 'paradigm' is used in the sense of T.S. Kuhn — as an over-arching, widely accepted framework of 'givens' that lends structure and shape to an area, providing in tacit fashion the ground rules for inquiry and also the criteria for adjudicating quality of work done. Three major background figures — who could be said to have pursued work within this educational research paradigm — are Willard Waller (1961), Jules Henry (1971), and Philip Jackson (1968).

The reference to 'social anthropology' is not meant to imply a close identity with anthropological theory and method. The paradigm so named provides only a general framework and research philosophy. The connection with anthropology is through the emphasis on interpreting; on building up explanatory models of existing practice; on drawing out patterns of coherence and inter-connectedness that otherwise go unnoticed. Like social anthropologists pursuing ethnographic fieldwork, illuminative researchers immerse themselves in the working worlds of those they are studying; they seek to build up an overall picture or model of the system in question, and they look for relationships between beliefs and practices, and between organizational patterns and customary response of individuals. The end product therefore is not a set of findings as such, nor a catalogue of facts and figures, nor even an extended description, but rather an interpretive commentary of a series of interconnected educational issues and phenomena that are carefully documented.

Parlett and Hamilton distinguish the social anthropology paradigm from the one that has dominated such educational research until recently — a paradigm whose roots are traceable to 'agricultural-botany'. Here the emphasis is on applying a structured design — one linked to a hypothetico-deductive methodology of the kind that characterizes the experimental and mental testing traditions in psychology, closely allied with statistical method (see Hamilton, 1974). The customary concerns of investigators working in the traditional paradigm are to operationalize variables, match samples, measure educational outcomes numerically, hold constant some variables and vary others in precise ways, or correlate sets of dimensions across different and usually large populations. Their operations parallel much work in social science research generally, and lie within its positivist tradition: they entail a search for 'underlying attributes, objective observables, and universal forces' (Stake, 1975).

The agricultural-botany paradigm has been described as 'appropriate for testing fertilisers on carefully tended fields of crops at agricultural research stations, but (as) inapplicable and incongruous for monitoring how innovations become absorbed and adopted in a diversity of school settings, by teachers with different perspectives, teaching separate and distinctive groups of children' (Parlett, 1974). Educational problems and processes seem strikingly more complicated than the agricultural-botany paradigm can naturally cater for. Often it seems to produce cumbersome research designs, to incorporate an unwieldy investigative technology, to take a very long time to do, and to end up with reports that are over-technical and little read, incorporating findings and discussions that are more narrowly conceived than practitioners and decision-makers would like. Research workers espousing the alternative paradigm are seeking to embrace more of the day-to-day complexities of educational phenomena and processes; they are examining structures, institutions, individuals, and educational practices in ways that preserve them intact: rather than thinking in terms of parameters, factors, variables, and the like, the researcher is concerned with reactions, theories, assumptions, and events.

Although the agricultural-botany praradigm has come under much fire in recent years, it still holds sway in many quarters. Although there has been in educational research generally a wider range of techniques and theoretical positions employed than would have seemed likely a few years ago, the predominant assumptions of most research are still heavily influenced by the traditional paradigm.

In summary so far, then, the illuminative approach represents a shift in the basic research paradigm and also seeks to extend that paradigm in the direction of applied research. It draws on and incorporates many ideas, methods, and traditions that already exist elsewhere in applied social research, evaluation theory, and other fields. But it differs in significant ways from other approaches in the way in which its various procedures and underlying goals are combined together to form what is intended as a closely linked series of basic strategies for investigating education.

Client-centred and Problem-orientated Applied Research

The term 'illuminative' has in some quarters become almost synonymous with 'small scale and non-quantitative'. This is inaccurate on two counts. First, illuminative researchers certainly do not eschew quantitative data and methods altogether. They have their place in the array of possibilities. Second, the most salient feature of the approach has to do with its being client-centred: it is applied research that concentrates on its 'clients' — used here in a very general way to include groups as diverse as innovators, project participants, advisers, local officials, related professional interest groups, governmental policy makers, and other constituencies within or related to the educational system defined as 'target audiences' in particular studies.

Illuminative researchers believe that educational research has, by and large, failed to have impact on the workings of educational institutions and on the ways in which teachers, policy makers, and other parties reflect upon their professional activities. These professionals, however, constantly have to make judgments, decide priorities, accommodate to changes, and conclude whether particular initiatives have been successful or not. By and large they are concerned and involved and sometimes perplexed by the inherent complexity of the issues. Yet educational research rarely does much to help. The illuminative approach, therefore, has developed as its central objective the investigation of educational problems as encountered in practice, developing recognizable portrayals and useful interpretations that relate directly to the underlying questions of policy and practice of concern to those within the educational system.

All the other features characterizing the illuminative approach ultimately derive from this primary concern. Thus, it is clearly important for researchers — in the early phases of each illuminative study — to identify issues and problems of perceived relevance, interest, or importance to the range of relevant constituencies and then to give priority to these concerns. Equally, the various descriptions, accounts, conclusions, and commentaries arising from the study need to be rendered into a form that will enhance understanding of the inherent issues and dilemmas, in a way that readers or recipients of reports will comprehend them and appreciate them.

As in all research there are certain underlying values incorporated. Those of illuminative educational research are essentially diagnostic-therapeutic. Early studies grew alongside a programme of social psychiatric research into higher education in the USA heavily influenced by assumptions drawn from psychotherapy: e.g. that diagnostic inquiry begins with a presented problem area, proceeds by exploratory investigation and the drawing of inferences, and culminates in the discovery of often unacknowledged and contextual determinants that form the basis for interpretations. If these are aptly and sensitively expressed they may change self-knowledge in beneficial ways: at the very least, the taken for granted may be viewed in a new light.

Illuminative researchers do not claim to be 'value-free' or to be capable of 'total objectivity'. But they hold as one of their strongest personal and professional values that, under usual circumstances, concerted effort must be made to represent different value positions, ideologies, and opinions that are encountered in the course of the research; and, moreover, to represent them in ways considered fair by those holding those positions. Commitment to being as judicious, non-partisan and impartial as possible is open to criticism from some, who favour a committed political stance; and from others, who believe it is impossible to be impartial so that one should not pretend to be. Illuminative researchers believe it is difficult but not impossible to be fair to differing points of view; and accept that this represents a stance that is itself 'political'.

Illuminative research can be regarded as applied and also as interventionist in that it seeks to lead to change. However, it is not 'action research' in the usual sense; and, generally but not invariably, it stops short of making policy recommendations — especially where to do so would be to advance the views of one interest group or constituency over those of others. The working assumption is that illuminative research can best improve quality of practice and effectiveness of decision-making and administration, by activities such as challenging conventional assumptions; disentangling complexities that are usually left in a muddle; isolating significant processes from others that are less so; and generally by raising consciousness as well as the level of sophistication of discussion and debate. It seeks to provoke thought and unsettle established ways of thinking.

A highly significant part of an illuminative evaluation or research study is the setting up of the initial contract. If there are sponsors or commissioners of the study, there is likely to be extended negotiation to ensure that it evolves in ways that are congruent with their concerns. The negotiation also permits clarification of value questions and what special role for the researchers is called for in this particular study: e.g. formative evaluators, recorders and archivists, policy analysts, or some other role. Establishing a contract reduces subsequent misunderstandings or possible confusion about the purposes and scope of the study and what the investigators are or are not going to do. Even in work that has not derived from a special commission, a process equivalent to contract-setting takes place — although in this case it is a 'negotiation' with imaginary parties; early decisions about the intended audience and the overall nature and purpose of the study are still required before decisions are reached about methods, interpretive framework, research design, and appropriate feedback or reporting procedures.

It is because all illuminative studies embody a strong commitment to pursuing applied concerns that the usual distinctions between 'evaluation' and 'research' are not heavily drawn: studies vary in their contractual arrangements — some are constituted as more evaluative inquiries, others with a less closely defined brief; some are designed to advance general understanding for a broad readership, others to provide pertinent feedback to a decision-making committee.

Methods and Theoretical Frameworks

Since illuminative studies take varied forms and respond to different client needs, both the range of methods and the theoretical approaches necessary also differ from study to study. Most illuminative research to date, however, has been based on fieldwork methods (Schatzman and Strauss, 1973), using observation (both participant and non-participant, structured and unstructured); interviewing (both non-directive and semi-structured, individual and group); analysis of documents (e.g. of memoranda, public statements, historical notes); question-naires (open-ended and categorized types); and a variety of other techniques — e.g. 'back translation' (Hamilton, 1973), in which respondents are briefly interviewed about their questionnaire responses, and various 'unobtrusive measures' (Webb *et al.*, 1966). Another distinctive procedural feature is the emphasis placed on circulating interim statements and successive drafts of reports to selected audiences for detailed appraisal, review, and correction. The re-drafting that follows this process represents a highly significant stage in formulating final interpretations.

Already noted has been that features of design and method follow logically from the central obligation to relate to the world views, interests, and problems of consumers and clients. It means, for instance, that illuminative investigations must often be briefer than usual research studies: clients do not usually want to wait for five or six years for the final report. To take client-centredness seriously, inevitably often forces illuminative investigators to work within shorter timespans than most researchers would consider acceptable. And if studies are to be brief they must make full use of flexible, rapid, loosely-structured, high yielding techniques of inquiry. These are already widely used in educational research generally, but are usually considered legitimate only in the pilot study phase, and not thereafter.

One of the most striking distinguishing features of illuminative studies is the way in which the design evolves. If the study is to be rapid and also open-ended, an elaborate research design set out in advance is clearly out of the question. Decisions are, therefore, constantly called for as the study is under way – about which techniques to use, how much time should be allocated to particular segments of study, and how total resources should be deployed to pursue leads that have been opened up or problems that have been newly discovered. In the course of a study, investigators 'focus progressively' on particular areas of concentration. In other words, they select among events, topics, questions, ideologies, and trends being discovered and allocate more attention to these. They also take strongly into account the needs and preoccupations of target audiences in establishing the priorities. Organizing and interpreting field data proceed concurrently with their collection. Clearly, studies will often grow in directions that have not been predicted, or sometimes even suspected, in advance. To sum up, in illuminative studies, problems define methods; discoveries up-date the design; and the expanding knowledge base defines the current strategy.

Just as methods are seen as being selected 'off the rack' to meet particular needs of the inquiry, there is similar flexibility in the theoretical frameworks applied in a particular study. Illuminative researchers take a lead from Willard Waller (1961):

'In our analysis of this material (life histories, case records, diaries, letters, and other personal documents) we shall be guided by such scientific concepts from the various fields of psychology, psychiatry, and sociology as seem to be clearly relevant, neither dragging any interpretation in by the heels nor failing to cross academic boundary lines in search of usable interpretations'.

Illuminative research does not fit in with any one existing speciality. It is an interdisciplinary approach that integrates features of method and theory from different fields in an unusual way.

As implied before, the approach leads to exploring a problem or set of issues in ways that are revealing to 'commonsense' modes of thinking rather than to an 'academic and theoretic' reference frame (*cf.* Olson, 1975). The main intention is, therefore, not to structure the study in order to test, apply, or even develop formal theory in the usual sense; instead, the idea is to develop appropriate interpretive frameworks in order to make the examined problem area more comprehensible to those concerned with it. Illuminative researchers seek to develop 'grounded theory' (Glaser and Strauss, 1967): they describe, document, and summarize; they identify commonalities and continuities; they formulate first order generalizations; they elucidate, abstract and explain the phenomena and problems explored. Beginning with observable and recognizable daily events and policy issues and only subsequently moving towards a more analytic and explanatory stance represents a deliberate strategy: by this means the all-important connection with 'lay' concerns and ways of thinking is maintained. A related concern, for illuminative research, is the obligation to discern and 'capture', summarize and formulate, the mass of practical knowledge, 'know-how', and everyday wisdom, that exists already throughout the educational system though often in unarticulated, fragmented and diffused forms. The wealth of knowledge of the seasoned practitioner deserves attention – for all the difficulties of assessing its validity and general utility.

At the same time, illuminative researchers and evaluators are not unconcerned with theoretical questions of a more formal kind. They acknowledge that their approach embodies a number of basic assumptions that derive from several fields in the social sciences (social psychology and symbolic interactionist sociology, in particular); and that these affect the kind of analyses and interpretations that are drawn. Several theoretical principles have also been defined and these are likely to be extended, elaborated, and refined. Perhaps they will form the beginning of a general body of theory about educational *practice* (as opposed to educational philosophy, educational psychology, and educational sociology, that all have different roots and purposes). Among these broad interpretive principles are the following (an extended treatment is not possible here):

(i) The institutions, traditions, and procedures of education embody certain structures, norms, theories, rule systems, ideologies, and ideas-in-currency, that pervade the management framework of organized pedagogy, define boundaries of teaching and learning activities and, as such, are rarely critically examined in everyday practice.

(ii) Teaching and learning involve far more than 'transmission and reception of knowledge' that can be elucidated by attending to 'inputs' and 'educational products' — students / pupils do not respond merely to presented content and to tasks assigned but, rather, they adapt to and work within a local teaching and learning milieu which embodies and transmits conventions, beliefs, and models of reality that are internalized, govern the total response to presented academic tasks, and influence profoundly the processes of socialization and intellectual development.

(iii) The 'actors' (e.g. teachers, pupils, administrators, parents) do not simply respond passively to the system they operate within — they are also scriptwriters, interpreters, and activists: 'The human being is not swept along as a neutral and indifferent unit by the operation of a system. As an organism capable of self-interaction he forges his actions out of a process of definition involving choice, appraisal, and decision . . . Cultural norms, status positions and role relationships are only frameworks inside of which that process (of formative transaction) goes on' (Blumer, 1953).

(iv) There are few, if any, educational 'absolutes'; and curricula, teaching methods, organizational policies, classroom procedures, and institutional philosophies have numerous social, historical, political and epistemological determinants.

(v) Educational systems are maintained in equilibrium by a process of constant negotiation between interest groups; and difficulties in instituting system changes arise because the system is self-correcting and maintaining, with established forms being 'naturally' perpetuated except in cases where there is far-reaching intervention at 'nodal' points.

Finally, in this brief discussion of theoretical questions, the illuminative approach also embodies what Schon and Argyris (1974) have termed a 'theory of practice' — a set of operating assumptions, procedures, and intentions, that underlie it as a field of professional activity. In this case, the theory of practice is a fairly elaborate one, and is of course the subject of the present account. Obviously, however, it is not presented in full.

Objectivity, Accuracy, and Validity

Criticisms of the illuminative style of work often take the form of questioning the objectivity and authenticity of its data and reports. It pays to remember that, methodologically speaking, its adopted parent disciplines are social anthropology, clinical psychiatric studies, and history — *not* educational psychology. Arguably, therefore, it is by criteria appropriate to the former rather than to the latter that its methodological standards should be appraised. It makes no pretence, for instance, of achieving high statistical reliability of its data, in the sense most usual to quantitative educational research. It is simply inappropriate to judge the 'quality' and treatment of information collected by such means − just as it would be inappropriate to judge the predictive power of meteorology or oceanography by the standards of physical chemistry.

In illuminative research, information comes in many varied forms − much of it disorderly and incomplete, unstructured, some of it impressionistic or nebulous; but it does not automatically mean that such information is insignificant, or that it reveals nothing, or that it is not worth collecting and analysing with appropriate care. Social anthropologists and historians are used to weighing and sifting a complex array of 'messy' or 'untidy' human evidence and drawing conclusions from it, and illuminative researchers have to do the same. This is not to deny that it is difficult to collect, order, systematize, validate, and present data of this type. But there is no alternative but to do as best as one can. Of course, one could aid the process by, for instance, instituting response formats that could be standardized; or by imposing strict codifications on qualitative data; or by operationalizing or simplifying phenomena *a priori*. But his would undercut the approach: important defining features − e.g. the flexibility to follow up leads, the speed of processing − would have to be discarded. In other words, in order to study practitioners' concerns, and to relate the investigation closely to the 'real life' of institutions, and to permit the design to evolve in the course of study, one requires other characteristics of the illuminative approach: the flexible methodology; the holistic treatment of phenomena and milieux; the willingness to collect material under less than ideal circumstances; and the great variety in the form and quality of data obtained.

This said, there is still a great deal of attention paid to investigators being as systematic, as orderly, as careful, and as circumspect as possible, in the collection and processing of information. Illuminative research stresses the need to observe and record accurately; to weigh the accuracy of material obtained; and to adopt checking procedures. Wherever possible, investigative techniques are used in combination, several methods being applied to yield data in various modalities; data of the most hard and fast kind are obtained wherever practicable; different investigators, operating semi-independently, cross-check each other's notes and information; reports and memoranda are circulated for checking for historical and technical accuracy; consultants or colleagues are encouraged to play 'devil's advocate', asking questions about the evidence underlying statements made. In reporting, there are established conventions; to make clear what is quoted opinion, what is public material and what is the author's interpretation. In deciding what to include in any report there is a highly selective criterion for inclusion, with no material entering the public realm without careful review and appraisal.

These procedures have become routine safeguards built into work of this kind. They involve application of particular skills to ensure that the highest standards pertain. The discovery of inaccuracies and distortions in a report would throw extreme doubt on the authenticity and value of the study generally. Since − as will be argued − reports are designed to be accessible and widely read, there is likely to be wide exposure to what is reported. While no one individual may be able to corroborate or check all that is reported, there are many separate readers who can do so for some section of the work.

Illuminative evaluation and research involve a high degree of interpretive work to be done by the investigators. This is sometimes held to be to its disadvantage. Yet it is not all that different from other kinds of social research: the possible ills of subjectivity are not excluded from more quantitative or experimental type educational research; even the most rigorous statistical survey study requires constant exercise of human judgment — e.g. in what questionnaire items to include; in what statistical comparisons will be made and how; and — most of all — in what light the findings will be presented or summarized for others. Often these judgments, and the reasons for them, are open to no more than cursory inspection by readers of reports. It is not usually the case either that even quantitative educational researches present all their raw data; summary tables are thus often no more 'publicly verifiable' than are summaries of field notes in qualitative studies.

Illuminative research regards the interpretive skills of the investigator as an important resource to draw upon. A high premium is put on making judicious selections throughout the study and on processes of abstracting, summarizing, highlighting, drawing together threads, and developing interpretations in reports. Given this orientation, it is important to ask what kinds of check are possible, for the reader or other outsider, on the ways in which the selections have been made and priorities established by the researchers, given that readers have little access directly to the raw data.

There are several precautions. Wherever possible, illuminative investigators should make explicit their procedures and criteria for selection, concentration, and focussing; their personal values and opinions if these are likely to introduce serious bias; how they went about the study and what they were trying to do; and what kind of report or outcome they were working towards. But there is another important kind of check that selections and explanations are appropriate and valid. Ultimately, the signal criterion must be whether those, for whom the research ostensibly is done, feel that what is portrayed is the same educational reality that they themselves know. If a piece of research, of whatever kind, fails to achieve this it is unlikely to be satisfactory from any point of view.

Presenting a recognizable reality becomes therefore a major means for testing the basic validity of the judgments made in the course of study. Shatzman and Strauss (1973) have differentiated two types of such validation: first, 'post-verification' i.e. do the participants in the documented enterprise regard the study as accurately depicting the world they know? Second, 'phenomenon recognition' by similar audiences — i.e. do those elsewhere find close parallels between what is described and their own experience?

There is a further extension of the recognizability principle: perhaps simple recognition is not enough; just as achieving a likeness in a portrait does not make it a great protrait. A more searching criterion for assessing the worth of illuminative studies is whether they help to increase sensitivity, understanding, and interest; change the way people look at things; or illuminate what was previously murky and confused. Here the criterion of the study's merit shifts to the market place, as it were: whether the study, at its end, is judged as having been worth doing and whether understanding of some portion of educational life has been advanced by it. These seem entirely appropriate questions to ask of a study, given the basic goals of the approach. It is important to add that if methodological standards of rigour were to slip, this would inevitably lead to the answers to those questions becoming negative.

Ethics, Politics, and Management

There are many potential hazards for research workers operating in illuminative style investigations. In general, they are using more intrusive methods of inquiry than in, say, a piece of survey research or even a study with structured interview schedules and formal observation check lists. It means that the ethical and professional dilemmas and responsibilities upon investigators are correspondingly greater. There are difficult questions to resolve, for a start, about how much an investigator should invade the privacy of individuals and institutions. That some invasion is necessary is almost a prerequisite in such research. There is an obligation to study 'the back of the shop' rather than just the display counter outside. At the same time, confidences have to be safeguarded and individuals protected; and one must consider carefully the implications of reporting certain material.

Illuminative researchers have to achieve fine balances: thus, while the public's 'right to know' is important, so is the upholding of individual and institutional rights to have a strong say in what happens to the information they provide for a study. There are many other questions: in interviewing, how pressing should the interviewer be? In school visiting, how much time should the investigator take up from busy professionals? In explaining the nature of the study in advance, to what extent is it possible to be completely frank and informative about its nature? While there is no way of making a study without minor disruption of the local milieu, it is important that investigators are not over-demanding, unduly obtrusive, or leave participating individuals — who are often nervous or defensive to begin with — feeling they have got nothing out of it for themselves.

At the reporting stage there are even greater problems — concerned with e.g. the extent to which it is appropriate to distort descriptions in order systematically to disguise the identity of individuals; how to report material that, quoted in isolation, could have pronounced negative repercussions; and how, generally, confidences can be preserved while reporting as fully as possible what has been found out.

As perhaps in all research there is obviously scope for abuse by the less scrupulous. Studies could degenerate into exploitation for private research purposes; researchers could increase conflict in unproductive ways; or misrepresent the study as impartial while working towards advancing a private political objective. While complicated codes of professional practice may have to be devised (and procedures for democratizing case-study type evaluations have already been advanced by Walker, 1974) there are probably no fully definable and adequate safeguards for all eventualities. What is required is a sense of responsibility and professionalism similar to that pertaining in the medical and other 'people' professions.

Again, concern about these issues — like those concerned with accuracy and usefulness — is not merely a minor, ancillary question of research methodology. The concern is central to the basically 'diagnostic', 'clinical', and 'client-centred' philosophies that underlie the approach. Illuminative researchers have to be reflexive about their activities, their work, their involvement, their motivations, and the personal impact they have on those they work with. Since a great deal of what they have to do cannot be found out through reading methodological texts, they need to learn by experience and example and to codify, for themselves and others, their procedures and working policies. There are perhaps four simple, yet cardinal guidelines that illuminative researchers have accepted: (i) investigators should not investigate others in ways they would not themselves like to be investigated; (ii) researchers should be understanding and open to differing points of view without becoming collusive and manipulative in the process; (iii) the worth and the rights of individual informants should be recognized at all times and they should be given full opportunity to express themselves about matters that concern them; (iv) those studied should afterwards feel they have been enhanced rather than diminished by having participated in the inquiry.

Reports and Writing up Illuminative Research

Although there are hopefully side benefits to the individuals participating in the course of an illuminative study, the main outcome and the most visible one is usually a report. These come in different shapes, sizes, and styles. The nature of the report is again determined by the perceived audience for whom it is being written. The style, the balance of contents, its length, and the assumptions made about what readers already know, have all to be decided in the light of who is regarded as constituting the particular audience. If the applied, client-centred philosophy is to be more than a pious platitude, these questions have to be addressed with extreme care. There is little point in doing a project if nobody reads its report; and therefore clarity and readability become primary concerns, not secondary ones. The choice of language and the degree of formality have to be carefully calibrated so as to be appropriate.

Writing up forms an intrinsic and important part of illuminative research method. It is not tacked on to the end of the study as an afterthought, but forms an integral part of the investigation. The stages of the study are not insulated but form a progression. Unlike other kinds of research, the data of the study are often not numerical, awaiting conversion to verbal summary; rather, they come already verbalized — as opinions, descriptions, stories, portrayals, and considered statements of policy. Data processing involves dealing with a complex array of evidence. Interview notes or transcripts, observation reports, personal memoranda, historical summaries, extracts from documents, have all to be organized and collated, summarized and selected from for quotation. It means, in practice, that handling the data and imposing some form upon it naturally merges with the assembling of the first draft.

Writing up also presents problems — as noted above — about what constitutes proper practice. For instance, the circulation of a draft to all who took part in the study for their comments may be appropriate for small-scale studies and desirable, even in larger studies, on 'democratic' grounds (MacDonald, 1976). But very wide circulation of a preliminary draft report also presents problems. It comes to assume primary place; the final version, with all the amendments and changes now decided upon, becomes of less interest, and people who have read first drafts rarely bother to read a later one. Deciding on who should see the report in draft and whose comments should be taken into account are two tricky professional and political dilemmas facing researchers.

Reports — according to the study — may or may not become political discussion pieces. What is certain is that writing has to be carried out with care. A hastily written, sloppy, poorly argued statement can easily lead to severe unintended consequences for both individuals or groups.

Conclusion

In conclusion, it is necessary to re-emphasize that the illuminative approach is not some minor rearrangement of methodological practice. Rather it constitutes a beginning attempt to rethink from scratch the nature of educational research as a specialized area of investigation into a particularly important professional and cultural endeavour. The particular features drawn attention to in this brief summary are closely interconnected — the grounding of the study in the phenomenal world of educators and other participants; the evolving design; the use of methods of research that can be fitted around studying issues that these groups themselves define (as well as others that the researchers unearth and unravel as they become more knowledgeable); the checking of observations and interpretations with experienced practitioners; the attempt to provide an account that is immediately recognizable and of genuine interest, that is fair and accurate, and which communicates the variety of different perspectives held; the need for lucidity and easy accessibility of reports for a non-research audience.

There are numerous other interdependencies. Thus, in order to write about a system of education in a way that is revealing for those who know it well, requires that the researchers themselves also have to come to know it well. This means they must immerse themselves in the life of the world they are charting; it means that they must become as near to being knowledgeable 'insiders' as they can. At the same time they have to be able to preserve their independent status as outsiders, keeping some distance, if they are to be able to ask suitable questions about the taken-for-granted local assumptions and beliefs, maintain their objectivity, and see the wood for the trees. To be absorbed into a working world or professional milieu and to be accepted there, and for those in it to be willing to talk freely with the outsider, requires investigators being accepted as having interest and tact. The 'cardinal guidelines' mentioned above are seen to be a methodological prerequisite, not merely a desirable extra.

The major features drawn attention to in this brief account have this in common: they have been discovered in the course of conducting illuminative studies as being necessary component parts of a total research strategy and philosophy. As Louis Smith has written, 'a methodology accrues'.

References to Appendix 1

BECKER, H.S., GEER, B. and HUGHES, C. (1968). *Making the Grade*. New York: Wiley and Sons.
BLUMER, H. (1953). 'Psychological import of the human group'. In: MUZAFER, S. and WILSON, M.O. (Eds) *Group Relations at the Crossroad*. New York: Harper.
CHANAN, G. and DELAMONT, S. (Eds) (1975). *Frontiers of Classroom Research*. Windsor: NFER.
GLASER, B. and STRAUSS, A. (1967). *The Discovery of Grounded Theory*. New York: Aldine.
HAMILTON, D.F. (1973). Doctoral Dissertation: University of Edinburgh.
HAMILTON, D.F. (1974). 'Educational research and the shadows of Francis Galton and Ronald Fisher'. (To be published in a reader on educational research edited by DOCKRELL, W.B. and HAMILTON, D.F. (1977).)
HAMILTON, D.F. and DELAMONT, S. (1974). 'Classroom research: a cautionary tale', *Research In Education*, 11, (May).
HAMILTON, D.F., JENKINS, D., KING, C., MACDONALD, B., and PARLETT, M.R. (1977). *Beyond the Numbers Game: A Reader in Educational Evaluation*. London: Macmillan; Berkeley: McCutchan.
HENRY, J. (1971). *Essays on Education*. Harmondsworth: Penguin.
JACKSON, P.W. (1968). *Life in Classrooms*. New York: Holt, Rinehart and Winston.
LACEY, C. (1970). *Hightown Grammar: The School as a Social System*. Manchester: Manchester U.P.
MACDONALD, B. (1976). 'Evaluation and the control of education'. In: TAWNEY, D. *Curriculum Evaluation Today: Trends and Implications*. London: Macmillan.
MACDONALD, B. and WALKER, R. (1975). 'Case study and the social philosophy of educational research', *Cambridge Journal of Education*, 5.
OLSON, D.R. (1975). 'The languages of experience: on natural language and formal education', *Bulletin, British Psychological Society*, 28.
PARLETT, M.R. (1974). 'The new evaluation', *Trends in Education*, 34.
PARLETT, M. and HAMILTON, D. (1972). 'Evaluation as illumination'. Reprinted in: TAWNEY, D. (Ed) (1976). *Curriculum Evaluation Today: Trends and Implications*. London: Macmillan.

SCHATZMAN, L. and STRAUSS, A.L. (1973). *Field Research: Strategies for a Natural Sociology*. Englewood Cliffs, N.J.: Prentice-Hall.

SCHON, D. and ARGYRIS, C. (1974). *Theories of Action*. New York: Jossey Bass.

SMITH, L.M. and POHLAND, P.A. (1974). 'Education, technology and the rural highlands'. In: KRAFT, R.H.P. *et al. Four Evaluation Examples: Anthropological, Economic, Narrative and Portrayal*. (American Educational Research Association Monograph on Curriculum Evaluation, No. 7) Chicago: Rand McNally.

STAKE, R.E. (1975). The Case Study Method in Social Enquiry. Unpublished paper presented at the Second Cambridge Conference on non-traditional evaluation and research in education.

STAKE, R.E. (1974). 'Responsive evaluation'. In: HAMILTON, D.F., JENKINS, D. *et al.* (Eds) (1977). *Beyond the Numbers Game: A Reader in Educational Évaluation*. London: Macmillan; Berkeley: McCutchan.

SYNDER, B.R. (1971). *The Hidden Curriculum*. New York: Knopf.

WALKER, R. (1974). 'The conduct of educational case study: ethics, theory and procedures'. In: SAFARI-PROJECT *Innovation, Evaluation, Research and the Problems of Control: Some Interim Papers*, University of East Anglia, Centre for Applied Research in Education.

WALLER, W. (1961). *The Sociology of Teaching*. (2nd Edn.) New York: Russell and Russell.

WEBB, E.J. *et al.* (1966). *Unobtrusive Measures: Non-Reactive Research in the Social Sciences*. Chicago: Rand McNally.

WILSON, S. *et al.* (1974). 'A review of the use of ethnographic techniques in educational research', Centre for New Schools. In: HAMILTON, D.F., JENKINS, D. *et al.* (Eds) (1977). *Beyond the Numbers Game: A Reader in Educational Evaluation*. London: Macmillan; Berkeley: McCutchan.

YOUNG, M. (Ed) (1971). *Knowledge and Control: New Directions for the Sociology of Education*. London: Collier-Macmillan.

APPENDIX 2

Details of the Study

This study was carried out between September 1974 and February 1976. We were a research team of three — one of us (MP) working half-time.

The investigation was divided into three main phases — the 'design phase' (September to December 1974); the 'fieldwork phase' (January to September 1975); and the 'reporting phase' (October 1975 to February 1976). During the first phase, we sought to become acquainted with the field of inquiry (see Chapter One) by visiting schools, associations and fellow researchers, attending meetings, and by reading the literature. One of our main tasks was to decide on the particular sub-investigations that were to form the second phase — the 'fieldwork phase'. Since we had only nine months (January to September 1975) for the crucial fieldwork phase, we clearly could not study everything with equal attention. Selections were required. The decisions made at the end of phase one seem to us, in retrospect, broadly correct.

Phase two involved a number of sub-projects, of varying weight and duration, that were usually the responsibility of one team member only and lasted several weeks. As integration of the visually impaired came in many different forms, we decided, to begin with, to study its varying guises. First, we examined the two open education schemes in Liverpool and Sheffield (see Chapter Six). A research colleague, commissioned by the team, spent one week at both St Vincent's and Tapton Mount. This work was carried out in November and December 1974. (At that time the permanent research team was one member short, hence the need to commission an outside researcher.) In addition to interviewing a total of 28 staff and pupils at the special and ordinary host schools, ex-pupils who had experienced open education were later (January to June 1975) interviewed in depth.

Second, we studied the work of a peripatetic advisory teacher responsible for all visually impaired integrated pupils in one local education authority (see Chapter Eight). Third, we visited units for the partially sighted, in order to observe their working at first hand (see Chapter Seven). Fourth, we studied integration in Sweden and Denmark, not in an attempt to draw formal comparisons between the Scandinavian and British experience, but rather to observe different varieties of integration scheme that were implemented abroad (see Chapter Nine). We were also able to pay a brief visit to a Braille Resource Program in the USA (see Chapter Six) during one of the team's visits to the USA on other business. Schemes of integration could not be studied in isolation from special school provision. So, fifth, we paid several visits to schools for the blind and partially sighted, both at home and abroad (see Appendix 3). Our intentions during these visits were several: to learn about special provision; to discuss integration, both in principle and in practice, with those intimately involved in and with special schooling; to observe classes and study the specialist equipment and techniques used in teaching the visually impaired; and to consider the perceived advantages and disadvantages of special education. We interviewed head teachers and members of staff (academic, pastoral and ancillary) and held long conversations with pupils, either individually or in groups.

In addition, we convened a one-day conference in May 1975 to which we invited the head teachers (or their representatives) of all the special schools, colleges and units that we were unable to visit personally. A total of 15 attended. We used the meeting as an opportunity to discuss our research at length and to seek the opinions of our audience on our areas of study.

Sixth, at the more administrative level, we consulted with local education authority officials and representatives of the Department of Education and Science whose main responsibility was educational provision for the blind and partially sighted. In this way we were able to gain both a nationwide and a local perspective.

Seventh, our work took us out of schools to the associations, societies and related bodies for and of the visually impaired. We were concerned to monitor the opinions of those who had a vested interest in education, even if they were not teaching in schools. Ophthalmologists, ophthalmic opticians, and social workers were also consulted.

One area of investigation — the eighth in this list — which occupied a good deal of our time was the study of children individually integrated in ordinary schools. The rationale for this part of the work was described in the introduction to Part IV, along with the difficulties encountered and procedures followed.

The main methods of research in this study were interviews, both formal and informal, conversations, meetings, discussions and 'ethnographic', usually unstructured, observation. Some interviews were conducted by one team member, others involved two or, occasionally, all three of us. We also made numerous inquiries by telephone and also by letter or 'written inquiry'. We spent a total of 160 person-days 'in the field'. Another 42 person-days were devoted to formal project meetings and discussions with consultants to the project. Every day in the field was complemented by at least one or two days for note-writing, annotation, reading other investigators' notes on related topics, and discussion where necessary. We took extensive notes during each interview, discussion (where practicable, we used a tape recorder), or observation period. At the end of each visit, our notes were carefully written up, recorded, and typed for distribution to all three team members. Each member had an identical set of stiff-backed ring folders, nine in all, of different colours, each containing notes according to categories of subject matter. Throughout the study we were organizing and reorganizing our data. Each set of annotated notes was further annotated and cross-referenced by other team members in the light of our increasing knowledge. Data were so ordered as to be easily retrievable. At intervals we held intensive day-long group meetings, sometimes with consultants, during which we immersed ourselves in the data, discussing it, 'progressively focussing' on areas of importance, and deciding what we did and did not know. We wrote interim papers and memoranda for private circulation or for fellow researchers to comment upon.

It is difficult in a study of this type to determine in advance the major areas of inquiry or to separate rigidly the various phases of the research. The emergence of areas of concentration and major interpretive themes began in phase one but continued throughout the research. Similarly, the process of structuring the mass of material and data obtained began in phase one but was still going on during the final drafting of the report.

Procedures for according 'major status' to certain themes and not to others and for deciding what particular selection of quotations or points of view should be included in the report, operated along the following lines.

First, there were three of us and the fieldwork and writing were divided up. Each investigator sought to develop his or her own points of view, interpretations, and assessment of what was most telling, revealing, or informative. These were then discussed at length. This meant that the independence was not complete — indeed it was not: we collaborated closely and shared information, notes, reports, drafts, and ideas; and — in the course of the project — developed a group 'point of view'. However, this was formed from three different sources, not one, and each investigator can cite examples of having been challenged and over-ruled by the other two. We encouraged disputation and were on guard against each other's sloppy thinking and unsubstantiated assertions, and were forced to come to terms with our own.

Second, we took opportunities to discuss our ideas, choice of themes, and priorities with a variety of professionals in the field; we circulated a summary discussion paper to a number of head teachers; we invited reactions to the synopsis of our report from several specialists in the field; and circulated our draft of the final report to a panel of 25 readers. In the course of interviews and discussions we would (routinely) calibrate the 'audience's reactions' when we indicated what we had done and were yet to do. At the beginning we were asking those we conversed with, what we should be concentrating upon; at the end what we had left out (and we tried to fill the gaps).

Third, as discussed in Appendix 1, considered judgments are required at every stage of an illuminative research investigation. But the judgments are tempered by reality testing and other methodological 'safeguards'. We have already discussed a number of them. Others included: (a) taking extensive notes of meetings and discussions and reviewing them at later times; (b) writing up some notes independently and comparing the records of the three investigators; (c) cross-questioning each other to expose points of confusion and ignorance; (d) extensive redrafting of the manuscript of this book; (e) criticizing each other's interviewing styles; (f) listening to taped interviews and reviewing them jointly; (g) not including anything in the report, finally, that had not been confirmed in *some* way by more than one source; (h) follow-up phone calls or occasionally re-visiting to sort out any remaining uncertainties; (i) writing up notes promptly after fieldwork; (j) reviewing periodically our working as a research team and making changes in procedures of deciding monthly strategies at group meetings.

In writing up, responsibility was shared between the three authors: first drafts usually grew out of discussions of the team. These were then distributed, edited, re-written, re-distributed, re-edited and so forth until they were acceptable to the three of us. In most cases final drafting was conducted by a different team member than the one who wrote about it first. The chapters in this book have been drafted and redrafted not less than twice, and some have gone through seven or eight drafts. Drafting and redrafting is an essential final step in progressive focussing and distillation and permits inaccuracies and poorly thought out arguments to be identified.

This is a brief account only of the methods of work. To write a full biography of the study — e.g. all the stages it went through, the mistakes made, the lucky breaks, the exact division of responsibilities, the lessons learned — would occupy another whole volume.

APPENDIX 3

Participants in the Research

During the course of our research, we visited the following special schools, colleges and units for the visually impaired in England and Wales:

Schools for the Blind and Partially Sighted
Blatchington Court School for the Partially Sighted, Seaford.
Bridgend School for the Blind and Partially Sighted, Wales.
Chorleywood School for the Blind, Rickmansworth.
Condover Hall School for the Blind, Shrewsbury.
Exhall Grange School for the Partially Sighted, Coventry.
John Aird School for the Partially Sighted, London.
Joseph Clarke School for the Partially Sighted, London.
Royal Normal College for the Blind and Partially Sighted, Shrewsbury (Further
    Education).
Royal School for the Blind, Liverpool.
St Vincent's School for the Blind and Partially Sighted, Liverpool.
Shawgrove School for the Partially Sighted, Manchester.
Tapton Mount School for the Blind, Sheffield.
Worcester College for the Blind, Worcester.

Partially Sighted Units
Dyfatty Infants School, Swansea.
Moseley Junior School, Coventry.
Springwood Primary School, Cardiff.
Stradbroke Primary School, Sheffield.

The following special schools and units overseas were also visited by the research team:
Braille Resource Program at Kennedy School, Medford, Massachusetts, USA.
Perkins School for the Blind, Watertown, Massachusetts, USA
Refnaes School, Kalundborg, Denmark.
Royal National Institute for the Blind and Partially Sighted, Copenhagen,
    Denmark.
Tomteboda School (at Johannesborgskolan), Gothenborg, Sweden.
Tomteboda School, Stockholm, Sweden.

In addition, we met representatives from the following schools, units and colleges at a conference convened by the project team in May 1975.
Dorton House School for the Blind, Kent.
George Auden School for the Partially Sighted, Birmingham.
Lickey Grange School for the Blind, Birmingham.
Nansen School for the Partially Sighted, London.
Newman School, Rotherham.
Priestley Smith School for the Partially Sighted, Birmingham.
Queen Alexandra College for the Blind, Birmingham (Further Education).
Rushton Hall School for the Blind, Kettering.
South Bristol Open Air School, Bristol.
Temple Bank School for the Partially Sighted, Bradford.
West of England School for the Partially Sighted, Exeter.

Members of the project team also visited the following ordinary schools:
Abbeydale Grange School, Sheffield
Alban Wood JMI, Watford.
Barnwell Comprehensive, Stevenage.
Bowmansgreen JMI, St Albans.
Carmel College, Hertfordshire.
Firs JMI School, Bishops Stortford.
Forrest School, London.
Furze Platt School, Berkshire.
Grove Middle School, Surrey.
Halsey Secondary School, Hemel Hempstead.
Hartley Brook School, Sheffield
Hartsbourne JMI School, Watford.
Heathfields Primary School, High Wycombe.
High Storrs Comprehensive School, Sheffield
Highams Park Senior High School, London.
Hillside Secondary School, Borehamwood.
Ickleford JMI School, Ickleford.
Nowton Court School, Bury St Edmunds.
Raynes Park Comprehensive, London.
Russell School, Bedfordshire.
St Julian's (Girls) School, St Albans.
Tinkers Wood Primary School, High Wycombe.
Virgo Fidelis Convent, London.

The following special schools were also visited:
Bents Green School, Sheffield
Breakspeare (ESN(S)) School, Watford.
Lonsdale School, Stevenage.
Ruggets (ESN(M)) School, Standon.
Vinio House (ESN(S)) School, High Wycombe.
Woolley Wood (ESN(S)) School, Sheffield

Representatives from the following organizations at home and abroad were consulted and/or visited:
American Federation of the Blind, New York.
American Foundation for the Overseas Blind, Paris.
Association of Blind and Partially Sighted Teachers and Students.
Boston University Low Vision Centre, Boston, USA.
College of Teachers for the Blind.
Danish School of Educational Studies, Copenhagen, Denmark.
Department of Child Development, University of Nottingham.
Department of Education and Science, London.
Department of Psychology, University College, London.
Disabled Living Foundation, London.
Hampstead Child Therapy Clinic, London.
Massachusetts Institute of Technology, Boston, USA.
Ministry of Education, Copenhagen, Denmark.
Moorfields Eye Hospital, London.
National Association for the Education of the Partially Sighted.
National Association of Social Workers for the Blind.
National Federation of the Blind.
Research Centre for the Visually Handicapped, Birmingham.
Research Centre, Uppsala University, Uppsala, Sweden.

Royal National Institute for the Blind, London.
Royal National Institute for the Blind and Partially Sighted, Copenhagen,
    Denmark.
School of Education, Birmingham University (Teachers' Diploma in Special
    Education (Visually Handicapped)).
Sheffield Local Education Authority.
Swedish Institute of the Blind, Stockholm, Sweden.
Teachers' College, Stockholm, Sweden.
The Ontario Institute for Studies in Education, Pre-School Blind Children's
    Project, Toronto, Canada.
Warnock Committee (Representative).
Welsh Education Office.

GLOSSARY

The definitions in this glossary are taken mainly from the following sources:

BBC (1973). *In Touch : Aids and Services for Blind and Partially Sighted People*. BBC: Kent.

BISHOP, V.E. (1971). *Teaching the Visually Limited Child*. Springfield, Ill.: Thomas.

COLLINS, K.T., DOWNES, L.W., GRIFFITHS, S.R., and SHAW, K.E. (1973). *Keywords in Education*. London: Longman.

DEPARTMENT OF EDUCATION AND SCIENCE (1972). *The Education of the Visually Handicapped*. (Vernon Report). London: HMSO.

FAYE, E.E. (1970). *The Low Vision Patient*. New York: Grune and Stratton.

LOWENFELD, B. (1974) (Ed). *The Visually Handicapped Child in School*. London: Constable.

MARTIN-DOYLE, J.L.C. and KEMP, M.H. (1975). *A Synopsis of Ophthalmology*. Bristol: John Wright and Sons Ltd.

THOMSON, W.A.R. (1965). *Black's Medical Dictionary*. London: Blacks.

ACCOMMODATION adjustment of the eye for seeing at different distances, accomplished by changing the shape of the crystalline lens through action of the ciliary muscle, thus focussing a clear image on the retina.

ADVENTITIOUSLY VISUALLY IMPAIRED visually impaired by accident.

ALBINISM an hereditary loss of pigment in the iris, skin and hair, usually associated with lowered visual acuity, nystagmus and photophobia and often accompanied by refractive errors.

ALTERNATING SQUINT a condition where the patient can fix an object with either eye at will, but the eye that is not fixing turns inwards (or occasionally outwards).

AMBLYOPIA dimness of vision without any apparent disease of the eye.

ANIRIDIA congenital absence of the iris.

APHAKIA absence of the lens of the eye.

AQUEOUS clear, watery fluid which fills the anterior and posterior chambers within the front part of the eye.

ASTIGMATISM refractive error which prevents the light rays from coming to a single focus on the retina because of different degrees of refraction in the various meridians of the eye.

ATROPHY a wasting away.

BD8 a form completed by a consultant ophthalmologist certifying blindness or partial sight. Form BD8 is also used for registration of the individual by the local authority. It is a confidential document.

BILATERAL pertaining to both sides, especially an eye condition which occurs in both eyes.

BINOCULAR TELESCOPIC SPECTACLES (BINOCULARS) these are used for near vision work; they enable both eyes to focus on the same object and to fuse the two images into a single one.

BINOCULAR VISION the ability to use two eyes simultaneously to focus on the same object and to fuse the two images into a single image which gives a correct interpretation of its solidity and its position in space.

BLINDISMS mannerisms displayed by blind persons, e.g. rocking back and forth, flapping of hands, gazing upward with head held back.

BLINDNESS (GREAT BRITAIN) in Great Britain, the official definition of a blind person is 'a person so blind as to be unable to perform any work for which eyesight is essential'. Visual acuity of 3/60 or less in the better eye usually constitutes blindness. However, where an individual's field of vision is markedly contracted, then a visual acuity of more than 3/60 can constitute blindness. Blindness is certified by an ophthalmologist. For educational purposes, the Education Act of 1944 defined the blind as 'pupils who have no sight or whose sight is or is likely to become so defective that they require education by methods not involving the use of sight'.

BLINDNESS (USA) in the United States, the legal definition of blindness is as follows: central visual acuity of 20/200 or less in the better eye after correction; or visual acuity of more than 20/200 if there is a field defect in which the widest diameter of the visual field subtends an angle distance no greater than 20 degrees. Some States include up to 30 degrees. (20/200 American is equivalent to 6/60 Snellen.)

BRAILLE the main reading and writing medium for blind children. It is a system based on six raised dots, various combinations of which denote letters, word contractions (signs standing for two or more letters in a word) and punctuation. The 63 possible permutations are assigned a total of 201 'meanings', some combinations being multi-purpose — thus, a sign may denote a letter, word, or contraction according to its position in the word. There are two grades: Grade II includes all the signs and contractions possible; Grade I uses 42 of them, each standing for either an alphabetical letter or a punctuation sign, carrying one interpretation, and no contractions are employed.

CATARACT a condition in which the crystalline lens of the eye, or its capsule, or both, become opaque, with consequent loss of visual acuity. There are two main types of cataract: (1) congenital or developmental and (2) acquired.

CENTRAL VISUAL ACUITY ability of the eye to perceive the shape of objects in the direct line of vision.

CEREBRAL PALSY term used to describe a group of conditions characterized by varying degrees of paralysis and occurring in infancy or early childhood. Paralysis depends upon disease of the brain, although the causation is still obscure: pre-natal, natal, and post-natal factors may all be responsible.

CHOROID the vascular, intermediate coat which furnishes nourishment to other parts of the eyeball.

COLOUR BLINDNESS diminished ability to perceive differences in colour, usually for red or green, rarely for blue or yellow.

CONES AND RODS two kinds of cells which form a layer of the retina and act as light-receiving media. Cones are concerned with visual acuity and colour discrimination; rods, with motion and vision at low degrees of illumination (night vision).

CONGENITAL present at birth.

CORNEA the clear, circular transparent portion of the outer coat of the eyeball, forming the covering of the aqueous chamber. The cornea is responsible for refraction of light rays, functioning as a convex lens.

CRYSTALLINE LENS a transparent, colourless body suspended behind the iris, the function of which is to bring the rays of light to a focus on the retina. It functions as a convex lens.

CSE Certificate of Secondary Education.

DETACHED RETINA see Retinal detachment.

DIABETIC RETINOPATHY an uncommon complication of diabetes affecting the retina. It is usually bilateral and can be 'simple' or 'malignant'. In retinopathy, the blood vessels in the retina haemorrhage.

DIAGNOSIS determination of the nature of an abnormality, disorder, or disease.

DISCISION (NEEDLING) a surgical procedure, in which the lens capsule is punctured or broken up with a knife-needle, so that the contents of the lens may be absorbed.

DISLOCATION OF THE LENS OR DISLOCATED LENSES a condition resulting from some defect in the suspensory ligaments, resulting in the lens being misplaced or not in its normal position; focus and accommodation are affected.

DISTANCE VISION a person's vision as measured by Snellen charts and similar tests — it refers to the resolving power of the eye when looking at an object over six metres from the eye when the accommodation mechanism is at rest and the eye focussed for infinity.

EDUCATIONALLY BLIND a braille-user.

ELECTRORETINOGRAM an electrical response of the retina indicating the functional capacity of the rods and cones (excluding the macula).

EMBRYOPATHIES those congenital abnormalities due to damage to the developing embryo from such varying sources as virus infection transmitted by the mother, to damage from X-rays.

FIELD OF VISION the monocular area from 60° nasally to 180° temporally — the entire area which can be seen without shifting the gaze.

FLAT-FIELD MAGNIFIER a magnifying instrument with one side of the glass made convex and the other flat. Useful for children but dependent on peripheral vision.

FOCUS point to which rays are converged after passing through a lens; focal distance is the distance rays travel after refraction before focus is reached.

FOVEA small depression in the retina at the back of the eye; the part of the macula adapted for most acute vision.

FUNCTIONAL VISION useful residual vision.

GLAUCOMA increased pressure inside the eye; 'hardening of the eyeball' caused by accumulation of aqueous fluid in the front portion.

HAND MAGNIFIERS these may be portable or mounted on a stand. When stand-mounted, the reading material is either slid underneath the magnifier or the instrument is pushed across the page. Many are bulky — some are self-illuminated. They are used for both near and distance vision.

HEREDITARY physical and mental characteristics transmitted from parents to offspring.

HYPEROPIA or HYPERMETROPIA (FARSIGHTEDNESS or LONG-SIGHTEDNESS) a refractive error in which, because the eyeball is short or the refractive power of the lens weak, the point of focus for rays of light from distant objects (parallel light rays) is behind the retina; thus, accommodation to increase the refractive power of the lens is necessary for distant as well as near vision.

INTRA-UTERINE INFECTIONS infections in the uterus.

IRIS the coloured circular membrane suspended behind the cornea and immediately in front of the lens. The iris regulates the amount of light entering the eye by changing the size of the pupil.

ITINERANT OR PERIPATETIC PROGRAMME an organizational pattern used in educating the visually impaired. The pupil is enrolled full time in an ordinary school and is visited regularly by a travelling teacher trained to teach or advise pupils with low vision.

ITINERANT TEACHER see Peripatetic teacher.

JAEGER TEST a test for near-vision; lines of reading matter printed in a series of various sizes of type.

KEELER AID a low vision aid made by the Keeler organization, London. This company has produced a whole system of aids for both near and distance vision.

LEA Local Education Authority.

LENS a refractive medium with one or both surfaces curved.

LIGHT PERCEPTION ability to distinguish light from dark.

LONG CANE a lightweight aluminium tube with a rounded hook at the top and a nylon tip at the end. Its length is tailored to the user's height and stride; it usually reaches to mid-chest height when held upright. The user holds the stick ahead of him at an angle of about 30° to the ground, and moves it from side to side in an arc roughly the width of his body to screen the ground ahead of him. The cane is swung to the left as the user steps out with his right foot, and vice versa. The technique requires training.

LOW VISION AIDS (LVAs) Any optical appliance that does more than correct a refractive error. There are two main types in current use: those which are hand-held or hand-manipulated, and those worn on a spectacle frame. (See Hand magnifiers and Spectacle-mounted LVAs)

LOW VISION CLINIC a medical centre where expert diagnosis of visual conditions is undertaken, and where low vision aids can be dispensed in an attempt to maximize the use that the individual makes of any residual vision.

MACULA the small area of the retina that surrounds the fovea and comprises the area of distinct vision.

MACULAR DEGENERATION a condition (very common among the elderly) affecting the fovea (small depression in the retina at the back of the eye — the part of the macula adapted for most acute vision). It is usually bilateral and results in a serious and progressive deterioration of central vision.

MAINSTREAMING the retention of handicapped children in ordinary schools.

MINISCOPE miniature monocular for partially sighted patients.

MOBILITY AIDS any instrument or technique that serves to facilitate the mobility of a severely visually impaired person. Includes a variety of things — long and short canes, guide dogs, ultrasonic torches, laser canes, etc.

MONOCULAR (1) one-eyed, of one eye.

MONOCULAR (2) a kind of hand-held telescopic lens, useful for tasks of short duration, e.g. reading bus numbers, street names. A monocular telescope can also fit over the lens of spectacles for long-vision tasks such as reading the blackboard.

MYOPIA (NEARSIGHTEDNESS) a refractive error in which, because the eyeball is too long in relation to its focussing power, the point of focus for rays of light from distant objects (parallel light rays) is in front of the retina. Thus, to obtain distinct vision, the object must be brought nearer to take advantage of divergent light rays (those from objects less than 20 feet away).

MYOPIC CHORIORETINAL ATROPHY atrophy tends to occur in every severe case of myopia. Choroiditis refers to inflammation of the choroid coat of the eye. When well advanced, it produces inflammation of the retina and interferes with sight in various ways e.g. black spots in the field of vision, loss of vision for particular colours. These degenerative patches thus formed alternate with normal retinal tissue.

N PRINT TEST a test of near vision using cards of differing sizes of print held by the reader at any convenient distance. Starting with the largest print, the reader reads progressively smaller print until the smallest print that is readable has been reached. The test is for corrected vision i.e. spectacles are worn if prescribed.

NEAR VISION the ability to perceive distinctly objects at normal reading distance, or about 14 inches from the eye.

NYSTAGMUS an involuntary, rapid movement of one or both eyes; it may be lateral, vertical, rotary, or mixed.

OPHTHALMOLOGIST OR OCULIST a physician, an MD who specializes in diagnosis and treatment of defects and diseases of the eye, performing surgery when necessary or prescribing other types of treatment, including glasses.

OPTACON (OPtical-to-TActile-CONverter) an electronic reading device which converts printed images into direct tactile representation which can be felt by the fingertip.

OPTIC ATROPHY a condition in which the optic nerve, which carries messages from the retina to the brain, degenerates or is damaged so that the fibres which make up this nerve become atrophied (wasted away). This wasting means that some of the information the fibres carry becomes indistinct.

OPTIC NERVE the special nerve of the sense of sight which carries messages from the retina to the brain.

OPHTHALMIC OPTICIAN a non-medical eye specialist who measures refractive errors of the eye and prescribes lenses, eye exercises and prisms.

PARTIAL SIGHT (GREAT BRITAIN) in Great Britain the official definition of a partially sighted person is one who is 'substantially or permanently handicapped by defective vision caused by congenital defect, or illness, or injury' but not 'so blind as to be unable to perform any work for which eyesight is essential'. Visual acuity of between 6/60 and 6/18 with good or contracted fields of vision can constitute partial sight. Partial sight is certified by an ophthalmologist. For educational purposes, the Education Act of 1944, defined the partially sighted as 'pupils who by reason of defective vision cannot follow the ordinary curriculum without detriment to their sight or to their educational development, but can be educated by special methods involving the use of sight'.

PARTIAL SIGHT (USA) for educational purposes, a partially sighted (seeing) child is one who has a visual acuity of 20 / 70 or less in the better eye after the best possible correction, and who can use vision as his chief channel of learning.

PERINATAL pertaining to the period between the seventh month of pregnancy and the first week of life.

PERIPATETIC TEACHER a teacher who is not attached permanently to any particular school but who moves from one school to another teaching some subject(s) or activities on a specialist basis.

PERIPHERAL VISION ability to perceive the presence, motion or colour of objects outside the direct line of vision.

PERKINS BRAILLER an upright braille typewriter.

PHOTOPHOBIA abnormal sensitivity to and discomfort from light.

PREMATURITY birth before the full term of pregnancy.

PROGNOSIS forecast of the probable course and outcome of a disease or disorder.

PUPIL the round hole (black centre) in the middle of the iris which corresponds roughly with the lens opening of a camera; permits light to enter the eye.

REFRACTION (1) deviation in the course of rays of light in passing from one transparent medium into another of different density; (2) determination of refraction errors of the eye and correction by glasses.

REFRACTIVE ERROR a defect in the eye that prevents light rays from being brought to a single focus exactly on the retina.

REGISTRATION registration as blind or partially sighted is carried out by the local authority, the County Council or County Borough, once a consultant ophthalmologist has completed a form (known as the BD8) reporting on a person's sight and once the patient has agreed to registration.

RESIDUAL VISION the amount of vision a visually impaired individual has left.

RESOURCE ROOM one of the organizational patterns for educating the visually impaired where the low vision pupil is enrolled in the ordinary classroom but may come for extra assistance to a special classroom which has special equipment and a teacher trained to teach the visually impaired.

RETINA a membrane of highly complex structure, lining the innermost surface of the eye, formed of sensitive nerve fibres and connected to the optic nerve. It collects visual stimuli whose impulses are then transmitted by the optic nerve to the brain.

RETINAL DETACHMENT or DETACHED RETINA varying degrees of separation of the retina from the choroid. Rents, tears, and holes produce areas of various sizes of detachment, and in these areas, vision is seriously reduced or possibly totally absent. With total detachment, the affected eye is blind.

RETINITIS inflammation of the retina.

RETINITIS PIGMENTOSA an hereditary degeneration and atrophy of the retina. There is usually misplaced pigment.

RETINOBLASTOMA the most common malignant intra-ocular tumour of childhood occurs usually under age five. It is probably always congenital.

RETROLENTAL FIBROPLASIA a disease of the retina in which a mass of scar tissue forms in the back of the lens of the eye. Both eyes are affected in most cases and it occurs chiefly in infants born prematurely who receive excessive oxygen.

RNIB Royal National Institute for the Blind.

SCOTOMA a blind spot or partially blind area in the visual field.

SE FORMS six forms exist for each child. The first three are completed by the head teacher, school doctor, and educational psychologist. The fourth form is a summary and action sheet describing the needs of the child requiring special education. The fifth certifies the category or categories of handicapped pupils (based on educational need rather than diagnostic label) in which a child is considered to fall and is completed by an experienced educational psychologist or adviser in special education. A sixth form ensures that the educational needs of children whose parents are serving in the Armed Forces are not overlooked.

SNELLEN CHART used for testing central visual acuity. It consists of lines of letters, numbers, or symbols in graded sizes drawn to Snellen measurements. Each line is labelled with the distance at which it can be read by the normal eye. Normal vision is expressed by the fraction 6 / 6.

SNELLEN TEST a distance test of central visual acuity. A reading of 6 / 6 means that the individual has 'normal' vision – that he can read at six metres what he ought to be able to read at six metres. There are various readings on a Snellen test, and the worst measured visual acuity is probably 3 / 60, which means that the individual can only read at three metres what he should be able to read at 60. Gradations on the Snellen chart are normally in multiples of 6: 6 / 6 is 'normal' vision, 6 / 12, 6 / 18, 6 / 24, 6 / 36, 6 / 60 are progressively 'worse' Snellen test readings. (See 'Blindness' and 'Partial sight'.)

SPECTACLE-MOUNTED LVAs simple magnifying lenses or compound lens systems, capable of considerably more magnification than hand magnifiers. They may be either uniocular or binocular, bifocal or trifocal; separate near and distance vision variants also exist.

SQUINT (STRABISMUS) failure of the two eyes simultaneously to direct their gaze at the same object because of muscle imbalance.

TALKING BOOK any book that has been recorded on tape or cassette so that the visually impaired may listen to it rather than read it.

TELESCOPIC GLASSES magnifying spectacles founded on the principles of a telescope; occasionally prescribed for improving very poor vision which cannot be helped by ordinary glasses. Consists of two telescopes mounted in standard spectacle frames, allowing no peripheral vision.

THERMOFORMING a method of reproducing braille copies using a modified tabletop vacuum-forming machine originally developed for 'blister-packing' of 3-dimensional objects in plastic film. The thermoforming method is particularly useful where copies of an already existing braille book are required, or where the number of copies requested is not sufficient to warrant making of a zinc press plate. Up to 50 copies can be made from a paper master.

TRAUMA injury, wound, shock, or the resulting condition.

TUNNEL VISION contraction of the visual field to such an extent that only a small area of central visual acuity remains, thus giving the affected individual the impression of looking through a tunnel.

VERNON COMMITTEE a committee appointed in 1968 by the Secretary of State 'to consider the organisation of education services for the blind and the partially sighted and to make recommendations'. There were 18 people on the Committee, covering a wide range of backgrounds — in special and ordinary education, psychology, medicine, training of teachers of handicapped children, and the administration of local education and health services. In addition, there were two parents of blind or otherwise handicapped children: two members of the Committee were themselves blind.

VERNON REPORT report of the Vernon Committee published in 1972 by the Department of Education and Science.

VISUAL ACUITY ability of the eye to perceive the shape of objects in the direct line of vision.

VISUAL PERCEPTION appreciation or interpretation of a physical situation through vision.

VITREOUS transparent, colourless mass of soft, gelatinous material filling the eyeball behind the lens.

WARNOCK COMMITTEE a committee of inquiry set up in 1974 by the Secretaries of State for England, Scotland and Wales to 'review educational provision in England, Scotland and Wales for children and young people handicapped by disabilities of body or mind, taking account of the medical aspects of their needs, together with arrangements to prepare them for entry into employment; to consider the most effective use of resources for these purposes; and to make recommendations'. The Committee has 25 members, representing a wide range of educational and medical backgrounds. Parents also sit on the Committee.

9384